1

THE HUMAN CYCLE

Ghose, Aurobindo
///

Sri Aurobindo

The Human Cycle:
The Psychology of Social Development

This edition is published and distributed in the United States by Lotus Light Publications, PO Box 325, Twin Lakes, WI 53181 USA, a division in arrangement with Sri Aurobindo Ashram Trust Publication Department, Pondicherry 605002, India.

ISBN 0-914955-44-6

Library of Congress Catalog Card Number 88-81717

Printed in India

LOTUS LIGHT PUBLICATIONS
Box 325, Twin Lakes, WI 53181
USA

First published in the philosophical review *Arya*
between August 1916 and July 1918

First American edition 1950
Second American edition 1999

This edition is published and distributed in the United States
by Lotus Light Publications, PO Box 325, Twin Lakes,
WI 53181 USA • www.lotuspress.com
by arrangement with Sri Aurobindo Ashram Trust,
Publication Departnment, Pondicherry 605002, India

ISBN 0-914955-44-6
Library of Congress Catalog Card Number 98-67017

Printed at Sri Aurobindo Ashram Press, Pondicherry, India
PRINTED IN INDIA

Publisher's Note

The Human Cycle was first published in monthly instalments in the *Arya* between August 1916 and July 1918 under the title *The Psychology of Social Development*. Each chapter was written immediately before its publication. The text was revised during the late 1930s and again, more lightly, in 1949. That year it was published as a book under the title *The Human Cycle*. The Publisher's Note to the first edition, which was dictated by Sri Aurobindo, is reproduced in the present edition.

In 1962 a combined edition of *The Human Cycle*, *The Ideal of Human Unity* and *War and Self-Determination* was published by the Sri Aurobindo International Centre of Education. In 1971 the three works were published under the title *Social and Political Thought* as volume 15 of the Sri Aurobindo Birth Centenary Library. This has been reprinted several times under the combined titles of the constituent works. A separate edition of *The Human Cycle* was published in 1977.

This edition of *The Human Cycle* has been thoroughly checked against the *Arya* and the texts of all revised editions.

CONTENTS

CONTENTS

The Human Cycle

Publisher's Note to the First Edition

The chapters constituting this book were written under the title "The Psychology of Social Development" from month to month in the philosophical monthly, "Arya", from August 15, 1916 to July 15, 1918 and used recent and contemporary events as well as illustrations from the history of the past in explanation of the theory of social evolution put forward in these pages. The reader has therefore to go back in his mind to the events of that period in order to follow the line of thought and the atmosphere in which it developed. At one time there suggested itself the necessity of bringing this part up to date, especially by some reference to later developments in Nazi Germany and the development of a totalitarian Communist regime in Russia. But afterwards it was felt that there was sufficient prevision and allusion to these events and more elaborate description or criticism of them was not essential; there was already without them an adequate working out and elucidation of this theory of the social cycle.

November, 1949

Chapter I
The Cycle of Society

MODERN Science, obsessed with the greatness of its physical discoveries and the idea of the sole existence of Matter, has long attempted to base upon physical data even its study of Soul and Mind and of those workings of Nature in man and animal in which a knowledge of psychology is as important as any of the physical sciences. Its very psychology founded itself upon physiology and the scrutiny of the brain and nervous system. It is not surprising therefore that in history and sociology attention should have been concentrated on the external data, laws, institutions, rites, customs, economic factors and developments, while the deeper psychological elements so important in the activities of a mental, emotional, ideative being like man have been very much neglected. This kind of science would explain history and social development as much as possible by economic necessity or motive, — by economy understood in its widest sense. There are even historians who deny or put aside as of a very subsidiary importance the working of the idea and the influence of the thinker in the development of human institutions. The French Revolution, it is thought, would have happened just as it did and when it did, by economic necessity, even if Rousseau and Voltaire had never written and the eighteenth-century philosophic movement in the world of thought had never worked out its bold and radical speculations.

Recently, however, the all-sufficiency of Matter to explain Mind and Soul has begun to be doubted and a movement of emancipation from the obsession of physical science has set in, although as yet it has not gone beyond a few awkward and rudimentary stumblings. Still there is the beginning of a perception that behind the economic motives and causes of social and historical development there are profound psychological, even perhaps soul factors; and in pre-war Germany, the metropolis of

rationalism and materialism but the home also, for a century and
a half, of new thought and original tendencies good and bad,
beneficent and disastrous, a first psychological theory of history
was conceived and presented by an original intelligence. The
earliest attempts in a new field are seldom entirely successful,
and the German historian, originator of this theory, seized on
a luminous idea, but was not able to carry it very far or probe
very deep. He was still haunted by a sense of the greater importance of the economic factor, and like most European science his
theory related, classified and organised phenomena much more
successfully than it explained them. Nevertheless, its basic idea
formulated a suggestive and illuminating truth, and it is worth
while following up some of the suggestions it opens out in the
light especially of Eastern thought and experience.

The theorist, Lamprecht, basing himself on European and
particularly on German history, supposed that human society
progresses through certain distinct psychological stages which
he terms respectively symbolic, typal and conventional, individualist and subjective. This development forms, then, a sort of
psychological cycle through which a nation or a civilisation is
bound to proceed. Obviously, such classifications are likely to
err by rigidity and to substitute a mental straight line for the coils
and zigzags of Nature. The psychology of man and his societies
is too complex, too synthetical of many-sided and intermixed
tendencies to satisfy any such rigorous and formal analysis. Nor
does this theory of a psychological cycle tell us what is the
inner meaning of its successive phases or the necessity of their
succession or the term and end towards which they are driving.
But still to understand natural laws whether of Mind or Matter
it is necessary to analyse their working into its discoverable
elements, main constituents, dominant forces, though these may
not actually be found anywhere in isolation. I will leave aside
the Western thinker's own dealings with his idea. The suggestive
names he has offered us, if we examine their intrinsic sense and
value, may yet throw some light on the thickly veiled secret of
our historic evolution, and this is the line on which it would be
most useful to investigate.

Undoubtedly, wherever we can seize human society in what to us seems its primitive beginnings or early stages, — no matter whether the race is comparatively cultured or savage or economically advanced or backward, — we do find a strongly symbolic mentality that governs or at least pervades its thought, customs and institutions. Symbolic, but of what? We find that this social stage is always religious and actively imaginative in its religion; for symbolism and a widespread imaginative or intuitive religious feeling have a natural kinship and especially in earlier or primitive formations they have gone always together. When man begins to be predominantly intellectual, sceptical, ratiocinative he is already preparing for an individualist society and the age of symbols and the age of conventions have passed or are losing their virtue. The symbol then is of something which man feels to be present behind himself and his life and his activities, — the Divine, the Gods, the vast and deep unnameable, a hidden, living and mysterious nature of things. All his religious and social institutions, all the moments and phases of his life are to him symbols in which he seeks to express what he knows or guesses of the mystic influences that are behind his life and shape and govern or at the least intervene in its movements.

If we look at the beginnings of Indian society, the far-off Vedic age which we no longer understand, for we have lost that mentality, we see that everything is symbolic. The religious institution of sacrifice governs the whole society and all its hours and moments, and the ritual of the sacrifice is at every turn and in every detail, as even a cursory study of the Brahmanas and Upanishads ought to show us, mystically symbolic. The theory that there was nothing in the sacrifice except a propitiation of Nature-gods for the gaining of worldly prosperity and of Paradise, is a misunderstanding by a later humanity which had already become profoundly affected by an intellectual and practical bent of mind, practical even in its religion and even in its own mysticism and symbolism, and therefore could no longer enter into the ancient spirit. Not only the actual religious worship but also the social institutions of the time were penetrated through and through with the symbolic spirit. Take the hymn of the Rig Veda which is supposed to be a marriage hymn for the union of a human couple and was certainly used as such in the later Vedic ages. Yet the whole sense of the hymn turns about the successive marriages of Suryā, daughter of the Sun, with different gods and the human marriage is quite a subordinate matter overshadowed and governed entirely by the divine and mystic figure and is spoken of in the terms of that figure. Mark, however, that the divine marriage here is not, as it would be in later ancient poetry, a decorative image or poetical ornamentation used to set off and embellish the human union; on the contrary, the human is an inferior figure and image of the divine. The distinction marks off the entire contrast between that more ancient mentality and our modern regard upon things. This symbolism influenced for a long time Indian ideas of marriage and is even now conventionally remembered though no longer understood or effective.

We may note also in passing that the Indian ideal of the relation between man and woman has always been governed by the symbolism of the relation between the Purusha and Prakriti (in the Veda Nri and Gna), the male and female divine Principles in the universe. Even, there is to some degree a practical correlation between the position of the female sex and this idea. In the earlier Vedic times when the female principle stood on a sort of equality with the male in the symbolic cult, though with a certain predominance for the latter, woman was as much the mate as the adjunct of man; in later times when the Prakriti has become subject in idea to the Purusha, the woman also depends entirely on the man, exists only for him and has hardly even a separate spiritual existence. In the Tantrik Shakta religion which puts the female principle highest, there is an attempt which could not get itself translated into social practice, — even as this Tantrik cult could never entirely shake off the subjugation of the Vedantic idea, — to elevate woman and make her an object of profound respect and even of worship.

Or let us take, for this example will serve us best, the Vedic institution of the fourfold order, *caturvarṇa*, miscalled the system of the four castes, — for caste is a conventional, *varṇa* a symbolic and typal institution. We are told that the institution of the four orders of society was the result of an economic evolution complicated by political causes. Very possibly;[1] but the important point is that it was not so regarded and could not be so regarded by the men of that age. For while we are satisfied when we have found the practical and material causes of a social phenomenon and do not care to look farther, they cared little or only subordinately for its material factors and looked always first and foremost for its symbolic, religious or psychological significance. This appears in the Purushasukta of the Veda, where the four orders are described as having sprung from the body of the creative Deity, from his head, arms, thighs and feet. To us this is merely a poetical image and its sense is that the Brahmins were the men of knowledge, the Kshatriyas the men of power, the Vaishyas the producers and support of society, the Shudras its servants. As if that were all, as if the men of those days would have so profound a reverence for mere poetical figures like this of the body of Brahma or that other of the marriages of Suryā, would have built upon them elaborate systems of ritual and sacred ceremony, enduring institutions, great demarcations of social type and ethical discipline. We read always our own mentality into that of these ancient forefathers and it is therefore that we can find in them nothing but imaginative barbarians. To us poetry is a revel of intellect and fancy, imagination a plaything and caterer for our amusement, our entertainer, the nautch-girl of the mind. But to the men of old the poet was a seer, a revealer of hidden truths, imagination no dancing courtesan but a priestess in God's house commissioned not to spin fictions but to image difficult and hidden truths; even the metaphor or simile in the Vedic style is used with a serious purpose and expected to convey a reality, not to suggest a pleasing artifice of thought. The image was to these seers a revelative symbol of the unrevealed and it was used because it could hint luminously to the mind what the precise intellectual

---

[1] It is at least doubtful. The Brahmin class at first seem to have exercised all sorts of economic functions and not to have confined themselves to those of the priesthood.

word, apt only for logical or practical thought or to express the
physical and the superficial, could not at all hope to manifest. To
them this symbol of the Creator's body was more than an image,
it expressed a divine reality. Human society was for them an
attempt to express in life the cosmic Purusha who has expressed
himself otherwise in the material and the supraphysical universe.
Man and the cosmos are both of them symbols and expressions
of the same hidden Reality.

From this symbolic attitude came the tendency to make
everything in society a sacrament, religious and sacrosanct, but
as yet with a large and vigorous freedom in all its forms, — a
freedom which we do not find in the rigidity of "savage" communities because these have already passed out of the symbolic into
the conventional stage though on a curve of degeneration instead
of a curve of growth. The spiritual idea governs all; the symbolic
religious forms which support it are fixed in principle; the social
forms are lax, free and capable of infinite development. One
thing, however, begins to progress towards a firm fixity and this
is the psychological type. Thus we have first the symbolic idea of
the four orders, expressing — to employ an abstractly figurative
language which the Vedic thinkers would not have used nor perhaps understood, but which helps best our modern understanding — the Divine as knowledge in man, the Divine as power,
the Divine as production, enjoyment and mutuality, the Divine
as service, obedience and work. These divisions answer to four
cosmic principles, the Wisdom that conceives the order and principle of things, the Power that sanctions, upholds and enforces it,
the Harmony that creates the arrangement of its parts, the Work
that carries out what the rest direct. Next, out of this idea there
developed a firm but not yet rigid social order based primarily upon temperament and psychic type[2] with a corresponding
ethical discipline and secondarily upon the social and economic
function.[3] But the function was determined by its suitability
to the type and its helpfulness to the discipline; it was not the

[2] *guṇa.*
[3] *karma.*

primary or sole factor. The first, the symbolic stage of this evolution is predominantly religious and spiritual; the other elements, psychological, ethical, economic, physical are there but subordinated to the spiritual and religious idea. The second stage, which we may call the typal, is predominantly psychological and ethical; all else, even the spiritual and religious, is subordinate to the psychological idea and to the ethical ideal which expresses it. Religion becomes then a mystic sanction for the ethical motive and discipline, Dharma; that becomes its chief social utility, and for the rest it takes a more and more other-worldly turn. The idea of the direct expression of the divine Being or cosmic Principle in man ceases to dominate or to be the leader and in the forefront; it recedes, stands in the background and finally disappears from the practice and in the end even from the theory of life.

This typal stage creates the great social ideals which remain impressed upon the human mind even when the stage itself is passed. The principal active contribution it leaves behind when it is dead is the idea of social honour; the honour of the Brahmin which resides in purity, in piety, in a high reverence for the things of the mind and spirit and a disinterested possession and exclusive pursuit of learning and knowledge; the honour of the Kshatriya which lives in courage, chivalry, strength, a certain proud self-restraint and self-mastery, nobility of character and the obligations of that nobility; the honour of the Vaishya which maintains itself by rectitude of dealing, mercantile fidelity, sound production, order, liberality and philanthropy; the honour of the Shudra which gives itself in obedience, subordination, faithful service, a disinterested attachment. But these more and more cease to have a living root in the clear psychological idea or to spring naturally out of the inner life of the man; they become a convention, though the most noble of conventions. In the end they remain more as a tradition in the thought and on the lips than a reality of the life.

For the typal passes naturally into the conventional stage. The conventional stage of human society is born when the external supports, the outward expressions of the spirit or the ideal become more important than the ideal, the body or even the

clothes more important than the person. Thus in the evolution
of caste, the outward supports of the ethical fourfold order, —
birth, economic function, religious ritual and sacrament, family
custom, — each began to exaggerate enormously its proportions
and its importance in the scheme. At first, birth does not seem to
have been of the first importance in the social order, for faculty
and capacity prevailed; but afterwards, as the type fixed itself, its
maintenance by education and tradition became necessary and
education and tradition naturally fixed themselves in a hereditary groove. Thus the son of a Brahmin came always to be
looked upon conventionally as a Brahmin; birth and profession
were together the double bond of the hereditary convention at
the time when it was most firm and faithful to its own character.
This rigidity once established, the maintenance of the ethical
type passed from the first place to a secondary or even a quite
tertiary importance. Once the very basis of the system, it came
now to be a not indispensable crown or pendent tassel, insisted
upon indeed by the thinker and the ideal code-maker but not
by the actual rule of society or its practice. Once ceasing to be
indispensable, it came inevitably to be dispensed with except as
an ornamental fiction. Finally, even the economic basis began to
disintegrate; birth, family custom and remnants, deformations,
new accretions of meaningless or fanciful religious sign and
ritual, the very scarecrow and caricature of the old profound
symbolism, became the riveting links of the system of caste in
the iron age of the old society. In the full economic period of
caste the priest and the Pundit masquerade under the name of
the Brahmin, the aristocrat and feudal baron under the name of
the Kshatriya, the trader and money-getter under the name of
the Vaishya, the half-fed labourer and economic serf under the
name of the Shudra. When the economic basis also breaks down,
then the unclean and diseased decrepitude of the old system has
begun; it has become a name, a shell, a sham and must either be
dissolved in the crucible of an individualist period of society or
else fatally affect with weakness and falsehood the system of life
that clings to it. That in visible fact is the last and present state
of the caste system in India.

The tendency of the conventional age of society is to fix, to arrange firmly, to formalise, to erect a system of rigid grades and hierarchies, to stereotype religion, to bind education and training to a traditional and unchangeable form, to subject thought to infallible authorities, to cast a stamp of finality on what seems to it the finished life of man. The conventional period of society has its golden age when the spirit and thought that inspired its forms are confined but yet living, not yet altogether walled in, not yet stifled to death and petrified by the growing hardness of the structure in which they are cased. That golden age is often very beautiful and attractive to the distant view of posterity by its precise order, symmetry, fine social architecture, the admirable subordination of its parts to a general and noble plan. Thus at one time the modern litterateur, artist or thinker looked back often with admiration and with something like longing to the mediaeval age of Europe; he forgot in its distant appearance of poetry, nobility, spirituality the much folly, ignorance, iniquity, cruelty and oppression of those harsh ages, the suffering and revolt that simmered below these fine surfaces, the misery and squalor that was hidden behind that splendid façade. So too the Hindu orthodox idealist looks back to a perfectly regulated society devoutly obedient to the wise yoke of the Shastra, and that is his golden age, — a nobler one than the European in which the apparent gold was mostly hard burnished copper with a thin gold-leaf covering it, but still of an alloyed metal, not the true Satya Yuga. In these conventional periods of society there is much indeed that is really fine and sound and helpful to human progress, but still they are its copper age and not the true golden; they are the age when the Truth we strive to arrive at is not realised, not accomplished,[4] but the exiguity of it eked out or its full appearance imitated by an artistic form, and what we have of the reality has begun to fossilise and is doomed to be lost in a hard mass of rule and order and convention.

For always the form prevails and the spirit recedes and

---

[4] The Indian names of the golden age are Satya, the Age of the Truth, and Krita, the Age when the law of the Truth is accomplished.

diminishes. It attempts indeed to return, to revive the form, to modify it, anyhow to survive and even to make the form survive; but the time-tendency is too strong. This is visible in the history of religion; the efforts of the saints and religious reformers become progressively more scattered, brief and superficial in their actual effects, however strong and vital the impulse. We see this recession in the growing darkness and weakness of India in her last millennium; the constant effort of the most powerful spiritual personalities kept the soul of the people alive but failed to resuscitate the ancient free force and truth and vigour or permanently revivify a conventionalised and stagnating society; in a generation or two the iron grip of that conventionalism has always fallen on the new movement and annexed the names of its founders. We see it in Europe in the repeated moral tragedy of ecclesiasticism and Catholic monasticism. Then there arrives a period when the gulf between the convention and the truth becomes intolerable and the men of intellectual power arise, the great "swallowers of formulas", who, rejecting robustly or fiercely or with the calm light of reason symbol and type and convention, strike at the walls of the prison-house and seek by the individual reason, moral sense or emotional desire the Truth that society has lost or buried in its whited sepulchres. It is then that the individualistic age of religion and thought and society is created; the Age of Protestantism has begun, the Age of Reason, the Age of Revolt, Progress, Freedom. A partial and external freedom, still betrayed by the conventional age that preceded it into the idea that the Truth can be found in outsides, dreaming vainly that perfection can be determined by machinery, but still a necessary passage to the subjective period of humanity through which man has to circle back towards the recovery of his deeper self and a new upward line or a new revolving cycle of civilisation.

Chapter II

The Age of Individualism
and Reason

A N INDIVIDUALISTIC age of human society comes as a
result of the corruption and failure of the conventional,
as a revolt against the reign of the petrified typal figure.
Before it can be born it is necessary that the old truths shall
have been lost in the soul and practice of the race and that even
the conventions which ape and replace them shall have become
devoid of real sense and intelligence; stripped of all practical
justification, they exist only mechanically by fixed idea, by the
force of custom, by attachment to the form. It is then that men
in spite of the natural conservatism of the social mind are compelled at last to perceive that the Truth is dead in them and that
they are living by a lie. The individualism of the new age is an
attempt to get back from conventionalism of belief and practice
to some solid bed-rock, no matter what, of real and tangible
Truth. And it is necessarily individualistic, because all the old
general standards have become bankrupt and can no longer give
any inner help; it is therefore the individual who has to become a
discoverer, a pioneer, and to search out by his individual reason,
intuition, idealism, desire, claim upon life or whatever other
light he finds in himself the true law of the world and of his own
being. By that, when he has found or thinks he has found it,
he will strive to rebase on a firm foundation and remould in a
more vital even if a poorer form religion, society, ethics, political
institutions, his relations with his fellows, his strivings for his
own perfection and his labour for mankind.

It is in Europe that the age of individualism has taken birth
and exercised its full sway; the East has entered into it only by
contact and influence, not from an original impulse. And it is to
its passion for the discovery of the actual truth of things and for

the governing of human life by whatever law of the truth it has found that the West owes its centuries of strength, vigour, light, progress, irresistible expansion. Equally, it is due not to any original falsehood in the ideals on which its life was founded, but to the loss of the living sense of the Truth it once held and its long contented slumber in the cramping bonds of a mechanical conventionalism that the East has found itself helpless in the hour of its awakening, a giant empty of strength, inert masses of men who had forgotten how to deal freely with facts and forces because they had learned only how to live in a world of stereotyped thought and customary action. Yet the truths which Europe has found by its individualistic age covered only the first more obvious, physical and outward facts of life and only such of their more hidden realities and powers as the habit of analytical reason and the pursuit of practical utility can give to man. If its rationalistic civilisation has swept so triumphantly over the world, it is because it found no deeper and more powerful truth to confront it; for all the rest of mankind was still in the inactivity of the last dark hours of the conventional age.

The individualistic age of Europe was in its beginning a revolt of reason, in its culmination a triumphal progress of physical Science. Such an evolution was historically inevitable. The dawn of individualism is always a questioning, a denial. The individual finds a religion imposed upon him which does not base its dogma and practice upon a living sense of ever verifiable spiritual Truth, but on the letter of an ancient book, the infallible dictum of a Pope, the tradition of a Church, the learned casuistry of schoolmen and Pundits, conclaves of ecclesiastics, heads of monastic orders, doctors of all sorts, all of them unquestionable tribunals whose sole function is to judge and pronounce, but none of whom seems to think it necessary or even allowable to search, test, prove, inquire, discover. He finds that, as is inevitable under such a regime, true science and knowledge are either banned, punished and persecuted or else rendered obsolete by the habit of blind reliance on fixed authorities; even what is true in old authorities is no longer of any value, because its words are learnedly or ignorantly repeated but its real sense is no longer lived except at most by a few. In politics he finds everywhere divine rights, established privileges, sanctified tyrannies which are evidently armed with an oppressive power and justify themselves by long prescription, but seem to have no real claim or title to exist. In the social order he finds an equally stereotyped reign of convention, fixed disabilities, fixed privileges, the self-regarding arrogance of the high, the blind prostration of the low, while the old functions which might have justified at one time such a distribution of status are either not performed at all or badly performed without any sense of obligation and merely as a part of caste pride. He has to rise in revolt; on every claim of authority he has to turn the eye of a resolute inquisition; when he is told that this is the sacred truth of things or the command of God or the immemorial order of human life, he has to reply, "But is it really so? How shall I know that this is the truth of things and not superstition and falsehood? When did God command it, or how do I know that this was the sense of His command and not your error or invention, or that the book on which you found yourself is His word at all, or that He has ever spoken His will to mankind? This immemorial order of which you speak, is it really immemorial, really a law of Nature or an imperfect result of Time and at present a most false convention? And of all you say, still I must ask, does it agree with the facts of the world, with my sense of right, with my judgment of truth, with my experience of reality?" And if it does not, the revolting individual flings off the yoke, declares the truth as he sees it and in doing so strikes inevitably at the root of the religious, the social, the political, momentarily perhaps even the moral order of the community as it stands, because it stands upon the authority he discredits and the convention he destroys and not upon a living truth which can be successfully opposed to his own. The champions of the old order may be right when they seek to suppress him as a destructive agency perilous to social security, political order or religious tradition; but he stands there and can no other, because to destroy is his mission, to destroy falsehood and lay bare a new foundation of truth.

But by what individual faculty or standard shall the innovator find out his new foundation or establish his new measures? Evidently, it will depend upon the available enlightenment of the time and the possible forms of knowledge to which he has access. At first it was in religion a personal illumination supported in the West by a theological, in the East by a philosophical reasoning. In society and politics it started with a crude primitive perception of natural right and justice which took its origin from the exasperation of suffering or from an awakened sense of general oppression, wrong, injustice and the indefensibility of the existing order when brought to any other test than that of privilege and established convention. The religious motive led at first; the social and political, moderating itself after the swift suppression of its first crude and vehement movements, took advantage of the upheaval of religious reformation, followed behind it as a useful ally and waited its time to assume the lead when the spiritual momentum had been spent and, perhaps by the very force of the secular influences it called to its aid, had missed its way. The movement of religious freedom in Europe took its stand first on a limited, then on an absolute right of the individual experience and illumined reason to determine the true sense of inspired Scripture and the true Christian ritual and order of the Church. The vehemence of its claim was measured by the vehemence of its revolt from the usurpations, pretensions and brutalities of the ecclesiastical power which claimed to withhold the Scripture from general knowledge and impose by moral authority and physical violence its own arbitrary interpretation of Sacred Writ, if not indeed another and substituted doctrine, on the recalcitrant individual conscience. In its more tepid and moderate forms the revolt engendered such compromises as the Episcopalian Churches, at a higher degree of fervour Calvinistic Puritanism, at white heat a riot of individual religious judgment and imagination in such sects as the Anabaptist, Independent, Socinian and countless others. In the East such a movement divorced from all political or any strongly iconoclastic social significance would have produced simply a series of religious reformers, illumined saints, new bodies of belief with their appropriate cultural and social practice; in the West atheism and secularism were its inevitable and predestined goal. At first questioning the conventional forms of religion, the mediation of the priesthood between God and the soul and the substitution of Papal authority for the authority of the Scripture, it could not fail to go forward and question the Scripture itself and then all supernaturalism, religious belief or suprarational truth no less than outward creed and institute.

For, eventually, the evolution of Europe was determined less by the Reformation than by the Renascence; it flowered by the vigorous return of the ancient Graeco-Roman mentality of the one rather than by the Hebraic and religio-ethical temperament of the other. The Renascence gave back to Europe on one hand the free curiosity of the Greek mind, its eager search for first principles and rational laws, its delighted intellectual scrutiny of the facts of life by the force of direct observation and individual reasoning, on the other the Roman's large practicality and his sense for the ordering of life in harmony with a robust utility and the just principles of things. But both these tendencies were pursued with a passion, a seriousness, a moral and almost religious ardour which, lacking in the ancient Graeco-Roman mentality, Europe owed to her long centuries of Judaeo-Christian discipline. It was from these sources that the individualistic age of Western society sought ultimately for that principle of order and control which all human society needs and which more ancient times attempted to realise first by the materialisation of fixed symbols of truth, then by ethical type and discipline, finally by infallible authority or stereotyped convention.

Manifestly, the unrestrained use of individual illumination or judgment without either any outer standard or any generally recognisable source of truth is a perilous experiment for our imperfect race. It is likely to lead rather to a continual fluctuation and disorder of opinion than to a progressive unfolding of the truth of things. No less, the pursuit of social justice through the stark assertion of individual rights or class interests and desires must be a source of continual struggle and revolution and may end in an exaggerated assertion of the will in each to

live his own life and to satisfy his own ideas and desires which
will produce a serious malaise or a radical trouble in the social
body. Therefore on every individualistic age of mankind there is
imperative the search for two supreme desiderata. It must find
a general standard of Truth to which the individual judgment
of all will be inwardly compelled to subscribe without physical
constraint or imposition of irrational authority. And it must
reach too some principle of social order which shall be equally
founded on a universally recognisable truth of things; an order is
needed that will put a rein on desire and interest by providing at
least some intellectual and moral test which these two powerful
and dangerous forces must satisfy before they can feel justified
in asserting their claims on life. Speculative and scientific reason
for their means, the pursuit of a practicable social justice and
sound utility for their spirit, the progressive nations of Europe
set out on their search for this light and this law.

They found and held it with enthusiasm in the discoveries of
physical Science. The triumphant domination, the all-shattering
and irresistible victory of Science in nineteenth-century Europe
is explained by the absolute perfection with which it at least
seemed for a time to satisfy these great psychological wants of
the Western mind. Science seemed to it to fulfil impeccably its
search for the two supreme desiderata of an individualistic age.
Here at last was a truth of things which depended on no doubtful
Scripture or fallible human authority but which Mother Nature
herself had written in her eternal book for all to read who had
patience to observe and intellectual honesty to judge. Here were
laws, principles, fundamental facts of the world and of our being
which all could verify at once for themselves and which must
therefore satisfy and guide the free individual judgment, deliver-
ing it equally from alien compulsion and from erratic self-will.
Here were laws and truths which justified and yet controlled
the claims and desires of the individual human being; here a
science which provided a standard, a norm of knowledge, a
rational basis for life, a clear outline and sovereign means for
the progress and perfection of the individual and the race. The
attempt to govern and organise human life by verifiable Science,

by a law, a truth of things, an order and principles which all can observe and verify in their ground and fact and to which therefore all may freely and must rationally subscribe, is the culminating movement of European civilisation. It has been the fulfilment and triumph of the individualistic age of human society; it has seemed likely also to be its end, the cause of the death of individualism and its putting away and burial among the monuments of the past.

For this discovery by individual free-thought of universal laws of which the individual is almost a by-product and by which he must necessarily be governed, this attempt actually to govern the social life of humanity in conscious accordance with the mechanism of these laws seems to lead logically to the suppression of that very individual freedom which made the discovery and the attempt at all possible. In seeking the truth and law of his own being the individual seems to have discovered a truth and law which is not of his own individual being at all, but of the collectivity, the pack, the hive, the mass. The result to which this points and to which it still seems irresistibly to be driving us is a new ordering of society by a rigid economic or governmental Socialism in which the individual, deprived again of his freedom in his own interest and that of humanity, must have his whole life and action determined for him at every step and in every point from birth to old age by the well-ordered mechanism of the State.[1] We might then have a curious new version, with very important differences, of the old Asiatic or even of the old Indian order of society. In place of the religio-ethical sanction there will be a scientific and rational or naturalistic motive and rule; instead of the Brahmin Shastrakara the scientific, administrative and economic expert. In the place of the King himself observing the law and compelling with the aid and consent of the society all to tread without deviation

---

[1] We already see a violent though incomplete beginning of this line of social evolution in Fascist Italy, Nazi Germany, Communist Russia. The trend is for more and more nations to accept this beginning of a new order, and the resistance of the old order is more passive than active — it lacks the fire, enthusiasm and self-confidence which animates the innovating Idea.

the line marked out for them, the line of the Dharma, there will stand the collectivist State similarly guided and empowered. Instead of a hierarchical arrangement of classes each with its powers, privileges and duties there will be established an initial equality of education and opportunity, ultimately perhaps with a subsequent determination of function by experts who shall know us better than ourselves and choose for us our work and quality. Marriage, generation and the education of the child may be fixed by the scientific State as of old by the Shastra. For each man there will be a long stage of work for the State superintended by collectivist authorities and perhaps in the end a period of liberation, not for action but for enjoyment of leisure and personal self-improvement, answering to the Vanaprastha and Sannyasa Asramas of the old Aryan society. The rigidity of such a social state would greatly surpass that of its Asiatic forerunner; for there at least there were for the rebel, the innovator two important concessions. There was for the individual the freedom of an early Sannyasa, a renunciation of the social for the free spiritual life, and there was for the group the liberty to form a sub-society governed by new conceptions like the Sikh or the Vaishnava. But neither of these violent departures from the norm could be tolerated by a strictly economic and rigorously scientific and unitarian society. Obviously, too, there would grow up a fixed system of social morality and custom and a body of socialistic doctrine which one could not be allowed to question practically, and perhaps not even intellectually, since that would soon shatter or else undermine the system. Thus we should have a new typal order based upon purely economic capacity and function, *gunakarma*, and rapidly petrifying by the inhibition of individual liberty into a system of rationalistic conventions. And quite certainly this static order would at long last be broken by a new individualist age of revolt, led probably by the principles of an extreme philosophical Anarchism.

On the other hand, there are in operation forces which seem likely to frustrate or modify this development before it can reach its menaced consummation. In the first place, rationalistic and physical Science has overpassed itself and must before long be overtaken by a mounting flood of psychological and psychic knowledge which cannot fail to compel quite a new view of the human being and open a new vista before mankind. At the same time the Age of Reason is visibly drawing to an end; novel ideas are sweeping over the world and are being accepted with a significant rapidity, ideas inevitably subversive of any premature typal order of economic rationalism, dynamic ideas such as Nietzsche's Will-to-live, Bergson's exaltation of Intuition above intellect or the latest German philosophical tendency to acknowledge a suprarational faculty and a suprarational order of truths. Already another mental poise is beginning to settle and conceptions are on the way to apply themselves in the field of practice which promise to give the succession of the individualistic age of society not to a new typal order, but to a subjective age which may well be a great and momentous passage to a very different goal. It may be doubted whether we are not already in the morning twilight of a new period of the human cycle.

Secondly, the West in its triumphant conquest of the world has awakened the slumbering East and has produced in its midst an increasing struggle between an imported Western individualism and the old conventional principle of society. The latter is here rapidly, there slowly breaking down, but something quite different from Western individualism may very well take its place. Some opine, indeed, that Asia will reproduce Europe's Age of Reason with all its materialism and secularist individualism while Europe itself is pushing onward into new forms and ideas; but this is in the last degree improbable. On the contrary, the signs are that the individualistic period in the East will be neither of long duration nor predominantly rationalistic and secularist in its character. If then the East, as the result of its awakening, follows its own bent and evolves a novel social tendency and culture, that is bound to have an enormous effect on the direction of the world's civilisation; we can measure its probable influence by the profound results of the first reflux of the ideas even of the unawakened East upon Europe. Whatever that effect may be, it will not be in favour of any re-ordering of society on the lines of the still current tendency towards a

mechanical economism which has not ceased to dominate mind
and life in the Occident. The influence of the East is likely to be
rather in the direction of subjectivism and practical spirituality,
a greater opening of our physical existence to the realisation of
ideals other than the strong but limited aims suggested by the
life and the body in their own gross nature.

But, most important of all, the individualistic age of Europe
has in its discovery of the individual fixed among the idea-forces
of the future two of a master potency which cannot be entirely
eliminated by any temporary reaction. The first of these, now
universally accepted, is the democratic conception of the right
of all individuals as members of the society to the full life and
the full development of which they are individually capable.
It is no longer possible that we should accept as an ideal any
arrangement by which certain classes of society should arrogate
development and full social fruition to themselves while assign-
ing a bare and barren function of service alone to others. It
is now fixed that social development and well-being mean the
development and well-being of all the individuals in the society
and not merely a flourishing of the community in the mass which
resolves itself really into the splendour and power of one or
two classes. This conception has been accepted in full by all
progressive nations and is the basis of the present socialistic
tendency of the world. But in addition there is this deeper truth
which individualism has discovered, that the individual is not
merely a social unit; his existence, his right and claim to live and
grow are not founded solely on his social work and function.
He is not merely a member of a human pack, hive or ant-hill;
he is something in himself, a soul, a being, who has to fulfil
his own individual truth and law as well as his natural or his
assigned part in the truth and law of the collective existence.[2] He
demands freedom, space, initiative for his soul, for his nature,
for that puissant and tremendous thing which society so much

---

[2] This is no longer recognised by the new order, Fascist or Communistic, — here the
individual is reduced to a cell or atom of the social body. "We have destroyed" proclaims
a German exponent "the false view that men are individual beings; there is no liberty of
individuals, there is only liberty of nations or races."

distrusts and has laboured in the past either to suppress altogether or to relegate to the purely spiritual field, an individual thought, will and conscience. If he is to merge these eventually, it cannot be into the dominating thought, will and conscience of others, but into something beyond into which he and all must be both allowed and helped freely to grow. That is an idea, a truth which, intellectually recognised and given its full exterior and superficial significance by Europe, agrees at its root with the profoundest and highest spiritual conceptions of Asia and has a large part to play in the moulding of the future.

Chapter III

The Coming of the Subjective Age

THE INHERENT aim and effort and justification, the psychological seed-cause, the whole tendency of development of an individualistic age of mankind, all go back to the one dominant need of rediscovering the substantial truths of life, thought and action which have been overlaid by the falsehood of conventional standards no longer alive to the truth of the ideas from which their conventions started. It would seem at first that the shortest way would be to return to the original ideas themselves for light, to rescue the kernel of their truth from the shell of convention in which it has become incrusted. But to this course there is a great practical obstacle; and there is another which reaches beyond the surface of things, nearer to the deeper principles of the development of the soul in human society. The recovery of the old original ideas now travestied by convention is open to the practical disadvantage that it tends after a time to restore force to the conventions which the Time-Spirit is seeking to outgrow and, if or when the deeper truth-seeking tendency slackens in its impulse, the conventions re-establish their sway. They revive, modified, no doubt, but still powerful; a new incrustation sets in, the truth of things is overlaid by a more complex falsity. And even if it were otherwise, the need of a developing humanity is not to return always to its old ideas. Its need is to progress to a larger fulfilment in which, if the old is taken up, it must be transformed and exceeded. For the underlying truth of things is constant and eternal, but its mental figures, its life forms, its physical embodiments call constantly for growth and change.

It is this principle and necessity that justify an age of individualism and rationalism and make it, however short it may be, an inevitable period in the cycle. A temporary reign of the critical reason largely destructive in its action is an imperative need for human progress. In India, since the great Buddhistic upheaval of the national thought and life, there has been a series of recurrent attempts to rediscover the truth of the soul and life and get behind the veil of stifling conventions; but these have been conducted by a wide and tolerant spiritual reason, a plastic soul-intuition and deep subjective seeking, insufficiently militant and destructive. Although productive of great internal and considerable external changes, they have never succeeded in getting rid of the predominant conventional order. The work of a dissolvent and destructive intellectual criticism, though not entirely absent from some of these movements, has never gone far enough; the constructive force, insufficiently aided by the destructive, has not been able to make a wide and free space for its new formation. It is only with the period of European influence and impact that circumstances and tendencies powerful enough to enforce the beginnings of a new age of radical and effective revaluation of ideas and things have come into existence. The characteristic power of these influences has been throughout — or at any rate till quite recently — rationalistic, utilitarian and individualistic. It has compelled the national mind to view everything from a new, searching and critical standpoint, and even those who seek to preserve the present or restore the past are obliged unconsciously or half-consciously to justify their endeavour from the novel point of view and by its appropriate standards of reasoning. Throughout the East, the subjective Asiatic mind is being driven to adapt itself to the need for changed values of life and thought. It has been forced to turn upon itself both by the pressure of Western knowledge and by the compulsion of a quite changed life-need and life-environment. What it did not do from within, has come on it as a necessity from without and this externality has carried with it an immense advantage as well as great dangers.

The individualistic age is, then, a radical attempt of mankind to discover the truth and law both of the individual being and of the world to which the individual belongs. It may begin, as it began in Europe, with the endeavour to get back, more especially in the sphere of religion, to the original truth which convention has overlaid, defaced or distorted; but from that first step it must proceed to others and in the end to a general questioning of the foundations of thought and practice in all the spheres of human life and action. A revolutionary reconstruction of religion, philosophy, science, art and society is the last inevitable outcome. It proceeds at first by the light of the individual mind and reason, by its demand on life and its experience of life; but it must go from the individual to the universal. For the effort of the individual soon shows him that he cannot securely discover the truth and law of his own being without discovering some universal law and truth to which he can relate it. Of the universe he is a part; in all but his deepest spirit he is its subject, a small cell in that tremendous organic mass: his substance is drawn from its substance and by the law of its life the law of his life is determined and governed. From a new view and knowledge of the world must proceed his new view and knowledge of himself, of his power and capacity and limitations, of his claim on existence and the high road and the distant or immediate goal of his individual and social destiny.

In Europe and in modern times this has taken the form of a clear and potent physical Science: it has proceeded by the discovery of the laws of the physical universe and the economic and sociological conditions of human life as determined by the physical being of man, his environment, his evolutionary history, his physical and vital, his individual and collective need. But after a time it must become apparent that the knowledge of the physical world is not the whole of knowledge; it must appear that man is a mental as well as a physical and vital being and even much more essentially mental than physical or vital. Even though his psychology is strongly affected and limited by his physical being and environment, it is not at its roots determined by them, but constantly reacts, subtly determines their action, effects even their new-shaping by the force of his psychological demand on life. His economic state and social institutions are themselves governed by his psychological demand on the possibilities, circumstances, tendencies created by the relation between the mind and soul of humanity and its life and body. Therefore to find the truth of things and the law of his being in relation to that truth he must go deeper and fathom the subjective secret of himself and things as well as their objective forms and surroundings.

This he may attempt to do for a time by the power of the critical and analytic reason which has already carried him so far; but not for very long. For in his study of himself and the world he cannot but come face to face with the soul in himself and the soul in the world and find it to be an entity so profound, so complex, so full of hidden secrets and powers that his intellectual reason betrays itself as an insufficient light and a fumbling seeker: it is successfully analytical only of superficialities and of what lies just behind the superficies. The need of a deeper knowledge must then turn him to the discovery of new powers and means within himself. He finds that he can only know himself entirely by becoming actively self-conscious and not merely self-critical, by more and more living in his soul and acting out of it rather than floundering on surfaces, by putting himself into conscious harmony with that which lies behind his superficial mentality and psychology and by enlightening his reason and making dynamic his action through this deeper light and power to which he thus opens. In this process the rationalistic ideal begins to subject itself to the ideal of intuitional knowledge and a deeper self-awareness; the utilitarian standard gives way to the aspiration towards self-consciousness and self-realisation; the rule of living according to the manifest laws of physical Nature is replaced by the effort towards living according to the veiled Law and Will and Power active in the life of the world and in the inner and outer life of humanity.

All these tendencies, though in a crude, initial and ill-developed form, are manifest now in the world and are growing from day to day with a significant rapidity. And their emergence and greater dominance means the transition from the rationalistic and utilitarian period of human development which individualism has created to a greater subjective age of society. The change began by a rapid turning of the current of thought into large and profound movements contradictory of the old intellectual standards, a swift breaking of the old tables. The materialism of the nineteenth century gave place first to a novel and profound vitalism which has taken various forms from Nietzsche's theory of the Will to be and Will to Power as the root and law of life to the new pluralistic and pragmatic philosophy which is pluralistic because it has its eye fixed on life rather than on the soul and pragmatic because it seeks to interpret being in the terms of force and action rather than of light and knowledge. These tendencies of thought, which had until yesterday a profound influence on the life and thought of Europe prior to the outbreak of the great War, especially in France and Germany, were not a mere superficial recoil from intellectualism to life and action, — although in their application by lesser minds they often assumed that aspect; they were an attempt to read profoundly and live by the Life-Soul of the universe and tended to be deeply psychological and subjective in their method. From behind them, arising in the void created by the discrediting of the old rationalistic intellectualism, there had begun to arise a new Intuitionalism, not yet clearly aware of its own drive and nature, which seeks through the forms and powers of Life for that which is behind Life and sometimes even lays as yet uncertain hands on the sealed doors of the Spirit.

The art, music and literature of the world, always a sure index of the vital tendencies of the age, have also undergone a profound revolution in the direction of an ever-deepening subjectivism. The great objective art and literature of the past no longer commands the mind of the new age. The first tendency was, as in thought so in literature, an increasing psychological vitalism which sought to represent penetratingly the most subtle psychological impulses and tendencies of man as they started to the surface in his emotional, aesthetic and vitalistic cravings and activities. Composed with great skill and subtlety but without any real insight into the law of man's being, these creations seldom got behind the reverse side of our surface emotions, sensations and actions which they minutely analysed in their details but without any wide or profound light of knowledge; they were perhaps more immediately interesting but ordinarily inferior as art to the old literature which at least seized firmly and with a large and powerful mastery on its province. Often they described the malady of Life rather than its health and power, or the riot and revolt of its cravings, vehement and therefore impotent and unsatisfied, rather than its dynamis of self-expression and self-possession. But to this movement which reached its highest creative power in Russia, there succeeded a turn towards a more truly psychological art, music and literature, mental, intuitional, psychic rather than vitalistic, departing in fact from a superficial vitalism as much as its predecessors departed from the objective mind of the past. This new movement aimed like the new philosophic Intuitionalism at a real rending of the veil, the seizure by the human mind of that which does not overtly express itself, the touch and penetration into the hidden soul of things. Much of it was still infirm, unsubstantial in its grasp on what it pursued, rudimentary in its forms, but it initiated a decisive departure of the human mind from its old moorings and pointed the direction in which it is being piloted on a momentous voyage of discovery, the discovery of a new world within which must eventually bring about the creation of a new world without in life and society. Art and literature seem definitely to have taken a turn towards a subjective search into what may be called the hidden inside of things and away from the rational and objective canon or motive.

Already in the practical dealing with life there are advanced progressive tendencies which take their inspiration from this profounder subjectivism. Nothing indeed has yet been firmly accomplished, all is as yet tentative initiation and the first feeling out towards a material shape for this new spirit. The dominant activities of the world, the great recent events such as the enormous clash of nations in Europe and the stirrings and changes within the nations which preceded and followed it, were rather the result of a confused half struggle half effort at accommodation between the old intellectual and materialistic and the new still superficial subjective and vitalistic impulses in the West. The latter unenlightened by a true inner growth of the soul were necessarily impelled to seize upon the former and utilise them for their unbridled demand upon life; the world was moving towards a monstrously perfect organisation of the Will-to-live and the Will-to-power and it was this that threw itself out in the clash of War and has now found or is finding new forms of life for itself which show better its governing idea and motive. The Asuric or even Rakshasic character of the recent world-collision was due to this formidable combination of a falsely enlightened vitalistic motive-power with a great force of servile intelligence and reasoning contrivance subjected to it as instrument and the genius of an accomplished materialistic Science as its Djinn, its giant worker of huge, gross and soulless miracles. The War was the bursting of the explosive force so created and, even though it strewed the world with ruins, its after results may well have prepared the collapse, as they have certainly produced a disintegrating chaos or at least poignant disorder, of the monstrous combination which produced it, and by that salutary ruin are emptying the field of human life of the principal obstacles to a truer development towards a higher goal.

Behind it all the hope of the race lies in those infant and as yet subordinate tendencies which carry in them the seed of a new subjective and psychic dealing of man with his own being, with his fellow-men and with the ordering of his individual and social life. The characteristic note of these tendencies may be seen in the new ideas about the education and upbringing of the child that became strongly current in the pre-war era. Formerly, education was merely a mechanical forcing of the child's nature into arbitrary grooves of training and knowledge in which his individual subjectivity was the last thing considered, and his family upbringing was a constant repression and compulsory shaping of his habits, his thoughts, his character into the mould fixed for them by the conventional ideas or individual interests and ideals of the teachers and parents. The discovery that education must be a bringing out of the child's own intellectual and moral capacities to their highest possible value and must be based on the psychology of the child-nature was a step forward towards a more healthy because a more subjective system; but it still fell short because it still regarded him as an object to be handled and moulded by the teacher, to be educated. But at least there was a glimmering of the realisation that each human being is a self-developing soul and that the business of both parent and teacher is to enable and to help the child to educate himself, to develop his own intellectual, moral, aesthetic and practical capacities and to grow freely as an organic being, not to be kneaded and pressured into form like an inert plastic material. It is not yet realised what this soul is or that the true secret, whether with child or man, is to help him to find his deeper self, the real psychic entity within. That, if we ever give it a chance to come forward, and still more if we call it into the foreground as "the leader of the march set in our front", will itself take up most of the business of education out of our hands and develop the capacity of the psychological being towards a realisation of its potentialities of which our present mechanical view of life and man and external routine methods of dealing with them prevent us from having any experience or forming any conception. These new educational methods are on the straight way to this truer dealing. The closer touch attempted with the psychical entity behind the vital and physical mentality and an increasing reliance on its possibilities must lead to the ultimate discovery that man is inwardly a soul and a conscious power of the Divine and that the evocation of this real man within is the right object of education and indeed of all human life if it would find and live according to the hidden Truth and deepest law of its own being. That was the knowledge which the ancients sought to express through religious and social symbolism, and subjectivism is a road of return to the lost knowledge. First deepening man's inner experience, restoring perhaps on an unprecedented scale insight and self-knowledge to the race, it must end by revolutionising his social and collective self-expression.

Meanwhile, the nascent subjectivism preparative of the new age has shown itself not so much in the relations of individuals or in the dominant ideas and tendencies of social development, which are still largely rationalistic and materialistic and only vaguely touched by the deeper subjective tendency, but in the new collective self-consciousness of man in that organic mass of his life which he has most firmly developed in the past, the nation. It is here that it has already begun to produce powerful results whether as a vitalistic or as a psychical subjectivism, and it is here that we shall see most clearly what is its actual drift, its deficiencies, its dangers as well as the true purpose and conditions of a subjective age of humanity and the goal towards which the social cycle, entering this phase, is intended to arrive in its wide revolution.

Chapter IV

The Discovery of the Nation-Soul

THE PRIMAL law and purpose of the individual life is to seek its own self-development. Consciously or half-consciously or with an obscure unconscious groping it strives always and rightly strives at self-formulation, — to find itself, to discover within itself the law and power of its own being and to fulfil it. This aim in it is fundamental, right, inevitable because, even after all qualifications have been made and caveats entered, the individual is not merely the ephemeral physical creature, a form of mind and body that aggregates and dissolves, but a being, a living power of the eternal Truth, a self-manifesting spirit. In the same way the primal law and purpose of a society, community or nation is to seek its own self-fulfilment; it strives rightly to find itself, to become aware within itself of the law and power of its own being and to fulfil it as perfectly as possible, to realise all its potentialities, to live its own self-revealing life. The reason is the same; for this too is a being, a living power of the eternal Truth, a self-manifestation of the cosmic Spirit, and it is there to express and fulfil in its own way and to the degree of its capacities the special truth and power and meaning of the cosmic Spirit that is within it. The nation or society, like the individual, has a body, an organic life, a moral and aesthetic temperament, a developing mind and a soul behind all these signs and powers for the sake of which they exist. One may say even that, like the individual, it essentially is a soul rather than has one; it is a group-soul that, once having attained to a separate distinctness, must become more and more self-conscious and find itself more and more fully as it develops its corporate action and mentality and its organic self-expressive life.

The parallel is just at every turn because it is more than a parallel; it is a real identity of nature. There is only this difference that the group-soul is much more complex because it has a great number of partly self-conscious mental individuals for the constituents of its physical being instead of an association of merely vital subconscious cells. At first, for this very reason, it seems more crude, primitive and artificial in the forms it takes; for it has a more difficult task before it, it needs a longer time to find itself, it is more fluid and less easily organic. When it does succeed in getting out of the stage of vaguely conscious self-formation, its first definite self-consciousness is objective much more than subjective. And so far as it is subjective, it is apt to be superficial or loose and vague. This objectiveness comes out very strongly in the ordinary emotional conception of the nation which centres round its geographical, its most outward and material aspect, the passion for the land in which we dwell, the land of our fathers, the land of our birth, *country, patria, vaterland, janma-bhūmi*. When we realise that the land is only the shell of the body, though a very living shell indeed and potent in its influences on the nation, when we begin to feel that its more real body is the men and women who compose the nation-unit, a body ever changing, yet always the same like that of the individual man, we are on the way to a truly subjective communal consciousness. For then we have some chance of realising that even the physical being of the society is a subjective power, not a mere objective existence. Much more is it in its inner self a great corporate soul with all the possibilities and dangers of the soul-life.

The objective view of society has reigned throughout the historical period of humanity in the West; it has been sufficiently strong though not absolutely engrossing in the East. Rulers, people and thinkers alike have understood by their national existence a political status, the extent of their borders, their economic well-being and expansion, their laws, institutions and the working of these things. For this reason political and economic motives have everywhere predominated on the surface and history has been a record of their operations and influence. The one subjective and psychological force consciously admitted and with difficulty deniable has been that of the individual. This predominance is so great that most modern historians and some political thinkers have concluded that objective necessities are by law of Nature the only really determining forces, all else is result or superficial accidents of these forces. Scientific history has been conceived as if it must be a record and appreciation of the environmental motives of political action, of the play of economic forces and developments and the course of institutional evolution. The few who still valued the psychological element have kept their eye fixed on individuals and are not far from conceiving of history as a mass of biographies. The truer and more comprehensive science of the future will see that these conditions only apply to the imperfectly self-conscious period of national development. Even then there was always a greater subjective force working behind individuals, policies, economic movements and the change of institutions; but it worked for the most part subconsciously, more as a subliminal self than as a conscious mind. It is when this subconscious power of the group-soul comes to the surface that nations begin to enter into possession of their subjective selves; they set about getting, however vaguely or imperfectly, at their souls.

Certainly, there is always a vague sense of this subjective existence at work even on the surface of the communal mentality. But so far as this vague sense becomes at all definite, it concerns itself mostly with details and unessentials, national idiosyncrasies, habits, prejudices, marked mental tendencies. It is, so to speak, an objective sense of subjectivity. As man has been accustomed to look on himself as a body and a life, the physical animal with a certain moral or immoral temperament, and the things of the mind have been regarded as a fine flower and attainment of the physical life rather than themselves anything essential or the sign of something essential, so and much more has the community regarded that small part of its subjective self of which it becomes aware. It clings indeed always to its idiosyncrasies, habits, prejudices, but in a blind objective fashion, insisting on their most external aspect and not at all going behind them to that for which they stand, that which they try blindly to express.

This has been the rule not only with the nation, but with

all communities. A Church is an organised religious community and religion, if anything in the world, ought to be subjective; for its very reason for existence — where it is not merely an ethical creed with a supernatural authority — is to find and realise the soul. Yet religious history has been almost entirely, except in the time of the founders and their immediate successors, an insistence on things objective, rites, ceremonies, authority, church governments, dogmas, forms of belief. Witness the whole external religious history of Europe, that strange sacrilegious tragi-comedy of discords, sanguinary disputations, "religious" wars, persecutions, State churches and all else that is the very negation of the spiritual life. It is only recently that men have begun seriously to consider what Christianity, Catholicism, Islam really mean and are in their soul, that is to say, in their very reality and essence.

But now we have, very remarkably, very swiftly coming to the surface this new psychological tendency of the communal consciousness. Now first we hear of the soul of a nation and, what is more to the purpose, actually see nations feeling for their souls, trying to find them, seriously endeavouring to act from the new sense and make it consciously operative in the common life and action. It is only natural that this tendency should have been, for the most part, most powerful in new nations or in those struggling to realise themselves in spite of political subjection or defeat. For these need more to feel the difference between themselves and others so that they may assert and justify their individuality as against the powerful superlife which tends to absorb or efface it. And precisely because their objective life is feeble and it is difficult to affirm it by its own strength in the adverse circumstances, there is more chance of their seeking for their individuality and its force of self-assertion in that which is subjective and psychological or at least in that which has a subjective or a psychological significance.

Therefore in nations so circumstanced this tendency of self-finding has been most powerful and has even created in some of them a new type of national movement, as in Ireland and India. This and no other was the root-meaning of Swadeshism in Bengal and of the Irish movement in its earlier less purely political stages. The emergence of Bengal as a sub-nation in India was throughout a strongly subjective movement and in its later development it became very consciously that. The movement of 1905 in Bengal pursued a quite new conception of the nation not merely as a country, but a soul, a psychological, almost a spiritual being and, even when acting from economical and political motives, it sought to dynamise them by this subjective conception and to make them instruments of self-expression rather than objects in themselves. We must not forget, however, that in the first stages these movements followed in their superficial thought the old motives of an objective and mostly political self-consciousness. The East indeed is always more subjective than the West and we can see the subjective tinge even in its political movements whether in Persia, India or China, and even in the very imitative movement of the Japanese resurgence. But it is only recently that this subjectivism has become self-conscious. We may therefore conclude that the conscious and deliberate subjectivism of certain nations was only the sign and precursor of a general change in humanity and has been helped forward by local circumstances, but was not really dependent upon them or in any sense their product.

This general change is incontestable; it is one of the capital phenomena of the tendencies of national and communal life at the present hour. The conception to which Ireland and India have been the first to give a definite formula, "to be ourselves", — so different from the impulse and ambition of dependent or unfortunate nations in the past which was rather to become like others, — is now more and more a generally accepted motive of national life. It opens the way to great dangers and errors, but it is the essential condition for that which has now become the demand of the Time-Spirit on the human race, that it shall find subjectively, not only in the individual, but in the nation and in the unity of the human race itself, its deeper being, its inner law, its real self and live according to that and no longer by artificial standards. This tendency was preparing itself everywhere and partly coming to the surface before the War, but most prominently, as we have said, in new nations like Germany or in dependent nations like Ireland and India. The shock of the war brought about from its earliest moments an immediate — and for the time being a militant — emergence of the same deeper self-consciousness everywhere. Crude enough were most of its first manifestations, often of a really barbarous and reactionary crudeness. Especially, it tended to repeat the Teutonic lapse, preparing not only "to be oneself", which is entirely right, but to live solely for and to oneself, which, if pushed beyond a certain point, becomes a disastrous error. For it is necessary, if the subjective age of humanity is to produce its best fruits, that the nations should become conscious not only of their own but of each other's souls and learn to respect, to help and to profit, not only economically and intellectually but subjectively and spiritually, by each other.

The great determining force has been the example and the aggression of Germany; the example, because no other nation has so self-consciously, so methodically, so intelligently, and from the external point of view so successfully sought to find, to dynamise, to live itself and make the most of its own power of being; its aggression, because the very nature and declared watchwords of the attack have tended to arouse a defensive self-consciousness in the assailed and forced them to perceive what was the source of this tremendous strength and to perceive too that they themselves must seek consciously an answering strength in the same deeper sources. Germany was for the time the most remarkable present instance of a nation preparing for the subjective stage because it had, in the first place, a certain kind of vision — unfortunately intellectual rather than illuminated — and the courage to follow it — unfortunately again a vital and intellectual rather than a spiritual hardihood, — and, secondly, being master of its destinies, was able to order its own life so as to express its self-vision. We must not be misled by appearances into thinking that the strength of Germany was created by Bismarck or directed by the Kaiser Wilhelm II. Rather the appearance of Bismarck was in many respects a misfortune for the growing nation because his rude and powerful hand precipitated its subjectivity into form and action at too early a stage; a longer period of incubation might have produced results less disastrous to itself, if less violently stimulative to humanity. The real source of this great subjective force which has been so much disfigured in its objective action, was not in Germany's statesmen and soldiers — for the most part poor enough types of men — but came from her great philosophers, Kant, Hegel, Fichte, Nietzsche, from her great thinker and poet Goethe, from her great musicians, Beethoven and Wagner, and from all in the German soul and temperament which they represented. A nation whose master achievement has lain almost entirely in the two spheres of philosophy and music, is clearly predestined to lead in the turn to subjectivism and to produce a profound result for good or evil on the beginnings of a subjective age.

This was one side of the predestination of Germany; the other is to be found in her scholars, educationists, scientists, organisers. It was the industry, the conscientious diligence, the fidelity to ideas, the honest and painstaking spirit of work for which the nation has been long famous. A people may be highly gifted in the subjective capacities, and yet if it neglects to culti-vate this lower side of our complex nature, it will fail to build that bridge between the idea and imagination and the world of facts, between the vision and the force, which makes realisation possible; its higher powers may become a joy and inspiration to the world, but it will never take possession of its own world until it has learned the humbler lesson. In Germany the bridge was there, though it ran mostly through a dark tunnel with a gulf underneath; for there was no pure transmission from the subjec-tive mind of the thinkers and singers to the objective mind of the scholars and organisers. The misapplication by Treitschke of the teaching of Nietzsche to national and international uses which would have profoundly disgusted the philosopher himself, is an example of this obscure transmission. But still a transmission there was. For more than a half-century Germany turned a deep eye of subjective introspection on herself and things and ideas in search of the truth of her own being and of the world, and for another half-century a patient eye of scientific research on the objective means for organising what she had or thought she had gained. And something was done, something indeed powerful and enormous, but also in certain directions, not in all, misshapen and disconcerting. Unfortunately, those directions were precisely the very central lines on which to go wrong is to miss the goal.

It may be said, indeed, that the last result of the something done — the war, the collapse, the fierce reaction towards the rigid, armoured, aggressive, formidable Nazi State, — is not only discouraging enough, but a clear warning to abandon that path and go back to older and safer ways. But the misuse of great powers is no argument against their right use. To go back is impossible; the attempt is always, indeed, an illusion; we have all to do the same thing which Germany has attempted, but to take care not to do it likewise. Therefore we must look beyond the red mist of blood of the War and the dark fuliginous confusion and chaos which now oppress the world to see why and where was the failure. For her failure which became evident by the turn her action took and was converted for the time being into total collapse, was clear even then to the dispassionate thinker who seeks only the truth. That befell her which sometimes befalls the seeker on the path of Yoga, the art of conscious self-finding, — a path exposed to far profounder perils than beset ordinarily the average man, — when he follows a false light to his spiritual ruin. She had mistaken her vital ego for herself; she had sought for her soul and found only her force. For she had said, like the Asura, "I am my body, my life, my mind, my temperament," and become attached with a Titanic force to these; especially she had said, "I am my life and body," and than that there can be no greater mistake for man or nation. The soul of man or nation is something more and diviner than that; it is greater than its instruments and cannot be shut up in a physical, a vital, a mental or a temperamental formula. So to confine it, even though the false formation be embodied in the armour-plated social body of a huge collective human dinosaurus, can only stifle the growth of the inner Reality and end in decay or the extinction that overtakes all that is unplastic and unadaptable.

It is evident that there is a false as well as a true subjectivism and the errors to which the subjective trend may be liable are as great as its possibilities and may well lead to capital disasters. This distinction must be clearly grasped if the road of this stage of social evolution is to be made safe for the human race.

Chapter V

True and False Subjectivism

THE SUBJECTIVE stage of human development is that critical juncture in which, having gone forward from symbols, types, conventions, having turned its gaze superficially on the individual being to discover his truth and right law of action and its relation to the superficial and external truth and law of the universe, our race begins to gaze deeper, to see and feel what is behind the outside and below the surface and therefore to live from within. It is a step towards self-knowledge and towards living in and from the self, away from knowledge of things as the not-self and from the living according to this objective idea of life and the universe. Everything depends on how that step is taken, to what kind of subjectivity we arrive and how far we go in self-knowledge; for here the dangers of error are as great and far-reaching as the results of right seeking. The symbolic, the typal, the conventional age avoid these dangers by building a wall of self-limitation against them; and it is because this wall becomes in the end a prison of self-ignorance that it has to be broken down and the perilous but fruitful adventure of subjectivism undertaken.

A psychic self-knowledge tells us that there are in our being many formal, frontal, apparent or representative selves and only one that is entirely secret and real; to rest in the apparent and to mistake it for the real is the one general error, root of all others and cause of all our stumbling and suffering, to which man is exposed by the nature of his mentality. We may apply this truth to the attempt of man to live by the law of his subjective being whether as an individual or as a social unit one in its corporate mind and body.

For this is the sense of the characteristic turn which modern civilisation is taking. Everywhere we are beginning, though still sparsely and in a groping tentative fashion, to approach things from the subjective standpoint. In education our object is to know the psychology of the child as he grows into man and to found our systems of teaching and training upon that basis. The new aim is to help the child to develop his intellectual, aesthetic, emotional, moral, spiritual being and his communal life and impulses out of his own temperament and capacities, — a very different object from that of the old education which was simply to pack so much stereotyped knowledge into his resisting brain and impose a stereotyped rule of conduct on his struggling and dominated impulses.[1] In dealing with the criminal the most advanced societies are no longer altogether satisfied with regarding him as a law-breaker to be punished, imprisoned, terrified, hanged or else tortured physically and morally, whether as a revenge for his revolt or as an example to others; there is a growing attempt to understand him, to make allowance for his heredity, environment and inner deficiencies and to change him from within rather than crush him from without. In the general view of society itself, we begin to regard the community, the nation or any other fixed grouping of men as a living organism with a subjective being of its own and a corresponding growth and natural development which it is its business to bring to perfection and fruition. So far, good; the greater knowledge, the truer depth, the wiser humanity of this new view of things are obvious. But so also are the limitations of our knowledge and experience on this new path and the possibility of serious errors and stumblings.

If we look at the new attempt of nations, whether subject or imperial, to fulfil themselves consciously and especially at the momentous experiment of the subjective German nationality, we shall see the starting-point of these possible errors. The first danger arises from the historical fact of the evolution of the subjective age out of the individualistic; and the first enormous stumble has accordingly been to transform the error

---

[1] There has been a rude set-back to this development in totalitarian States whose theory is that the individual does not exist and only the life of the community matters, but this new larger view still holds its own in freer countries.

of individualistic egoism into the more momentous error of a great communal egoism. The individual seeking for the law of his being can only find it safely if he regards clearly two great psychological truths and lives in that clear vision. First, the ego is not the self; there is one self of all and the soul is a portion of that universal Divinity. The fulfilment of the individual is not the utmost development of his egoistic intellect, vital force, physical well-being and the utmost satisfaction of his mental, emotional, physical cravings, but the flowering of the divine in him to its utmost capacity of wisdom, power, love and universality and through this flowering his utmost realisation of all the possible beauty and delight of existence.

The will to be, the will to power, the will to know are perfectly legitimate, their satisfaction the true law of our existence and to discourage and repress them improperly is to mutilate our being and dry up or diminish the sources of life and growth. But their satisfaction must not be egoistic, — not for any other reason moral or religious, but simply because they cannot so be satisfied. The attempt always leads to an eternal struggle with other egoisms, a mutual wounding and hampering, even a mutual destruction in which if we are conquerors today, we are the conquered or the slain tomorrow; for we exhaust ourselves and corrupt ourselves in the dangerous attempt to live by the destruction and exploitation of others. Only that which lives in its own self-existence can endure. And generally, to devour others is to register oneself also as a subject and predestined victim of Death.

No doubt, so long as we live without self-knowledge, we can do no other; men and nations have to act and think egoistically, because in their self-ignorance that is the only life known to them, and to live is their God-given impulse; therefore they must live egoistically rather than not at all, with whatever curb of law, ethics and practical common sense of self-restraint nature and experience have taught them. But subjectivism is in its very nature an attempt at self-knowledge and at living by a true self-knowledge and by an inner strength, and there is no real gain in it if we only repeat the old error in new terms.

Therefore we must find out that the true individual is not the ego, but the divine individuality which is through our evolution preparing to emerge in us; its emergence and satisfaction and not the satisfaction of the mere egoistic will-to-live for the sake of one's lower members is the true object at which a humanity subjectively seeking to know and fulfil its own deepest law and truth should increasingly aim.

The second psychic truth the individual has to grasp is this, that he is not only himself, but is in solidarity with all of his kind, — let us leave aside for the moment that which seems to be not of his kind. That which we are has expressed itself through the individual, but also through the universality, and though each has to fulfil itself in its own way, neither can succeed independently of the other. The society has no right to crush or efface the individual for its own better development or self-satisfaction; the individual, so long at least as he chooses to live in the world, has no right to disregard for the sake of his own solitary satisfaction and development his fellow-beings and to live at war with them or seek a selfishly isolated good. And when we say, no right, it is from no social, moral or religious standpoint, but from the most positive and simply with a view to the law of existence itself. For neither the society nor the individual can so develop to their fulfilment. Every time the society crushes or effaces the individual, it is inflicting a wound on itself and depriving its own life of priceless sources of stimulation and growth. The individual too cannot flourish by himself; for the universal, the unity and collectivity of his fellow-beings, is his present source and stock; it is the thing whose possibilities he individually expresses, even when he transcends its immediate level, and of which in his phenomenal being he is one result. Its depression strikes eventually at his own sources of life, by its increasing he also increases. This is what a true subjectivism teaches us, — first, that we are a higher self than our ego or our members, secondly, that we are in our life and being not only ourselves but all others; for there is a secret solidarity which our egoism may kick at and strive against, but from which we cannot escape. It is the old Indian discovery that our real "I" is a Supreme Being which is our true self and which it is our business to discover and consciously become and, secondly, that that Being is one in all, expressed in the individual and in the collectivity,[2] and only by admitting and realising our unity with others can we entirely fulfil our true self-being.[3]

Of these two truths mankind has had some vague vision in the principle with regard to the individual, though it has made only a very poor and fragmentary attempt to regard them in practice and in nine-tenths of its life has been busy departing from them — even where it outwardly professed something of the law. But they apply not only to the individual but to the nation. Here was the first error of the German subjectivism. Reasoning of the Absolute and the individual and the universal, it looked into itself and saw that in fact, as a matter of life, That seemed to express itself as the ego and, reasoning from the conclusions of modern Science, it saw the individual merely as a cell of the collective ego. This collective ego was, then, the greatest actual organised expression of life and to that all ought to be subservient, for so could Nature and its evolution best be assisted and affirmed. The greater human collectivity exists, but it is an inchoate and unorganised existence, and its growth can best be developed by the better development of the most efficient organised collective life already existing; practically, then, by the growth, perfection and domination of the most advanced nations, or possibly of the one most advanced nation, the collective ego which has best realised the purpose of Nature and whose victory and rule is therefore the will of God. For all organised lives, all self-conscious egos are in a state of war, sometimes overt, sometimes covert, sometimes complete, sometimes partial, and by the survival of the best is secured the highest advance of the race. And where was the best, which was the most advanced, self-realising, efficient, highest-cultured nation,

---

[2] *vyaṣṭi* and *samaṣṭi*.
[3] There is another side of the truth in which this interdependence is not so imperative, but that is a phenomenon of spiritual evolution which has nothing to do with the present subject.

if not, by common admission as well as in Germany's own self-vision, Germany itself? To fulfil then the collective German ego and secure its growth and domination was at once the right law of reason, the supreme good of humanity and the mission of the great and supreme Teutonic race.[4]

From this egoistic self-vision flowed a number of logical consequences, each in itself a separate subjective error. First, since the individual is only a cell of the collectivity, his life must be entirely subservient to the efficient life of the nation. He must be made efficient indeed, — the nation should see to his education, proper living, disciplined life, carefully trained and subordinated activity, — but as a part of the machine or a disciplined instrument of the national Life. Initiative must be the collectivity's, execution the individual's. But where was that vague thing, the collectivity, and how could it express itself not only as a self-conscious, but an organised and efficient collective will and self-directing energy? The State, there was the secret. Let the State be perfect, dominant, all-pervading, all-seeing, all-effecting; so only could the collective ego be concentrated, find itself, and its life be brought to the highest pitch of strength, organisation and efficiency. Thus Germany founded and established the growing modern error of the cult of the State and the growing subordination driving in the end towards the efface-ment of the individual. We can see what it gained, an immense collective power and a certain kind of perfection and scientific adjustment of means to end and a high general level of economic, intellectual and social efficiency, — apart from the tremendous momentary force which the luminous fulfilment of a great idea gives to man or nation. What it had begun to lose is as yet only slightly apparent, — all that deeper life, vision, intuitive power, force of personality, psychical sweetness and largeness which the free individual brings as his gift to the race.

Secondly, since the State is supreme, the representative of the

---

[4] The emphasis has somewhat shifted now and taken its stand more upon the crude vitalistic notions of blood, race, life-room, but the old idea is there giving more force to the later formulation.

Divine or the highest realised functioning of human existence, and has a divine right to the obedience, the unquestioning service and the whole activity of the individual, the service of State and community is the only absolute rule of morality. Within the State this may include and sanction all other moral rules because there no rebel egoism can be allowed, for the individual ego must be lost in that of the State or become part of it and all condition of covert or overt war must be abrogated in obedience to the collective good as determined by the collective will. But in relation to other States, to other collective egos the general condition, the effective law is still that of war, of strife between sharply divided egoisms each seeking to fulfil itself, each hampered and restricted in its field by the others. War then is the whole business of the State in its relation to other States, a war of arms, a war of commerce, a war of ideas and cultures, a war of collective personalities each seeking to possess the world or at least to dominate and be first in the world. Here there can enter no morality except that of success, though the pretence of morality may be a useful stratagem of war. To serve the State, the German collectivity which is his greater and real self is the business of the German individual whether at home or abroad, and to that end everything which succeeds is justifiable. Inefficiency, incompetence, failure are the only immorality. In war every method is justified which leads to the military success of the State, in peace every method which prepares it; for peace between nations is only a covert state of war. And as war is the means of physical survival and domination, so commerce is the means of economic survival and domination; it is in fact only another kind of war, another department of the struggle to live, one physical, the other vital. And the life and the body are, so Science has assured us, the whole of existence.

Thirdly, since the survival of the best is the highest good of mankind and the survival of the best is secured by the elimination of the unfit and the assimilation of the less fit, the conquest of the world by German culture is the straight path of human progress. But culture is not, in this view, merely a state of knowledge or a system or cast of ideas and moral and aesthetic tendencies;

culture is life governed by ideas, but by ideas based on the truths of life and so organised as to bring it to its highest efficiency. Therefore all life not capable of this culture and this efficiency must be eliminated or trodden down, all life capable of it but not actually reaching to it must be taken up and assimilated. But capacity is always a matter of genus and species and in humanity a matter of race. Logically, then, the Teutonic[5] race is alone entirely capable, and therefore all Teutonic races must be taken into Germany and become part of the German collectivity; races less capable but not wholly unfit must be Germanised; others, hopelessly decadent like the Latins of Europe and America or naturally inferior like the vast majority of the Africans and Asiatics, must be replaced where possible, like the Hereros, or, where not possible, dominated, exploited and treated according to their inferiority. So evolution would advance, so the human race grow towards its perfection.[6]

We need not suppose that all Germany thought in this strenuous fashion, as it was too long represented, or that the majority thought thus consciously; but it is sufficient that an energetic minority of thinkers and strong personalities should seize upon the national life and impress certain tendencies upon it for these to prevail practically or at the least to give a general trend subconsciously even where the thought itself is not actually proposed in the conscious mind. And the actual events of the present hour seem to show that it was this gospel that partly consciously, partly subconsciously or half articulately had taken possession of the collective German mind. It is easy to deride the rigidity of this terrible logic or riddle it with the ideas and truths it has ignored, and it is still easier to abhor, fear, hate and spew at it while practically following its principles in our own action with less openness, thoroughness and courage. But it is more profitable to begin by seeing that behind it there was and is a tremendous sincerity which is the secret of its force, and a

---

[5] "Nordic" is now the established term.
[6] This was written more than thirty years ago, but later developments have emphasised and brought out the truth of the description which was indeed much less apparent then.

sort of perverse honesty in its errors; the sincerity which tries to look straight at one's own conduct and the facts of life and the honesty to proclaim the real principles of that conduct and not — except as an occasional diplomacy — profess others with the lips while disregarding them in the practice. And if this ideal is to be defeated not merely for a time in the battle-field and in the collective person of the nation or nations professing it, as happened abortively in the War, but in the mind of man and in the life of the human race, an equal sincerity and a less perverse honesty has to be practised by those who have arrived at a better law.

The German gospel has evidently two sides, the internal and the external, the cult of the State, nation or community and the cult of international egoism. In the first, Germany, even if for a time entirely crushed in the battle-field, seems to have already secured the victory in the moral sense of the human race. The unsparing compulsion as against the assistance of the individual by the State[7] — for his and the common good, of course, but who professes to compel for harm? — is almost everywhere either dominant or else growing into a strong and prevailing current of opinion; the champions of individual freedom are now a morally defeated and dwindling army who can only fight on in the hope of a future reaction or of saving something of their principle from the wreck. On the external side, the international, the battle of ideas still goes on, but there were from the beginning ominous signs;[8] and now after the physical war with its first psychological results is well over, we are already able to see in which direction the tide is likely to flow. War is a dangerous teacher and physical victory leads often to a moral defeat. Germany, defeated in the war, has won in the after war; the German gospel rearisen in a sterner and fiercer avatar threatens to sweep over all Europe.

---

[7] Not always in the form of Socialism, Bolshevik Communism or Fascism. Other forms of government that are nominally based on the principles of individualistic democracy and freedom have begun to follow the same trend under the disguise or the mere profession of its opposite.

[8] The League of Nations was at no time a contrary sign. Whatever incidental or temporary good it might achieve, it could only be an instrument for the domination of the rest of the earth by Europe and of all by two or three major nations.

It is necessary, if we are not to deceive ourselves, to note that even in this field what Germany has done is to systematise certain strong actual tendencies and principles of international action to the exclusion of all that either professed to resist or did actually modify them. If a sacred egoism — and the expression did not come from Teutonic lips — is to govern international relations, then it is difficult to deny the force of the German position. The theory of inferior and decadent races was loudly proclaimed by other than German thinkers and has governed, with whatever assuaging scruples, the general practice of military domination and commercial exploitation of the weak by the strong; all that Germany has done is to attempt to give it a wider extension and more rigorous execution and apply it to European as well as to Asiatic and African peoples. Even the severity or brutality of her military methods or of her ways of colonial or internal political repression, taken at their worst, for much once stated against her has been proved and admitted to be deliberate lies manufactured by her enemies, was only a crystallising of certain recent tendencies towards the revival of ancient and mediaeval hardheartedness in the race. The use and even the justification of massacre and atrocious cruelty in war on the ground of military exigency and in the course of commercial exploitation or in the repression of revolt and disorder has been quite recently witnessed in the other continents, to say nothing of certain outskirts of Europe.[9] From one point of view, it is well that terrible examples of the utmost logic of these things should be prominently forced on the attention of mankind; for by showing the evil stripped of all veils the choice between good and evil instead of a halting between the two will be forced on the human conscience. Woe to the race if it blinds its conscience and buttresses up its animal egoism with the old justifications; for the gods have shown that Karma is not a jest.

But the whole root of the German error lies in its mistaking life and the body for the self. It has been said that this gospel

---

[9] Witness Egypt, Ireland, India, and afterwards Abyssinia, Spain, China — wherever still man tries to dominate by force over man or nation over nation.

is simply a reversion to the ancient barbarism of the religion of Odin; but this is not the truth. It is a new and a modern gospel born of the application of a metaphysical logic to the conclusions of materialistic Science, of a philosophic subjectivism to the objective pragmatic positivism of recent thought. Just as Germany applied the individualistic position to the realisation of her communal subjective existence, so she applied the materialistic and vitalistic thought of recent times and equipped it with a subjective philosophy. Thus she arrived at a bastard creed, an objective subjectivism which is miles apart from the true goal of a subjective age. To show the error it is necessary to see wherein lies the true individuality of man and of the nation. It lies not in its physical, economic, even its cultural life which are only means and adjuncts, but in something deeper whose roots are not in the ego, but in a Self one in difference which relates the good of each, on a footing of equality and not of strife and domination, to the good of the rest of the world.

Chapter VI

The Objective and Subjective Views of Life

THE PRINCIPLE of individualism is the liberty of the human being regarded as a separate existence to develop himself and fulfil his life, satisfy his mental tendencies, emotional and vital needs and physical being according to his own desire governed by his reason; it admits no other limit to this right and this liberty except the obligation to respect the same individual liberty and right in others. The balance of this liberty and this obligation is the principle which the individualistic age adopted in its remodelling of society; it adopted in effect a harmony of compromises between rights and duties, liberty and law, permissions and restraints as the scheme both of the personal life and the life of the society. Equally, in the life of nations the individualistic age made liberty the ideal and strove though with less success than in its own proper sphere to affirm a mutual respect for each other's freedom as the proper conduct of nations to one another. In this idea of life, as with the individual, so with the nation, each has the inherent right to manage its own affairs freely or, if it wills, to mismanage them freely and not to be interfered with in its rights and liberties so long as it does not interfere with the rights and liberties of other nations. As a matter of fact, the egoism of individual and nation does not wish to abide within these bounds; therefore the social law of the nation has been called in to enforce the violated principle as between man and man and it has been sought to develop international law in the same way and with the same object. The influence of these ideas is still powerful. In the recent European struggle the liberty of nations was set forth as the ideal for which the war was being waged, — in defiance of the patent fact that it had come about by nothing better than a clash of interests. The development of international law into an effective force which will restrain the egoism of nations as the social law restrains the egoism of individuals, is the solution which still attracts and seems the most practicable to most when they seek to deal with the difficulties of the future.[1]

The growth of modern Science has meanwhile created new ideas and tendencies, on one side an exaggerated individualism or rather vitalistic egoism, on the other the quite opposite ideal of collectivism. Science investigating life discovered that the root nature of all living is a struggle to take the best advantage of the environment for self-preservation, self-fulfilment, self-aggrandisement. Human thought seizing in its usual arbitrary and trenchant fashion upon this aspect of modern knowledge has founded on it theories of a novel kind which erect into a gospel the right for each to live his own life not merely by utilising others, but even at the expense of others. The first object of life in this view is for the individual to survive as long as he may, to become strong, efficient, powerful, to dominate his environment and his fellows and to raise himself on this strenuous and egoistic line to his full stature of capacity and reap his full measure of enjoyment. Philosophies like Nietzsche's, certain forms of Anarchism, — not the idealistic Anarchism of the thinker which is rather the old individualism of the ideal reason carried to its logical conclusion, — certain forms too of Imperialism have been largely influenced and strengthened by this type of ideas, though not actually created by them.

On the other hand, Science investigating life has equally discovered that not only is the individual life best secured and made efficient by association with others and subjection to a law of communal self-development rather than by aggressive self-affirmation, but that actually what Nature seeks to preserve is not the individual but the type and that in her scale of values the pack, herd, hive or swarm takes precedence over the individual

---

[1] No longer perhaps now, except with a dwindling minority — now that the League of Nations, constantly misused or hampered from its true functioning by the egoism and insincerity of its greater members, has collapsed into impotence and failure.

animal or insect and the human group over the individual human being. Therefore in the true law and nature of things the individual should live for all and constantly subordinate and sacrifice himself to the growth, efficiency and progress of the race rather than live for his own self-fulfilment and subordinate the race-life to his own needs. Modern collectivism derives its victorious strength from the impression made upon human thought by this opposite aspect of modern knowledge. We have seen how the German mind took up both these ideas and combined them on the basis of the present facts of human life: it affirmed the entire subordination of the individual to the community, nation or State; it affirmed, on the other hand, with equal force the egoistic self-assertion of the individual nation as against others or against any group or all the groups of nations which constitute the totality of the human race.

But behind this conflict between the idea of a nationalistic and imperialistic egoism and the old individualistic doctrine of individual and national liberty and separateness, there is striving to arise a new idea of human universalism or collectivism for the race which, if it succeeds in becoming a power, is likely to overcome the ideal of national separatism and liberty as it has overcome within the society itself the ideal of individual freedom and separate self-fulfilment. This new idea demands of the nation that it shall subordinate, if not merge and sacrifice, its free separateness to the life of a larger collectivity, whether that of an imperialistic group or a continental or cultural unity, as in the idea of a united Europe, or the total united life of the human race.

The principle of subjectivism entering into human thought and action, while necessarily it must make a great difference in the view-point, the motive-power and the character of our living, does not at first appear to make any difference in its factors. Subjectivism and objectivism start from the same data, the individual and the collectivity, the complex nature of each with its various powers of the mind, life and body and the search for the law of their self-fulfilment and harmony. But objectivism proceeding by the analytical reason takes an external and mechanical view of the whole problem. It looks at the world as a thing, an object, a process to be studied by an observing reason which places itself abstractly outside the elements and the sum of what it has to consider and observes it thus from outside as one would an intricate mechanism. The laws of this process are considered as so many mechanical rules or settled forces acting upon the individual or the group which, when they have been observed and distinguished by the reason, have by one's will or by some will to be organised and applied fully much as Science applies the laws it discovers. These laws or rules have to be imposed on the individual by his own abstract reason and will isolated as a ruling authority from his other parts or by the reason and will of other individuals or of the group, and they have to be imposed on the group itself either by its own collective reason and will embodied in some machinery of control which the mind considers as something apart from the life of the group or by the reason and will of some other group external to it or of which it is in some way a part. So the State is viewed in modern political thought as an entity in itself, as if it were something apart from the community and its individuals, something which has the right to impose itself on them and control them in the fulfilment of some idea of right, good or interest which is inflicted on them by a restraining and fashioning power rather than developed in them and by them as a thing towards which their self and nature are impelled to grow. Life is to be managed, harmonised, perfected by an adjustment, a manipulation, a machinery through which it is passed and by which it is shaped. A law outside oneself, — outside even when it is discovered or determined by the individual reason and accepted or enforced by the individual will, — this is the governing idea of objectivism; a mechanical process of management, ordering, perfection, this is its conception of practice.

Subjectivism proceeds from within and regards everything from the point of view of a containing and developing self-consciousness. The law here is within ourselves; life is a self-creating process, a growth and development at first subconscious, then half-conscious and at last more and more fully conscious of that which we are potentially and hold within ourselves; the principle of its progress is an increasing self-recognition, self-realisation and a resultant self-shaping. Reason and will are only effective movements of the self, reason a process in self-recognition, will a force for self-affirmation and self-shaping. Moreover, reason and intellectual will are only a part of the means by which we recognise and realise ourselves. Subjectivism tends to take a large and complex view of our nature and being and to recognise many powers of knowledge, many forces of effectuation. Even, we see it in its first movement away from the external and objective method discount and belittle the importance of the work of the reason and assert the supremacy of the life-impulse or the essential Will-to-be in opposition to the claims of the intellect or else affirm some deeper power of knowledge, called nowadays the intuition, which sees things in the whole, in their truth, in their profundities and harmonies while intellectual reason breaks up, falsifies, affirms superficial appearances and harmonises only by a mechanical adjustment. But substantially we can see that what is meant by this intuition is the self-consciousness feeling, perceiving, grasping in its substance and aspects rather than analysing in its mechanism its own truth and nature and powers. The whole impulse of subjectivism is to get at the self, to live in the self, to see by the self, to live out the truth of the self internally and externally, but always from an internal initiation and centre.

But still there is the question of the truth of the self, what it is, where is its real abiding-place; and here subjectivism has to deal with the same factors as the objective view of life and existence. We may concentrate on the individual life and consciousness as the self and regard its power, freedom, increasing light and satisfaction and joy as the object of living and thus arrive at a subjective individualism. We may, on the other hand, lay stress on the group consciousness, the collective self; we may see man only as an expression of this group-self necessarily incomplete in his individual or separate being, complete only by that larger entity, and we may wish to subordinate the life of the individual man to the growing power, efficiency, knowledge, happiness, self-fulfilment of the race or even sacrifice it and consider it as nothing except in so far as it lends itself to the life and growth of the community or the kind. We may claim to exercise a righteous oppression on the individual and teach him intellectually and practically that he has no claim to exist, no right to fulfil himself except in his relations to the collectivity. These alone then are to determine his thought, action and existence and the claim of the individual to have a law of his own being, a law of his own nature which he has a right to fulfil and his demand for freedom of thought involving necessarily the freedom to err and for freedom of action involving necessarily the freedom to stumble and sin may be regarded as an insolence and a chimera. The collective self-consciousness will then have the right to invade at every point the life of the individual, to refuse to it all privacy and apartness, all self-concentration and isolation, all independence and self-guidance and determine everything for it by what it conceives to be the best thought and highest will and rightly dominant feeling, tendency, sense of need, desire for self-satisfaction of the collectivity.

But also we may enlarge the idea of the self and, as objective Science sees a universal force of Nature which is the one reality and of which everything is the process, we may come subjectively to the realisation of a universal Being or Existence which fulfils itself in the world and the individual and the group with an impartial regard for all as equal powers of its self-manifestation. This is obviously the self-knowledge which is most likely to be right, since it most comprehensively embraces and accounts for the various aspects of the world-process and the eternal tendencies of humanity. In this view neither the separate growth of the individual nor the all-absorbing growth of the group can be the ideal, but an equal, simultaneous and, as far as may be, parallel development of both, in which each helps to fulfil the other. Each being has his own truth of independent self-realisation and his truth of self-realisation in the life of others and should feel, desire, help, participate more and more, as he grows in largeness and power, in the harmonious and natural growth of all the individual selves and all the collective selves of the one universal Being. These two, when properly viewed, would not be separate, opposite or really conflicting lines of tendency, but the same impulse of the one common existence, companion movements separating only to return upon each other in a richer and larger unity and mutual consequence.

Similarly, the subjective search for the self may, like the objective, lean preponderantly to identification with the conscious physical life, because the body is or seems to be the frame and determinant here of the mental and vital movements and capacities. Or it may identify itself with the vital being, the life-soul in us and its emotions, desires, impulses, seekings for power and growth and egoistic fulfilment. Or it may rise to a conception of man as a mental and moral being, exalt to the first place his inner growth, power and perfection, individual and collective, and set it before us as the true aim of our existence. A sort of subjective materialism, pragmatic and outward-going, is a possible standpoint; but in this the subjective tendency cannot long linger. For its natural impulse is to go always inward and it only begins to feel itself and have satisfaction of itself when it gets to the full conscious life within and feels all its power, joy and forceful potentiality pressing for fulfilment. Man at this stage regards himself as a profound, vital Will-to-be which uses body as its instrument and to which the powers of mind are servants and ministers. This is the cast of that vitalism which in various striking forms has played recently so great a part and still exercises a considerable influence on human thought. Beyond it we get to a subjective idealism now beginning to emerge and become prominent, which seeks the fulfilment of man in the satisfaction of his inmost religious, aesthetic, intuitive, his highest intellectual and ethical, his deepest sympathetic and emotional nature and, regarding this as the fullness of our being and the whole object of our being, tries to subject to it the physical and vital existence. These come to be considered rather as a possible symbol and instrument of the subjective life flowing out into forms than as having any value in themselves. A certain tendency to mysticism, occultism and the search for a self independent of the life and the body accompanies this new movement — new to modern life after the reign of individualism and objective intellectualism — and emphasises its real trend and character.

But here also it is possible for subjectivism to go beyond and to discover the true Self as something greater even than mind. Mind, life and body then become merely an instrumentation for the increasing expression of this Self in the world, — instruments not equal in their hierarchy, but equal in their necessity to the whole, so that their complete perfection and harmony and unity as elements of our self-expression become essential to the true aim of our living. And yet that aim would not be to perfect life, body and mind in themselves, but to develop them so as to make a fit basis and fit instruments for the revelation in our inner and outer life of the luminous Self, the secret Godhead who is one and yet various in all of us, in every being and existence, thing and creature. The ideal of human existence personal and social would be its progressive transformation into a conscious outflowering of the joy, power, love, light, beauty of the transcendent and universal Spirit.

Chapter VII

The Ideal Law of Social Development

THE TRUE law of our development and the entire object of our social existence can only become clear to us when we have discovered not only, like modern Science, what man has been in his past physical and vital evolution, but his future mental and spiritual destiny and his place in the cycles of Nature. This is the reason why the subjective periods of human development must always be immeasurably the most fruitful and creative. In the others he either seizes on some face, image, type of the inner reality Nature in him is labouring to manifest or else he follows a mechanical impulse or shapes himself in the mould of her external influences; but here in his subjective return inward he gets back to himself, back to the root of his living and infinite possibilities, and the potentiality of a new and perfect self-creation begins to widen before him. He discovers his real place in Nature and opens his eyes to the greatness of his destiny.

Existence is an infinite and therefore indefinable and illimitable Reality which figures itself out in multiple values of life. It begins, at least in our field of existence, with a material figure of itself, a mould of firm substance into which and upon which it can build, — worlds, the earth, the body. Here it stamps firmly and fixes the essential law of its movement. That law is that all things are one in their being and origin, one in their general law of existence, one in their interdependence and the universal pattern of their relations; but each realises this unity of purpose and being on its own lines and has its own law of variation by which it enriches the universal existence. In Matter variation is limited; there is variation of type, but, on the whole, uniformity of the individuals of the type. These individuals have a separate movement, but yet the same movement; subject to some minute differences, they adhere to one particular pattern and have the same assemblage of properties. Variety within the type, apart from minor unicities of detail, is gained by variation of group sub-types belonging to one general kind, species and sub-species of the same genus. In the development of Life, before mind has become self-conscious, the same law predominates; but, in proportion as life grows and still more when mind emerges, the individual also arrives at a greater and more vital power of variation. He acquires the freedom to develop according, no doubt, to the general law of Nature and the general law of his type, but also according to the individual law of his being.

Man, the mental being in Nature, is especially distinguished from her less developed creatures by a greater power of individuality, by the liberation of the mental consciousness which enables him finally to understand more and more himself and his law of being and his development, by the liberation of the mental will which enables him under the secret control of the universal Will to manage more and more the materials and lines of his development and by the capacity in the end to go beyond himself, beyond his mentality and open his consciousness into that from which mind, life and body proceed. He can even, however imperfectly at present, get at his highest to some consciousness of the Reality which is his true being and possess consciously also, as nothing else in terrestrial Nature can possess, the Self, the Idea, the Will which have constituted him and can become by that the master of his own nature and increasingly, not as now he is, a wrestler with dominant circumstance but the master of Nature. To do this, to arrive through mind and beyond mind at the Self, the Spirit which expresses itself in all Nature and, becoming one with it in his being, his force, his consciousness, his will, his knowledge, to possess at once humanly and divinely — according to the law and nature of human existence, but of human existence fulfilled in God and fulfilling God in the world — both himself and the world is the destiny of man and the object of his individual and social existence.[1]

This is done primarily through the individual man; for this end man has become an individual soul, that the One may find and manifest Himself in each human being. That end is not indeed achieved by the individual human being in his unaided mental force. He needs the help of the secret Divine above his mentality in his superconscient self; he needs the help also of the secret Divine around him in Nature and in his fellow-men. Everything in Nature is an occasion for him to develop his divine potentiality, an occasion which he has a certain relative freedom to use or to misuse, although in the end both his use and misuse of his materials are overruled in their results by the universal Will so as to assist eventually the development of his law of being and his destiny. All life around him is a help towards the divine purpose in him; every human being is his fellow-worker and assists him whether by association and union or by strife and opposition. Nor does he achieve his destiny as the individual Man for the sake of the individual soul alone, — a lonely salvation is not his complete ideal, — but for the world also or rather for God in the world, for God in all as well as above all and not for God solely and separately in one. And he achieves it by the stress, not really of his separate individual Will, but of the universal Will in its movement towards the goal of its cycles.

The object of all society should be, therefore, and must become, as man grows conscious of his real being, nature and destiny and not as now only of a part of it, first to provide the conditions of life and growth by which individual Man, — not isolated men or a class or a privileged race, but all individual men according to their capacity, — and the race through the growth

---

[1] It may be said that since man is a mental being limited by the mind, life and body, this development and organisation of a power beyond mind, a supramental power, would be the creation of a new superhuman race and that the use of the words human and humanly would no longer be in place. This is no doubt true, but the possibility for the race still remains, if not for all in the same degree or at the same time, yet in an eventual fulfilment.

of its individuals may travel towards this divine perfection. It must be, secondly, as mankind generally more and more grows near to some figure of the Divine in life and more and more men arrive at it, — for the cycles are many and each cycle has its own figure of the Divine in man, — to express in the general life of mankind, the light, the power, the beauty, the harmony, the joy of the Self that has been attained and that pours itself out in a freer and nobler humanity. Freedom and harmony express the two necessary principles of variation and oneness, — freedom of the individual, the group, the race, coordinated harmony of the individual's forces and of the efforts of all individuals in the group, of all groups in the race, of all races in the kind, — and these are the two conditions of healthy progression and successful arrival. To realise them and to combine them has been the obscure or half-enlightened effort of mankind throughout its history, — a task difficult indeed and too imperfectly seen and too clumsily and mechanically pursued by the reason and desires to be satisfactorily achieved until man grows by self-knowledge and self-mastery to the possession of a spiritual and psychical unity with his fellow-men. As we realise more and more the right conditions, we shall travel more luminously and spontaneously towards our goal and, as we draw nearer to a clear sight of our goal, we shall realise better and better the right conditions. The Self in man enlarging light and knowledge and harmonising will with light and knowledge so as to fulfil in life what he has seen in his increasing vision and idea of the Self, this is man's source and law of progress and the secret of his impulse towards perfection.

Mankind upon earth is one foremost self-expression of the universal Being in His cosmic self-unfolding; he expresses, under the conditions of the terrestrial world he inhabits, the mental power of the universal existence. All mankind is one in its nature, physical, vital, emotional, mental and ever has been in spite of all differences of intellectual development ranging from the poverty of the Bushman and negroid to the rich cultures of Asia and Europe, and the whole race has, as the human totality, one destiny which it seeks and increasingly approaches in the cycles of progression and retrogression it describes through the countless millenniums of its history. Nothing which any individual race or nation can triumphantly realise, no victory of their self-aggrandisement, illumination, intellectual achievement or mastery over the environment, has any permanent meaning or value except in so far as it adds something or recovers something or preserves something for this human march. The purpose which the ancient Indian scripture offers to us as the true object of all human action, *lokasaṅgraha*, the holding together of the race in its cyclic evolution, is the constant sense, whether we know it or know it not, of the sum of our activities.

But within this general nature and general destiny of mankind each individual human being has to follow the common aim on the lines of his own nature and to arrive at his possible perfection by a growth from within. So only can the race itself attain to anything profound, living and deep-rooted. It cannot be done brutally, heavily, mechanically in the mass; the group self has no true right to regard the individual as if he were only a cell of its body, a stone of its edifice, a passive instrument of its collective life and growth. Humanity is not so constituted. We miss the divine reality in man and the secret of the human birth if we do not see that each individual man is that Self and sums up all human potentiality in his own being. That potentiality he has to find, develop, work out from within. No State or legislator or reformer can cut him rigorously into a perfect pattern; no Church or priest can give him a mechanical salvation; no order, no class life or ideal, no nation, no civilisation or creed or ethical, social or religious Shastra can be allowed to say to him permanently, "In this way of mine and thus far shalt thou act and grow and in no other way and no farther shall thy growth be permitted." These things may help him temporarily or they may curb and he grows in proportion as he can use them and then exceed them, train and teach his individuality by them, but assert it always in the end in its divine freedom. Always he is the traveller of the cycles and his road is forward.

True, his life and growth are for the sake of the world, but he can help the world by his life and growth only in proportion as he can be more and more freely and widely his own real self.

True, he has to use the ideals, disciplines, systems of cooperation which he finds upon his path; but he can only use them well, in their right way and to their right purpose if they are to his life means towards something beyond them and not burdens to be borne by him for their own sake or despotic controls to be obeyed by him as their slave or subject; for though laws and disciplines strive to be the tyrants of the human soul, their only purpose is to be its instruments and servants and when their use is over they have to be rejected and broken. True it is, too, that he has to gather in his material from the minds and lives of his fellow-men around him and to make the most of the experience of humanity's past ages and not confine himself in a narrow mentality; but this he can only do successfully by making all this his own through assimilation of it to the principle of his own nature and through its subservience to the forward call of his enlarging future. The liberty claimed by the struggling human mind for the individual is no mere egoistic challenge and revolt, however egoistically or with one-sided exaggeration and misapplication it may sometimes be advanced; it is the divine instinct within him, the law of the Self, its claim to have room and the one primary condition for its natural self-unfolding.

Individual man belongs not only to humanity in general, his nature is not only a variation of human nature in general, but he belongs also to his race-type, his class-type, his mental, vital, physical, spiritual type in which he resembles some, differs from others. According to these affinities he tends to group himself in Churches, sects, communities, classes, coteries, associations whose life he helps, and by them he enriches the life of the large economic, social and political group or society to which he belongs. In modern times this society is the nation. By his enrichment of the national life, though not in that way only, he helps the total life of humanity. But it must be noted that he is not limited and cannot be limited by any of these groupings; he is not merely the noble, merchant, warrior, priest, scholar, artist, cultivator or artisan, not merely the religionist or the worldling or the politician. Nor can he be limited by his nationality; he is not merely the Englishman or the Frenchman, the Japanese or the Indian; if by a part of himself he belongs to the nation, by another he exceeds it and belongs to humanity. And even there is a part of him, the greatest, which is not limited by humanity; he belongs by it to God and to the world of all beings and to the godheads of the future. He has indeed the tendency of self-limitation and subjection to his environment and group, but he has also the equally necessary tendency of expansion and transcendence of environment and groupings. The individual animal is dominated entirely by his type, subordinated to his group when he does group himself; individual man has already begun to share something of the infinity, complexity, free variation of the Self we see manifested in the world. Or at least he has it in possibility even if there be as yet no sign of it in his organised surface nature. There is here no principle of a mere shapeless fluidity; it is the tendency to enrich himself with the largest possible material constantly brought in, constantly assimilated and changed by the law of his individual nature into stuff of his growth and divine expansion.

Thus the community stands as a mid-term and intermediary value between the individual and humanity and it exists not merely for itself, but for the one and the other and to help them to fulfil each other. The individual has to live in humanity as well as humanity in the individual; but mankind is or has been too large an aggregate to make this mutuality a thing intimate and powerfully felt in the ordinary mind of the race, and even if humanity becomes a manageable unit of life, intermediate groups and aggregates must still exist for the purpose of mass-differentiation and the concentration and combination of varying tendencies in the total human aggregate. Therefore the community has to stand for a time to the individual for humanity even at the cost of standing between him and it and limiting the reach of his universality and the wideness of his sympathies. Still the absolute claim of the community, the society or the nation to make its growth, perfection, greatness the sole object of human life or to exist for itself alone as against the individual and the rest of humanity, to take arbitrary possession of the one and make the hostile assertion of itself against the other, whether defensive or offensive, the law of its action in the world — and not, as it unfortunately is, a temporary necessity, — this attitude of societies, races, religions, communities, nations, empires is evidently an aberration of the human reason, quite as much as the claim of the individual to live for himself egoistically is an aberration and the deformation of a truth.

The truth deformed into this error is the same with the community as with the individual. The nation or community is an aggregate life that expresses the Self according to the general law of human nature and aids and partially fulfils the development and the destiny of mankind by its own development and the pursuit of its own destiny according to the law of its being and the nature of its corporate individuality. It has like the individual the right to be itself, and its just claim, as against any attempt at domination by other nations or of attack upon its separate development by any excessive tendency of human uniformity and regimentation, is to defend its existence, to insist on being itself, to persist in developing according to the secret Idea within it or, as we say, according to the law of its own nature. This right it must assert not only or even principally for its own sake, but in the interests of humanity. For the only things that we can really call our rights are those conditions which are necessary to our free and sound development, and that again is our right because it is necessary to the development of the world and the fulfilment of the destiny of mankind.

Nor does this right to be oneself mean with the nation or community any more than with the individual that it should roll itself up like a hedgehog, shut itself up in its dogmas, prejudices, limitations, imperfections, in the form and mould of its past or its present achievement and refuse mental or physical commerce and interchange or spiritual or actual commingling with the rest of the world. For so it cannot grow or perfect itself. As the individual lives by the life of other individuals, so does the nation by the life of other nations, by accepting from them material for its own mental, economic and physical life; but it has to assimilate this material, subject it to the law of its own nature, change it into stuff of itself, work upon it by its own free will and consciousness, if it would live securely and grow soundly. To have the principle or rule of another nature imposed upon it by force or a de-individualising pressure is a menace to its existence, a wound to its being, a fetter upon its march. As the free development of individuals from within is the best condition for the growth and perfection of the community, so the free development of the community or nation from within is the best condition for the growth and perfection of mankind.

Thus the law for the individual is to perfect his individuality by free development from within, but to respect and to aid and be aided by the same free development in others. His law is to harmonise his life with the life of the social aggregate and to pour himself out as a force for growth and perfection on humanity. The law for the community or nation is equally to perfect its corporate existence by a free development from within, aiding and taking full advantage of that of the individual, but to respect and to aid and be aided by the same free development of other communities and nations. Its law is to harmonise its life with that of the human aggregate and to pour itself out as a force for growth and perfection on humanity. The law for humanity is to pursue its upward evolution towards the finding and expression of the Divine in the type of mankind, taking full advantage of the free development and gains of all individuals and nations and groupings of men, to work towards the day when mankind may be really and not only ideally one divine family, but even then, when it has succeeded in unifying itself, to respect, aid and be aided by the free growth and activity of its individuals and constituent aggregates.

Naturally, this is an ideal law which the imperfect human race has never yet really attained and it may be very long before it can attain to it. Man, not possessing, but only seeking to find himself, not knowing consciously, obeying only in the rough subconsciously or half-consciously the urge of the law of his own nature with stumblings and hesitations and deviations and a series of violences done to himself and others, has had to advance by a tangle of truth and error, right and wrong, compulsion and revolt and clumsy adjustments, and he has as yet neither the

wideness of knowledge nor the flexibility of mind nor the purity
of temperament which would enable him to follow the law of
liberty and harmony rather than the law of discord and regimentation, compulsion and adjustment and strife. Still it is the very
business of a subjective age when knowledge is increasing and
diffusing itself with an unprecedented rapidity, when capacity
is generalising itself, when men and nations are drawn close
together and partially united though in an inextricable, confused
entanglement of chaotic unity, when they are being compelled
to know each other and impelled to know more profoundly
themselves, mankind, God and the world and when the idea of
self-realisation for men and nations is coming consciously to the
surface, — it is the natural work and should be the conscious
hope of man in such an age to know himself truly, to find the
ideal law of his being and his development and, if he cannot
even then follow it ideally owing to the difficulties of his egoistic
nature, still to hold it before him and find out gradually the way
by which it can become more and more the moulding principle
of his individual and social existence.

Chapter VIII

Civilisation and Barbarism

ONCE WE have determined that this rule of perfect individuality and perfect reciprocity is the ideal law for
the individual, the community and the race and that a
perfect union and even oneness in a free diversity is its goal, we
have to try to see more clearly what we mean when we say that
self-realisation is the sense, secret or overt, of individual and of
social development. As yet we have not to deal with the race,
with mankind as a unity; the nation is still our largest compact
and living unit. And it is best to begin with the individual, both
because of his nature we have a completer and nearer knowledge
and experience than of the aggregate soul and life and because
the society or nation is, even in its greater complexity, a larger, a
composite individual, the collective Man. What we find valid of
the former is therefore likely to be valid in its general principle
of the larger entity. Moreover, the development of the free individual is, we have said, the first condition for the development
of the perfect society. From the individual, therefore, we have to
start; he is our index and our foundation.

The Self of man is a thing hidden and occult; it is not his
body, it is not his life, it is not — even though he is in the scale
of evolution the mental being, the Manu, — his mind. Therefore
neither the fullness of his physical, nor of his vital, nor of his
mental nature can be either the last term or the true standard
of his self-realisation; they are means of manifestation, subordinate indications, foundations of his self-finding, values, practical
currency of his self, what you will, but not the thing itself which
he secretly is and is obscurely groping or trying overtly and
self-consciously to become. Man has not possessed as a race
this truth about himself, does not now possess it except in the
vision and self-experience of the few in whose footsteps the
race is unable to follow, though it may adore them as Avatars,

seers, saints or prophets. For the Oversoul who is the master of
our evolution, has his own large steps of Time, his own great
eras, tracts of slow and courses of rapid expansion, which the
strong, semi-divine individual may overleap, but not the still
half-animal race. The course of evolution proceeding from the
vegetable to the animal, from the animal to the man, starts in
the latter from the subhuman; he has to take up into him the
animal and even the mineral and vegetable: they constitute his
physical nature, they dominate his vitality, they have their hold
upon his mentality. His proneness to many kinds of inertia, his
readiness to vegetate, his attachment to the soil and clinging
to his roots, to safe anchorages of all kinds, and on the other
hand his nomadic and predatory impulses, his blind servility
to custom and the rule of the pack, his mob-movements and
openness to subconscious suggestions from the group-soul, his
subjection to the yoke of rage and fear, his need of punishment
and reliance on punishment, his inability to think and act for
himself, his incapacity for true freedom, his distrust of novelty,
his slowness to seize intelligently and assimilate, his downward
propensity and earthward gaze, his vital and physical subjection
to his heredity, all these and more are his heritage from the
subhuman origins of his life and body and physical mind. It is
because of this heritage that he finds self-exceeding the most
difficult of lessons and the most painful of endeavours. Yet it
is by exceeding of the lower self that Nature accomplishes the
great strides of her evolutionary process. To learn by what he
has been, but also to know and increase to what he can be, is
the task that is set for the mental being.

The time is passing away, permanently — let us hope — for
this cycle of civilisation, when the entire identification of the self
with the body and the physical life was possible for the general
consciousness of the race. That is the primary characteristic of
complete barbarism. To take the body and the physical life as the
one thing important, to judge manhood by the physical strength,
development and prowess, to be at the mercy of the instincts
which rise out of the physical inconscient, to despise knowledge
as a weakness and inferiority or look on it as a peculiarity and

no necessary part of the conception of manhood, this is the mentality of the barbarian. It tends to reappear in the human being in the atavistic period of boyhood, — when, be it noted, the development of the body is of the greatest importance, — but to the adult man in civilised humanity it is ceasing to be possible. For, in the first place, by the stress of modern life even the vital attitude of the race is changing. Man is ceasing to be so much of a physical and becoming much more of a vital and economic animal. Not that he excludes or is intended to exclude the body and its development or the right maintenance of and respect for the animal being and its excellences from his idea of life; the excellence of the body, its health, its soundness, its vigour and harmonious development are necessary to a perfect manhood and are occupying attention in a better and more intelligent way than before. But the first rank in importance can no longer be given to the body, much less that entire predominance assigned to it in the mentality of the barbarian.

Moreover, although man has not yet really heard and understood the message of the sages, "know thyself", he has accepted the message of the thinker, "educate thyself", and, what is more, he has understood that the possession of education imposes on him the duty of imparting his knowledge to others. The idea of the necessity of general education means the recognition by the race that the mind and not the life and the body are the man and that without the development of the mind he does not possess his true manhood. The idea of education is still primarily that of intelligence and mental capacity and knowledge of the world and things, but secondarily also of moral training and, though as yet very imperfectly, of the development of the aesthetic faculties. The intelligent thinking being, moralised, controlling his instincts and emotions by his will and his reason, acquainted with all that he should know of the world and his past, capable of organising intelligently by that knowledge his social and economic life, ordering rightly his bodily habits and physical being, this is the conception that now governs civilised humanity. It is, in essence, a return to and a larger development of the old Hellenic ideal, with a greater stress on capacity and utility and a very diminished stress on beauty and refinement. We may suppose, however, that this is only a passing phase; the lost elements are bound to recover their importance as soon as the commercial period of modern progress has been overpassed, and with that recovery, not yet in sight but inevitable, we shall have all the proper elements for the development of man as a mental being.

The old Hellenic or Graeco-Roman civilisation perished, among other reasons, because it only imperfectly generalised culture in its own society and was surrounded by huge masses of humanity who were still possessed by the barbarian habit of mind. Civilisation can never be safe so long as, confining the cultured mentality to a small minority, it nourishes in its bosom a tremendous mass of ignorance, a multitude, a proletariate. Either knowledge must enlarge itself from above or be always in danger of submergence by the ignorant night from below. Still more must it be unsafe, if it allows enormous numbers of men to exist outside its pale uninformed by its light, full of the natural vigour of the barbarian, who may at any moment seize upon the physical weapons of the civilised without undergoing an intellectual transformation by their culture. The Graeco-Roman culture perished from within and from without, from without by the floods of Teutonic barbarism, from within by the loss of its vitality. It gave the proletariate some measure of comfort and amusement, but did not raise it into the light. When light came to the masses, it was from outside in the form of the Christian religion which arrived as an enemy of the old culture. Appealing to the poor, the oppressed and the ignorant, it sought to capture the soul and the ethical being, but cared little or not at all for the thinking mind, content that that should remain in darkness if the heart could be brought to feel religious truth. When the barbarians captured the Western world, it was in the same way content to Christianise them, but made it no part of its function to intellectualise. Distrustful even of the free play of intelligence, Christian ecclesiasticism and monasticism became anti-intellectual and it was left to the Arabs to reintroduce the beginnings of scientific and philosophical knowledge into a semi-barbarous Christendom and to the half-pagan spirit of the Renaissance and a long struggle between religion and science to complete the return of a free intellectual culture in the re-emerging mind of Europe. Knowledge must be aggressive, if it wishes to survive and perpetuate itself; to leave an extensive ignorance either below or around it, is to expose humanity to the perpetual danger of a barbaric relapse.

The modern world does not leave room for a repetition of the danger in the old form or on the old scale. Science is there to prevent it. It has equipped culture with the means of self-perpetuation. It has armed the civilised races with weapons of organisation and aggression and self-defence which cannot be successfully utilised by any barbarous people, unless it ceases to be uncivilised and acquires the knowledge which Science alone can give. It has learned too that ignorance is an enemy it cannot afford to despise and has set out to remove it wherever it is found. The ideal of general education, at least to the extent of some information of the mind and the training of capacity, owes to it, if not its birth, at least much of its practical possibility. It has propagated itself everywhere with an irresistible force and driven the desire for increasing knowledge into the mentality of three continents. It has made general education the indispensable condition of national strength and efficiency and therefore imposed the desire of it not only on every free people, but on every nation that desires to be free and to survive, so that the universalisation of knowledge and intellectual activity in the human race is now only a question of Time; for it is only certain political and economic obstacles that stand in its way and these the thought and tendencies of the age are already labouring to overcome. And, in sum, Science has already enlarged for good the intellectual horizons of the race and raised, sharpened and intensified powerfully the general intellectual capacity of mankind.

It is true that the first tendencies of Science have been materialistic and its indubitable triumphs have been confined to the knowledge of the physical universe and the body and the physical life. But this materialism is a very different thing from the old identification of the self with the body. Whatever its apparent tendencies, it has been really an assertion of man the mental being and of the supremacy of intelligence. Science in its very nature is knowledge, is intellectuality, and its whole work has been that of the Mind turning its gaze upon its vital and physical frame and environment to know and conquer and dominate Life and Matter. The scientist is Man the thinker mastering the forces of material Nature by knowing them. Life and Matter are after all our standing-ground, our lower basis and to know their processes and their own proper possibilities and the opportunities they give to the human being is part of the knowledge necessary for transcending them. Life and the body have to be exceeded, but they have also to be utilised and perfected. Neither the laws nor the possibilities of physical Nature can be entirely known unless we know also the laws and possibilities of supraphysical Nature; therefore the development of new and the recovery of old mental and psychic sciences have to follow upon the perfection of our physical knowledge, and that new era is already beginning to open upon us. But the perfection of the physical sciences was a prior necessity and had to be the first field for the training of the mind of man in his new endeavour to know Nature and possess his world.

Even in its negative work the materialism of Science had a task to perform which will be useful in the end to the human mind in its exceeding of materialism. But Science in its heyday of triumphant Materialism despised and cast aside Philosophy; its predominance discouraged by its positive and pragmatic turn the spirit of poetry and art and pushed them from their position of leadership in the front of culture; poetry entered into an era of decline and decadence, adopted the form and rhythm of a versified prose and lost its appeal and the support of all but a very limited audience, painting followed the curve of Cubist extravagance and espoused monstrosities of shape and suggestion; the ideal receded and visible matter of fact was enthroned in its place and encouraged an ugly realism and utilitarianism; in its war against religious obscurantism Science almost succeeded in slaying religion and the religious spirit. But philosophy had become too much a thing of abstractions, a seeking for abstract truths in a world of ideas and words rather than what it should be, a discovery of the real reality of things by which human existence can learn its law and aim and the principle of its perfection. Poetry and art had become too much cultured pursuits to be ranked among the elegances and ornaments of life, concerned with beauty of words and forms and imaginations, rather than a concrete seeing and significant presentation of truth and beauty and of the living idea and the secret divinity in things concealed by the sensible appearances of the universe. Religion itself had become fixed in dogmas and ceremonies, sects and churches and had lost for the most part, except for a few individuals, direct contact with the living founts of spirituality. A period of negation was necessary. They had to be driven back and in upon themselves, nearer to their own eternal sources. Now that the stress of negation is past and they are raising their heads, we see them seeking for their own truth, reviving by virtue of a return upon themselves and a new self-discovery. They have learned or are learning from the example of Science that Truth is the secret of life and power and that by finding the truth proper to themselves they must become the ministers of human existence.

But if Science has thus prepared us for an age of wider and deeper culture and if in spite of and even partly by its materialism it has rendered impossible the return of the true materialism, that of the barbarian mentality, it has encouraged more or less indirectly both by its attitude to life and its discoveries another kind of barbarism, — for it can be called by no other name, — that of the industrial, the commercial, the economic age which is now progressing to its culmination and its close. This economic barbarism is essentially that of the vital man who mistakes the vital being for the self and accepts its satisfaction as the first aim of life. The characteristic of Life is desire and the instinct of possession. Just as the physical barbarian makes the excellence of the body and the development of physical force, health and prowess his standard and aim, so the vitalistic or economic barbarian makes the satisfaction of wants and desires and the accumulation of possessions his standard

and aim. His ideal man is not the cultured or noble or thought-
ful or moral or religious, but the successful man. To arrive, to
succeed, to produce, to accumulate, to possess is his existence.
The accumulation of wealth and more wealth, the adding of
possessions to possessions, opulence, show, pleasure, a cumbrous inartistic luxury, a plethora of conveniences, life devoid
of beauty and nobility, religion vulgarised or coldly formalised,.
politics and government turned into a trade and profession,
enjoyment itself made a business, this is commercialism. To the
natural unredeemed economic man beauty is a thing otiose or
a nuisance, art and poetry a frivolity or an ostentation and
a means of advertisement. His idea of civilisation is comfort,
his idea of morals social respectability, his idea of politics the
encouragement of industry, the opening of markets, exploitation
and trade following the flag, his idea of religion at best a pietistic
formalism or the satisfaction of certain vitalistic emotions. He
values education for its utility in fitting a man for success in
a competitive or, it may be, a socialised industrial existence,
science for the useful inventions and knowledge, the comforts,
conveniences, machinery of production with which it arms him,
its power for organisation, regulation, stimulus to production.
The opulent plutocrat and the successful mammoth capitalist
and organiser of industry are the supermen of the commercial
age and the true, if often occult rulers of its society.

The essential barbarism of all this is its pursuit of vital
success, satisfaction, productiveness, accumulation, possession,
enjoyment, comfort, convenience for their own sake. The vital
part of the being is an element in the integral human existence as
much as the physical part; it has its place but must not exceed its
place. A full and well-appointed life is desirable for man living
in society, but on condition that it is also a true and beautiful
life. Neither the life nor the body exist for their own sake, but
as vehicle and instrument of a good higher than their own.
They must be subordinated to the superior needs of the mental
being, chastened and purified by a greater law of truth, good and
beauty before they can take their proper place in the integrality
of human perfection. Therefore in a commercial age with its

ideal, vulgar and barbarous, of success, vitalistic satisfaction, productiveness and possession the soul of man may linger a while for certain gains and experiences, but cannot permanently rest. If it persisted too long, Life would become clogged and perish of its own plethora or burst in its straining to a gross expansion. Like the too massive Titan it will collapse by its own mass, *mole ruet sua.*

Chapter IX
Civilisation and Culture

NATURE starts from Matter, develops out of it its hidden Life, releases out of involution in life all the crude material of Mind and, when she is ready, turns Mind upon itself and upon Life and Matter in a great mental effort to understand all three in their phenomena, their obvious action, their secret laws, their normal and abnormal possibilities and powers so that they may be turned to the richest account, used in the best and most harmonious way, elevated to their highest as well as extended to their widest potential aims by the action of that faculty which man alone of terrestrial creatures clearly possesses, the intelligent will. It is only in this fourth stage of her progress that she arrives at humanity. The atoms and the elements organise brute Matter, the plant develops the living being, the animal prepares and brings to a certain kind of mechanical organisation the crude material of Mind, but the last work of all, the knowledge and control of all these things and self-knowledge and self-control, — that has been reserved for Man, Nature's mental being. That he may better do the work she has given him, she compels him to repeat physically and to some extent mentally stages of her animal evolution and, even when he is in possession of his mental being, she induces him continually to dwell with an interest and even a kind of absorption upon Matter and Life and his own body and vital existence. This is necessary to the largeness of her purpose in him. His first natural absorption in the body and the life is narrow and unintelligent; as his intelligence and mental force increase, he disengages himself to some extent, is able to mount higher, but is still tied to his vital and material roots by need and desire and has to return upon them with a larger curiosity, a greater power of utilisation, a more and more highly mental and, in the end, a more and more spiritual aim in the return. For his cycles are circles of a growing, but still imperfect harmony and synthesis, and she brings him back violently to her original principles, sometimes even to something like her earlier conditions so that he may start afresh on a larger curve of progress and self-fulfilment.

It would seem at first sight that since man is pre-eminently the mental being, the development of the mental faculties and the richness of the mental life should be his highest aim, — his preoccupying aim, even, as soon as he has got rid of the obsession of the life and body and provided for the indispensable satisfaction of the gross needs which our physical and animal nature imposes on us. Knowledge, science, art, thought, ethics, philosophy, religion, this is man's real business, these are his true affairs. To be is for him not merely to be born, grow up, marry, get his livelihood, support a family and then die, — the vital and physical life, a human edition of the animal round, a human enlargement of the little animal sector and arc of the divine circle; rather to become and grow mentally and live with knowledge and power within himself as well as from within outward is his manhood. But there is here a double motive of Nature, an insistent duality in her human purpose. Man is here to learn from her how to control and create; but she evidently means him not only to control, create and constantly re-create in new and better forms himself, his own inner existence, his mentality, but also to control and re-create correspondingly his environment. He has to turn Mind not only on itself, but on Life and Matter and the material existence; that is very clear not only from the law and nature of the terrestrial evolution, but from his own past and present history. And there comes from the observation of these conditions and of his highest aspirations and impulses the question whether he is not intended, not only to expand inwardly and outwardly, but to grow upward, wonderfully exceeding himself as he has wonderfully exceeded his animal beginnings, into something more than mental, more than human, into a being spiritual and divine. Even if he cannot do that, yet he may have to open his mind to what is beyond it and to govern his life more and more by the light and power that he receives from something greater than himself. Man's consciousness of the divine within himself and the world is the supreme fact of his existence and to grow into that may very well be the intention of his nature. In any case the fullness of Life is his evident object, the widest life and the highest life possible to him, whether that be a complete humanity or a new and divine race. We must recognise both his need of integrality and his impulse of self-exceeding if we would fix rightly the meaning of his individual existence and the perfect aim and norm of his society.

The pursuit of the mental life for its own sake is what we ordinarily mean by culture; but the word is still a little equivocal and capable of a wider or a narrower sense according to our ideas and predilections. For our mental existence is a very complex matter and is made up of many elements. First, we have its lower and fundamental stratum, which is in the scale of evolution nearest to the vital. And we have in that stratum two sides, the mental life of the senses, sensations and emotions in which the subjective purpose of Nature predominates although with the objective as its occasion, and the active or dynamic life of the mental being concerned with the organs of action and the field of conduct in which her objective purpose predominates although with the subjective as its occasion. We have next in the scale, more sublimated, on one side the moral being and its ethical life, on the other the aesthetic; each of them attempts to possess and dominate the fundamental mind stratum and turn its experiences and activities to its own benefit, one for the culture and worship of Right, the other for the culture and worship of Beauty. And we have, above all these, taking advantage of them, helping, forming, trying often to govern them entirely, the intellectual being. Man's highest accomplished range is the life of the reason or ordered and harmonised intelligence with its dynamic power of intelligent will, the *buddhi*, which is or should be the driver of man's chariot.

But the intelligence of man is not composed entirely and exclusively of the rational intellect and the rational will; there enters into it a deeper, more intuitive, more splendid and powerful, but much less clear, much less developed and as yet hardly at all self-possessing light and force for which we have not even a name. But, at any rate, its character is to drive at a kind of illumination, — not the dry light of the reason, nor the moist and suffused light of the heart, but a lightning and a solar splendour. It may indeed subordinate itself and merely help the reason and heart with its flashes; but there is another urge in it, its natural urge, which exceeds the reason. It tries to illuminate the intellectual being, to illuminate the ethical and aesthetic, to illuminate the emotional and the active, to illuminate even the senses and the sensations. It offers in words of revelation, it unveils as if by lightning flashes, it shows in a sort of mystic or psychic glamour or brings out into a settled but for mental man almost a supernatural light a Truth greater and truer than the knowledge given by Reason and Science, a Right larger and more divine than the moralist's scheme of virtues, a Beauty more profound, universal and entrancing than the sensuous or imaginative beauty worshipped by the artist, a joy and divine sensibility which leaves the ordinary emotions poor and pallid, a Sense beyond the senses and sensations, the possibility of a diviner Life and action which man's ordinary conduct of life hides away from his impulses and from his vision. Very various, very fragmentary, often very confused and misleading are its effects upon all the lower members from the reason downward, but this in the end is what it is driving at in the midst of a hundred deformations. It is caught and killed or at least diminished and stifled in formal creeds and pious observances; it is unmercifully traded in and turned into poor and base coin by the vulgarity of conventional religions; but it is still the light of which the religious spirit and the spirituality of man is in pursuit and some pale glow of it lingers even in their worst degradations.

This very complexity of his mental being, with the absence of any one principle which can safely dominate the others, the absence of any sure and certain light which can guide and fix in their vacillations the reason and the intelligent will, is man's great embarrassment and stumbling-block. All the hostile distinctions, oppositions, antagonisms, struggles, conversions, reversions, perversions of his mentality, all the chaotic war of ideas and impulses and tendencies which perplex his efforts, have arisen from the natural misunderstandings and conflicting claims of his many members. His reason is a judge who gives conflicting verdicts and is bribed and influenced by the suitors; his intelligent will is an administrator harassed by the conflicts of the different estates of his realm and by the sense of his own partiality and final incompetence. Still in the midst of it all he has formed certain large ideas of culture and the mental life, and his conflicting notions about them follow certain definite lines determined by the divisions of his nature and shaped into a general system of curves by his many attempts to arrive either at an exclusive standard or an integral harmony.

We have first the distinction between civilisation and barbarism. In its ordinary, popular sense civilisation means the state of civil society, governed, policed, organised, educated, possessed of knowledge and appliances as opposed to that which has not or is not supposed to have these advantages. In a certain sense the Red Indian, the Basuto, the Fiji islander had their civilisation; they possessed a rigorously, if simply organised society, a social law, some ethical ideas, a religion, a kind of training, a good many virtues in some of which, it is said, civilisation is sadly lacking; but we are agreed to call them savages and barbarians, mainly it seems, because of their crude and limited knowledge, the primitive rudeness of their appliances and the bare simplicity of their social organisation. In the more developed states of society we have such epithets as semi-civilised and semi-barbarous which are applied by different types of civilisation to each other, — the one which is for a time dominant and physically successful has naturally the loudest and most self-confident say in the matter. Formerly men were more straightforward and simpleminded and frankly expressed their standpoint by stigmatising all peoples different in general culture from themselves as barbarians or Mlechchhas. The word civilisation so used comes to have a merely relative significance or hardly any fixed sense at all. We must therefore get rid in it of all that is temporary or accidental and fix it upon this distinction that barbarism is the state of society in which man is almost entirely preoccupied with his life and body, his economic and physical existence, — at first with their sufficient maintenance, not as yet their greater or richer well-being, — and has few means and little inclination to develop his mentality, while civilisation is the more evolved state of society in which to a sufficient social and economic organisation is added the activity of the mental life in most if not all of its parts; for sometimes some of these parts are left aside or discouraged or temporarily atrophied by their inactivity, yet the society may be very obviously civilised and even highly civilised. This conception will bring in all the civilisations historic and prehistoric and put aside all the barbarism, whether of Africa or Europe or Asia, Hun or Goth or Vandal or Turcoman. It is obvious that in a state of barbarism the rude beginnings of civilisation may exist; it is obvious too that in a civilised society a great mass of barbarism or numerous relics of it may exist. In that sense all societies are semi-civilised. How much of our present-day civilisation will be looked back upon with wonder and disgust by a more developed humanity as the superstitions and atrocities of an imperfectly civilised era! But the main point is this that in any society which we can call civilised the mentality of man must be active, the mental pursuits developed and the regulation and improvement of his life by the mental being a clearly self-conscious concept in his better mind.

But in a civilised society there is still the distinction between the partially, crudely, conventionally civilised and the cultured. It would seem therefore that the mere participation in the ordinary benefits of civilisation is not enough to raise a man into the mental life proper; a farther development, a higher elevation is needed. The last generation drew emphatically the distinction between the cultured man and the Philistine and got a fairly clear idea of what was meant by it. Roughly, the Philistine was for them the man who lives outwardly the civilised life, possesses all its paraphernalia, has and mouths the current stock of opinions, prejudices, conventions, sentiments, but is impervious to ideas, exercises no free intelligence, is innocent of beauty and art, vulgarises everything that he touches, religion, ethics, literature, life. The Philistine is in fact the modern civilised barbarian; he is often the half-civilised physical and vital barbarian by his unintelligent attachment to the life of the body, the life of the vital needs and impulses and the ideal of the merely domestic and economic human animal; but essentially and commonly he is the mental barbarian, the average sensational man. That is to say, his mental life is that of the lower substratum of the mind, the life of the senses, the life of the sensations, the life of the emotions, the life of practical conduct — the first status of the mental being. In all these he may be very active, very vigorous, but he does not govern them by a higher light or seek to uplift them to a freer and nobler eminence; rather he pulls the higher faculties down to the level of his senses, his sensations, his unenlightened and unchastened emotions, his gross utilitarian practicality. His aesthetic side is little developed; either he cares nothing for beauty or has the crudest aesthetic tastes which help to lower and vulgarise the general standard of aesthetic creation and the aesthetic sense. He is often strong about morals, far more particular usually about moral conduct than the man of culture, but his moral being is as crude and undeveloped as the rest of him; it is conventional, unchastened, unintelligent, a mass of likes and dislikes, prejudices and current opinions, attachment to social conventions and respectabilities and an obscure dislike — rooted in the mind of sensations and not in the intelligence — of any open defiance or departure from the generally accepted standard of conduct. His ethical bent is a habit of the sense-mind; it is the morality of the average sensational man. He has a reason and the appearance of an intelligent will, but they are not his own, they are part of the group-mind, received from his environment; or so far as they are his own, merely a practical, sensational, emotional reason and will, a mechanical repetition of habitual notions and rules of conduct, not a play of real thought and intelligent determination. His use of them no more makes him a developed mental being than the daily movement to and from his place of business makes the average Londoner a developed physical being or his quotidian contributions to the economic life of the country make the bank-clerk a developed economic man. He is not mentally active, but mentally reactive, — a very different matter.

The Philistine is not dead, — quite the contrary, he abounds, — but he no longer reigns. The sons of Culture have not exactly conquered, but they have got rid of the old Goliath and replaced him by a new giant. This is the sensational man who has got awakened to the necessity at least of some intelligent use of the higher faculties and is trying to be mentally active. He has been whipped and censured and educated into that activity and he lives besides in a maelstrom of new information, new intellectual fashions, new ideas and new movements to which he can no longer be obstinately impervious. He is open to new ideas, he can catch at them and hurl them about in a rather confused fashion; he can understand or misunderstand ideals, organise to get them carried out and even, it would appear, fight and die for them. He knows he has to think about ethical problems, social problems, problems of science and religion, to welcome new political developments, to look with as understanding an eye as he can attain to at all the new movements of thought and inquiry and action that chase each other across the modern field or clash upon it. He is a reader of poetry as well as a devourer of fiction and periodical literature, — you will find in him perhaps a student of Tagore or an admirer of Whitman; he has perhaps no very clear ideas about beauty and aesthetics, but he has heard that Art is a not altogether unimportant part of life. The shadow of this new colossus is everywhere. He is the great reading public; the newspapers and weekly and monthly reviews are his; fiction and poetry and art are his mental caterers, the theatre and the cinema and the radio exist for him: Science hastens to bring her knowledge and discoveries to his doors and equip his life with endless machinery; politics are shaped in his image. It is he who opposed and then brought about the enfranchisement of women, who has been evolving syndicalism, anarchism, the war of classes, the uprising of labour, waging what we are told are wars of ideas or of cultures, — a ferocious type of conflict made in the very image of this new barbarism, — or bringing about in a few days Russian revolutions which the century-long efforts and sufferings of the intelligentsia failed to achieve. It is his coming which has been the precipitative agent for the reshaping of the modern world. If a Lenin, a Mussolini, a Hitler have achieved their rapid and almost stupefying success, it was because this driving force, this responsive quick-acting mass was there to carry them to victory — a force lacking to their less fortunate predecessors.

The first results of this momentous change have been inspiriting to our desire of movement, but a little disconcerting to the thinker and to the lover of a high and fine culture; for if it has to some extent democratised culture or the semblance of culture, it does not seem at first sight to have elevated or strengthened it by this large accession of the half-redeemed from below. Nor does the world seem to be guided any more directly by the reason and intelligent will of her best minds than before. Commercialism is still the heart of modern civilisation; a sensational activism is still its driving force. Modern education has not in the mass redeemed the sensational man; it has only made necessary to him things to which he was not formerly accustomed, mental activity and occupations, intellectual and even aesthetic sensations, emotions of idealism. He still lives in the vital substratum, but he wants it stimulated from above. He requires an army of writers to keep him mentally occupied and provide some sort of intellectual pabulum for him; he has a thirst for general information of all kinds which he does not care or has not time to coordinate or assimilate, for popularised scientific knowledge, for such new ideas as he can catch, provided they are put before him with force or brilliance, for mental sensations and excitation of many kinds, for ideals which he likes to think of as actuating his conduct and which do give it sometimes a certain colour. It is still the activism and sensationalism of the crude mental being, but much more open and free. And the cultured, the intelligentsia find that they can get a hearing from him such as they never had from the pure Philistine, provided they can first stimulate or amuse him; their ideas have now a chance of getting executed such as they never had before. The result has been to cheapen thought and art and literature, to make talent and even genius run in the grooves of popular success, to put the writer and thinker and scientist very much in a position like that of the cultured Greek slave in a Roman household where he has to work for, please, amuse and instruct his master while keeping a careful eye on his tastes and preferences and repeating trickily the manner and the points that have caught his fancy. The higher mental life, in a word, has been democratised, sensationalised, activised with both good and bad results. Through it all the eye of faith can see perhaps that a yet crude but an enormous change has begun. Thought and Knowledge, if not yet Beauty, can get a hearing and even produce rapidly some large, vague, yet in the end effective will for their results; the mass of culture and of men who think and strive seriously to appreciate and to know has enormously increased behind all this surface veil of sensationalism, and even the sensational man has begun to undergo a process of transformation. Especially, new methods of education, new principles of society are beginning to come into the range of practical possibility which will create perhaps one day that as yet unknown phenomenon, a race of men — not only a class — who have to some extent found and developed their mental selves, a cultured humanity.

Chapter X

Aesthetic and Ethical Culture

T HE IDEA of culture begins to define itself for us a little more clearly, or at least it has put away from it in a clear contrast its natural opposites. The unmental, the purely physical life is very obviously its opposite, it is barbarism; the unintellectualised vital, the crude economic or the grossly domestic life which looks only to money-getting, the procreation of a family and its maintenance, are equally its opposites; they are another and even uglier barbarism. We agree to regard the individual who is dominated by them and has no thought of higher things as an uncultured and undeveloped human being, a prolongation of the savage, essentially a barbarian even if he lives in a civilised nation and in a society which has arrived at the general idea and at some ordered practice of culture and refinement. The societies or nations which bear this stamp we agree to call barbarous or semi-barbarous. Even when a nation or an age has developed within itself knowledge and science and arts, but still in its general outlook, its habits of life and thought is content to be governed not by knowledge and truth and beauty and high ideals of living, but by the gross vital, commercial, economic view of existence, we say that that nation or age may be civilised in a sense, but for all its abundant or even redundant appliances and apparatus of civilisation it is not the realisation or the promise of a cultured humanity. Therefore upon even the European civilisation of the nineteenth century with all its triumphant and teeming production, its great developments of science, its achievement in the works of the intellect we pass a certain condemnation, because it has turned all these things to commercialism and to gross uses of vitalistic success. We say of it that this was not the perfection to which humanity ought to aspire and that this trend travels away from and not towards the higher curve of human evolution. It must be our definite verdict upon it that it was inferior as an age of culture to ancient Athens, to Italy of the Renascence, to ancient or classical India. For great as might be the deficiencies of social organisation in those eras and though their range of scientific knowledge and material achievement was immensely inferior, yet they were more advanced in the art of life, knew better its object and aimed more powerfully at some clear ideal of human perfection.

In the range of the mind's life itself, to live in its merely practical and dynamic activity or in the mentalised emotional or sensational current, a life of conventional conduct, average feelings, customary ideas, opinions and prejudices which are not one's own but those of the environment, to have no free and open play of mind, but to live grossly and unthinkingly by the unintelligent rule of the many, to live besides according to the senses and sensations controlled by certain conventions, but neither purified nor enlightened nor chastened by any law of beauty, — all this too is contrary to the ideal of culture. A man may so live with all the appearance or all the pretensions of a civilised existence, enjoy successfully all the plethora of its appurtenances, but he is not in the real sense a developed human being. A society following such a rule of life may be anything else you will, vigorous, decent, well-ordered, successful, religious, moral, but it is a Philistine society; it is a prison which the human soul has to break. For so long as it dwells there, it dwells in an inferior, uninspired and unexpanding mental status; it vegetates infructuously in the lower stratum and is governed not by the higher faculties of man, but by the crudities of the unuplifted sense-mind. Nor is it enough for it to open windows in this prison by which it may get draughts of agreeable fresh air, something of the free light of the intellect, something of the fragrance of art and beauty, something of the large breath of wider interests and higher ideals. It has yet to break out of its prison altogether and live in that free light, in that fragrance and large breath; only then does it breathe the natural atmosphere of the developed mental being. Not to live principally in the activities of the sense-mind, but in the activities of knowledge and reason and a wide intellectual curiosity, the activities of the cultivated aesthetic being, the activities of the enlightened will which make for character and high ethical ideals and a large human action, not to be governed by our lower or our average mentality but by truth and beauty and the self-ruling will is the ideal of a true culture and the beginning of an accomplished humanity.

We get then by elimination to a positive idea and definition of culture. But still on this higher plane of the mental life we are apt to be pursued by old exclusivenesses and misunderstandings. We see that in the past there seems often to have been a quarrel between culture and conduct; yet according to our definition conduct also is a part of the cultured life and the ethical ideality one of the master impulses of the cultured being. The opposition which puts on one side the pursuit of ideas and knowledge and beauty and calls that culture and on the other the pursuit of character and conduct and exalts that as the moral life must start evidently from an imperfect view of human possibility and perfection. Yet that opposition has not only existed, but is a naturally strong tendency of the human mind and therefore must answer to some real and important divergence in the very composite elements of our being. It is the opposition which Arnold drew between Hebraism and Hellenism. The trend of the Jewish nation which gave us the severe ethical religion of the Old Testament, — crude, conventional and barbarous enough in the Mosaic law, but rising to undeniable heights of moral exaltation when to the Law were added the Prophets, and finally exceeding itself and blossoming into a fine flower of spirituality in Judaic Christianity,[1] — was dominated by the preoccupation of a terrestrial and ethical righteousness and the promised rewards of right worship and right doing, but innocent of science and philosophy, careless of knowledge,

---

[1] The epithet is needed, for European Christianity has been something different, even at its best of another temperament, Latinised, Graecised, Celticised or else only a rough Teutonic imitation of the old-world Hebraism.

indifferent to beauty. The Hellenic mind was less exclusively but still largely dominated by a love of the play of reason for its own sake, but even more powerfully by a high sense of beauty, a clear aesthetic sensibility and a worship of the beautiful in every activity, in every creation, in thought, in art, in life, in religion. So strong was this sense that not only manners, but ethics were seen by it to a very remarkable extent in the light of its master idea of beauty; the good was to its instinct largely the becoming and the beautiful. In philosophy itself it succeeded in arriving at the conception of the Divine as Beauty, a truth which the metaphysician very readily misses and impoverishes his thought by missing it. But still, striking as is this great historical contrast and powerful as were its results on European culture, we have to go beyond its outward manifestation if we would understand in its source this psychological opposition.

The conflict arises from that sort of triangular disposition of the higher or more subtle mentality which we have already had occasion to indicate. There is in our mentality a side of will, conduct, character which creates the ethical man; there is another side of sensibility to the beautiful, — understanding beauty in no narrow or hyper-artistic sense, — which creates the artistic and aesthetic man. Therefore there can be such a thing as a predominantly or even exclusively ethical culture; there can be too, evidently, a predominantly or even exclusively aesthetic culture. There are at once created two conflicting ideals which must naturally stand opposed and look askance at each other with a mutual distrust or even reprobation. The aesthetic man tends to be impatient of the ethical rule; he feels it to be a barrier to his aesthetic freedom and an oppression on the play of his artistic sense and his artistic faculty; he is naturally hedonistic, — for beauty and delight are inseparable powers, — and the ethical rule tramples on pleasure, even very often on quite innocent pleasures, and tries to put a strait waistcoat on the human impulse to delight. He may accept the ethical rule when it makes itself beautiful or even seize on it as one of his instruments for creating beauty, but only when he can subordinate it to the aesthetic principle of his nature, — just as

he is often drawn to religion by its side of beauty, pomp, magnificent ritual, emotional satisfaction, repose or poetic ideality and
aspiration, — we might almost say, by the hedonistic aspects
of religion. Even when fully accepted, it is not for their own
sake that he accepts them. The ethical man repays this natural
repulsion with interest. He tends to distrust art and the aesthetic
sense as something lax and emollient, something in its nature
undisciplined and by its attractive appeals to the passions and
emotions destructive of a high and strict self-control. He sees
that it is hedonistic and he finds that the hedonistic impulse is
non-moral and often immoral. It is difficult for him to see how
the indulgence of the aesthetic impulse beyond a very narrow
and carefully guarded limit can be combined with a strict ethical
life. He evolves the puritan who objects to pleasure on principle;
not only in his extremes — and a predominant impulse tends to
become absorbing and leads towards extremes — but in the core
of his temperament he remains fundamentally the puritan. The
misunderstanding between these two sides of our nature is an
inevitable circumstance of our human growth which must try
them to their fullest separate possibilities and experiment in
extremes in order that it may understand the whole range of its
capacities.

Society is only an enlargement of the individual; therefore
this contrast and opposition between individual types repro-
duces itself in a like contrast and opposition between social and
national types. We must not go for the best examples to social
formulas which do not really illustrate these tendencies but are
depravations, deformations or deceptive conformities. We must
not take as an instance of the ethical turn the middle-class puritanism touched with a narrow, tepid and conventional religiosity
which was so marked an element in nineteenth-century England;
that was not an ethical culture, but simply a local variation of the
general type of bourgeois respectability you will find everywhere
at a certain stage of civilisation, — it was Philistinism pure and
simple. Nor should we take as an instance of the aesthetic any
merely Bohemian society or such examples as London of the
Restoration or Paris in certain brief periods of its history; that,

whatever some of its pretensions, had for its principle, always, the indulgence of the average sensational and sensuous man freed from the conventions of morality by a superficial intellectualism and aestheticism. Nor even can we take Puritan England as the ethical type; for although there was there a strenuous, an exaggerated culture of character and the ethical being, the determining tendency was religious, and the religious impulse is a phenomenon quite apart from our other subjective tendencies, though it influences them all; it is *sui generis* and must be treated separately. To get at real, if not always quite pure examples of the type we must go back a little farther in time and contrast early republican Rome or, in Greece itself, Sparta with Periclean Athens. For as we come down the stream of Time in its present curve of evolution, humanity in the mass, carrying in it its past collective experience, becomes more and more complex and the old distinct types do not recur or recur precariously and with difficulty.

Republican Rome — before it was touched and finally taken captive by conquered Greece — stands out in relief as one of the most striking psychological phenomena of human history. From the point of view of human development it presents itself as an almost unique experiment in high and strong character-building divorced as far as may be from the sweetness which the sense of beauty and the light which the play of the reason brings into character and uninspired by the religious temperament; for the early Roman creed was a superstition, a superficial religiosity and had nothing in it of the true religious spirit. Rome was the human will oppressing and disciplining the emotional and sensational mind in order to arrive at the self-mastery of a definite ethical type; and it was this self-mastery which enabled the Roman republic to arrive also at the mastery of its environing world and impose on the nations its public order and law. All supremely successful imperial nations have had in their culture or in their nature, in their formative or expansive periods, this predominance of the will, the character, the impulse to self-discipline and self-mastery which constitutes the very basis of the ethical tendency. Rome and Sparta like other ethical civilisations

had their considerable moral deficiencies, tolerated or deliber-
ately encouraged customs and practices which we should call
immoral, failed to develop the gentler and more delicate side
of moral character, but this is of no essential importance. The
ethical idea in man changes and enlarges its scope, but the kernel of the true ethical being remains always the same, — will,
character, self-discipline, self-mastery.

Its limitations at once appear, when we look back at its
prominent examples. Early Rome and Sparta were barren of
thought, art, poetry, literature, the larger mental life, all the
amenity and pleasure of human existence; their art of life excluded or discouraged the delight of living. They were distrustful, as the exclusively ethical man is always distrustful, of free
and flexible thought and the aesthetic impulse. The earlier spirit
of republican Rome held at arm's length as long as possible
the Greek influences that invaded her, closed the schools of the
Greek teachers, banished the philosophers, and her most typical
minds looked upon the Greek language as a peril and Greek
culture as an abomination: she felt instinctively the arrival at
her gates of an enemy, divined a hostile and destructive force
fatal to her principle of living. Sparta, though a Hellenic city,
admitted as almost the sole aesthetic element of her deliberate
ethical training and education a martial music and poetry, and
even then, when she wanted a poet of war, she had to import an
Athenian. We have a curious example of the repercussion of this
instinctive distrust even on a large and aesthetic Athenian mind
in the utopian speculations of Plato who felt himself obliged in
his Republic first to censure and then to banish the poets from his
ideal polity. The end of these purely ethical cultures bears witness
to their insufficiency. Either they pass away leaving nothing or
little behind them by which the future can be attracted and satisfied, as Sparta passed, or they collapse in a revolt of the complex
nature of man against an unnatural restriction and repression,
as the early Roman type collapsed into the egoistic and often
orgiastic licence of later republican and imperial Rome. The
human mind needs to think, feel, enjoy, expand; expansion is its
very nature and restriction is only useful to it in so far as it helps

to steady, guide and strengthen its expansion. It readily refuses the name of culture to those civilisations or periods, however noble their aim or even however beautiful in itself their order, which have not allowed an intelligent freedom of development.

On the other hand, we are tempted to give the name of a full culture to all those periods and civilisations, whatever their defects, which have encouraged a freely human development and like ancient Athens have concentrated on thought and beauty and the delight of living. But there were in the Athenian development two distinct periods, one of art and beauty, the Athens of Phidias and Sophocles, and one of thought, the Athens of the philosophers. In the first period the sense of beauty and the need of freedom of life and the enjoyment of life are the determining forces. This Athens thought, but it thought in the terms of art and poetry, in figures of music and drama and architecture and sculpture; it delighted in intellectual discussion, but not so much with any will to arrive at truth as for the pleasure of thinking and the beauty of ideas. It had its moral order, for without that no society can exist, but it had no true ethical impulse or ethical type, only a conventional and customary morality; and when it thought about ethics, it tended to express it in the terms of beauty, *to kalon, to epieikes*, the beautiful, the becoming. Its very religion was a religion of beauty and an occasion for pleasant ritual and festivals and for artistic creation, an aesthetic enjoyment touched with a superficial religious sense. But without character, without some kind of high or strong discipline there is no enduring power of life. Athens exhausted its vitality within one wonderful century which left it enervated, will-less, unable to succeed in the struggle of life, uncreative. It turned indeed for a time precisely to that which had been lacking to it, the serious pursuit of truth and the evolution of systems of ethical self-discipline; but it could only think, it could not successfully practise. The later Hellenic mind and Athenian centre of culture gave to Rome the great Stoic system of ethical discipline which saved her in the midst of the orgies of her first imperial century, but could not itself be stoical in its practice; for to Athens and to the characteristic temperament of Hellas, this thought was a straining to something it had not and could not have; it was the opposite of its nature and not its fulfilment.

This insufficiency of the aesthetic view of life becomes yet more evident when we come down to its other great example, Italy of the Renascence. The Renascence was regarded at one time as pre-eminently a revival of learning, but in its Mediterranean birth-place it was rather the efflorescence of art and poetry and the beauty of life. Much more than was possible even in the laxest times of Hellas, aesthetic culture was divorced from the ethical impulse and at times was even anti-ethical and reminiscent of the licence of imperial Rome. It had learning and curiosity, but gave very little of itself to high thought and truth and the more finished achievements of the reason, although it helped to make free the way for philosophy and science. It so corrupted religion as to provoke in the ethically minded Teutonic nations the violent revolt of the Reformation, which, though it vindicated the freedom of the religious mind, was an insurgence not so much of the reason, — that was left to Science, — but of the moral instinct and its ethical need. The subsequent prostration and loose weakness of Italy was the inevitable result of the great defect of its period of fine culture, and it needed for its revival the new impulse of thought and will and character given to it by Mazzini. If the ethical impulse is not sufficient by itself for the development of the human being, yet are will, character, self-discipline, self-mastery indispensable to that development. They are the backbone of the mental body.

Neither the ethical being nor the aesthetic being is the whole man, nor can either be his sovereign principle; they are merely two powerful elements. Ethical conduct is not the whole of life; even to say that it is three-fourths of life is to indulge in a very doubtful mathematics. We cannot assign to it its position in any such definite language, but can at best say that its kernel of will, character and self-discipline are almost the first condition for human self-perfection. The aesthetic sense is equally indispensable, for without that the self-perfection of the mental being cannot arrive at its object, which is on the mental plane the right and harmonious possession and enjoyment of the truth, power, beauty and delight of human existence. But neither can be the highest principle of the human order. We can combine them; we can enlarge the sense of ethics by the sense of beauty and delight and introduce into it to correct its tendency of hardness and austerity the element of gentleness, love, amenity, the hedonistic side of morals; we can steady, guide and strengthen the delight of life by the introduction of the necessary will and austerity and self-discipline which will give it endurance and purity. These two powers of our psychological being, which represent in us the essential principle of energy and the essential principle of delight, — the Indian terms are more profound and expressive, Tapas and Ananda,[2] — can be thus helped by each other, the one to a richer, the other to a greater self-expression. But that even this much reconciliation may come about they must be taken up and enlightened by a higher principle which must be capable of understanding and comprehending both equally and of disengaging and combining disinterestedly their purposes and potentialities. That higher principle seems to be provided for us by the human faculty of reason and intelligent will. Our crowning capacity, it would seem to be by right the crowned sovereign of our nature.

---

[2] Tapas is the energising conscious-power of cosmic being by which the world is created, maintained and governed; it includes all concepts of force, will, energy, power, everything dynamic and dynamising. Ananda is the essential nature of bliss of the cosmic consciousness and, in activity, its delight of self-creation and self-experience.

Chapter XI

The Reason as Governor of Life

REASON using the intelligent will for the ordering of the inner and the outer life is undoubtedly the highest developed faculty of man at his present point of evolution; it is the sovereign, because the governing and self-governing faculty in the complexities of our human existence. Man is distinguished from other terrestrial creatures by his capacity for seeking after a rule of life, a rule of his being and his works, a principle of order and self-development, which is not the first instinctive, original, mechanically self-operative rule of his natural existence. The principle he looks to is neither the unchanging, unprogressive order of the fixed natural type, nor in its process of change the mechanical evolution we see in the lower life, an evolution which operates in the mass rather than in the individual, imperceptibly to the knowledge of that which is being evolved and without its conscious cooperation. He seeks for an intelligent rule of which he himself shall be the governor and master or at least a partially free administrator. He can conceive a progressive order by which he shall be able to evolve and develop his capacities far beyond their original limits and workings; he can initiate an intelligent evolution which he himself shall determine or at least be in it a conscious instrument, more, a cooperating and constantly consulted party. The rest of terrestrial existence is helplessly enslaved and tyrannised over by its nature, but the instinct of man when he finds his manhood is to be master of his nature and free.

No doubt all is work of Nature and this too is Nature; it proceeds from the principle of being which constitutes his humanity and by the processes which that principle permits and which are natural to it. But still it is a second kind of Nature, a stage of being in which Nature becomes self-conscious in the individual, tries to know, modify, alter and develop, utilise, consciously experiment with herself and her potentialities. In this change a momentous self-discovery intervenes; there appears something that is hidden in matter and in the first disposition of life and has not clearly emerged in the animal in spite of its possession of a mind; there appears the presence of the Soul in things which at first was concealed in its own natural and outward workings, absorbed and on the surface at least self-oblivious. Afterwards it becomes, as in the animal, conscious to a certain degree on the surface, but is still helplessly given up to the course of its natural workings and, not understanding, cannot govern itself and its movements. But finally, in man, it turns its consciousness upon itself, seeks to know, endeavours to govern in the individual the workings of his nature and through the individual and the combined reason and energy of many individuals to govern too as far as possible the workings of Nature in mankind and in things. This turning of the consciousness upon itself and on things, which man represents, has been the great crisis, a prolonged and developing crisis, in the terrestrial evolution of the soul in Nature. There have been others before it in the past of the earth, such as that which brought about the appearance of the conscious life of the animal; there must surely be another in its future in which a higher spiritual and supramental consciousness shall emerge and be turned upon the works of the mind. But at present it is this which is at work; a self-conscious soul in mind, mental being, *manomaya puruṣa*, struggles to arrive at some intelligent ordering of its self and life and some indefinite, perhaps infinite development of the powers and potentialities of the human instrument.

The intellectual reason is not man's only means of knowledge. All action, all perception, all aesthesis and sensation, all impulse and will, all imagination and creation imply a universal, many-sided force of knowledge at work and each form or power of this knowledge has its own distinct nature and law, its own principle of order and arrangement, its own logic proper to itself, and need not follow, still less be identical with the law of nature, order and arrangement which the intellectual reason would assign to it or itself follow if it had control of all these movements. But the intellect has this advantage over the others that it can disengage itself from the work, stand back from it to study and understand it disinterestedly, analyse its processes, disengage its principles. None of the other powers and faculties of the living being can do this: for each exists for its own action, is confined by the work it is doing, is unable to see beyond it, around it, into it as the reason can; the principle of knowledge inherent within each force is involved and carried along in the action of the force, helps to shape it, but is also itself limited by its own formulations. It exists for the fulfilment of the action, not for knowledge, or for knowledge only as part of the action. Moreover, it is concerned only with the particular action or working of the moment and does not look back reflectively or forward intelligently or at other actions and forces with a power of clear coordination. No doubt, the other evolved powers of the living being, as for instance the instinct whether animal or human, — the latter inferior precisely because it is disturbed by the questionings and seekings of reason, — carry in themselves their own force of past experience, of instinctive self-adaptation, all of which is really accumulated knowledge, and they hold sometimes this store so firmly that they are transmitted as a sure inheritance from generation to generation. But all this, just because it is instinctive, not turned upon itself reflectively, is of great use indeed to life for the conduct of its operations, but of none — so long as it is not taken up by the reason — for the particular purpose man has in view, a new order of the dealings of the soul in Nature, a free, rational, intelligently coordinating, intelligently self-observing, intelligently experimenting mastery of the workings of force by the conscious spirit.

Reason, on the other hand, exists for the sake of knowledge, can prevent itself from being carried away by the action, can stand back from it, intelligently study, accept, refuse, modify, alter, improve, combine and recombine the workings and capacities of the forces in operation, can repress here, indulge there, strive towards an intelligent, intelligible, willed and organised perfection. Reason is science, it is conscious art, it is invention. It is observation and can seize and arrange truth of facts; it is speculation and can extricate and forecast truth of potentiality. It is the idea and its fulfilment, the ideal and its bringing to fruition. It can look through the immediate appearance and unveil the hidden truths behind it. It is the servant and yet the master of all utilities; and it can, putting away all utilities, seek disinterestedly Truth for its own sake and by finding it reveal a whole world of new possible utilities. Therefore it is the sovereign power by which man has become possessed of himself, student and master of his own forces, the godhead on which the other godheads in him have leaned for help in their ascent; it has been the Prometheus of the mythical parable, the helper, instructor, elevating friend, civiliser of mankind.

Recently, however, there has been a very noticeable revolt of the human mind against this sovereignty of the intellect, a dissatisfaction, as we might say, of the reason with itself and its own limitations and an inclination to give greater freedom and a larger importance to other powers of our nature. The sovereignty of the reason in man has been always indeed imperfect, in fact, a troubled, struggling, resisted and often defeated rule; but still it has been recognised by the best intelligence of the race as the authority and law-giver. Its only widely acknowledged rival has been faith. Religion alone has been strongly successful in its claim that reason must be silent before it or at least that there are fields to which it cannot extend itself and where faith alone ought to be heard; but for a time even Religion has had to forego or abate its absolute pretension and to submit to the sovereignty of the intellect. Life, imagination, emotion, the ethical and the aesthetic need have often claimed to exist for their own sake and to follow their own bent, practically they have often enforced their claim, but they have still been obliged in general to work under the inquisition and partial control of reason and to refer to it as arbiter and judge. Now, however, the thinking mind of the race has become more disposed to question itself and to ask whether existence is not too large, profound, complex and mysterious a thing to be entirely seized and governed by the powers of the intellect. Vaguely it is felt that there is some greater godhead than the reason.

To some this godhead is Life itself or a secret Will in life; they claim that this must rule and that the intelligence is only useful in so far as it serves that and that Life must not be repressed, minimised and mechanised by the arbitrary control of reason. Life has greater powers in it which must be given a freer play; for it is they alone that evolve and create. On the other hand, it is felt that reason is too analytical, too arbitrary, that it falsifies life by its distinctions and set classifications and the fixed rules based upon them and that there is some profounder and larger power of knowledge, intuition or another, which is more deeply in the secrets of existence. This larger intimate power is more one with the depths and sources of existence and more able to give us the indivisible truths of life, its root realities and to work them out, not in an artificial and mechanical spirit but with a divination of the secret Will in existence and in a free harmony with its large, subtle and infinite methods. In fact, what the growing subjectivism of the human mind is beginning obscurely to see is that the one sovereign godhead is the soul itself which may use reason for one of its ministers, but cannot subject itself to its own intellectuality without limiting its potentialities and artificialising its conduct of existence.

The highest power of reason, because its pure and characteristic power, is the disinterested seeking after true knowledge. When knowledge is pursued for its own sake, then alone are we likely to arrive at true knowledge. Afterwards we may utilise that knowledge for various ends; but if from the beginning we have only particular ends in view, then we limit our intellectual gain, limit our view of things, distort the truth because we cast it into the mould of some particular idea or utility and ignore or deny all that conflicts with that utility or that set idea. By so doing we may indeed make the reason act with great immediate power within the limits of the idea or the utility we have in view, just as instinct in the animal acts with great power within certain limits, for a certain end, yet finds itself helpless outside those limits. It is so indeed that the ordinary man uses his reason — as the animal uses his hereditary, transmitted instinct — with an absorbed devotion of it to the securing of some particular utility or with a useful but hardly luminous application of a customary and transmitted reasoning to the necessary practical interests of his life. Even the thinking man ordinarily limits his reason to the working out of certain preferred ideas; he ignores or denies all that is not useful to these or does not assist or justify or actually contradicts or seriously modifies them, — except in so far as life itself compels or cautions him to accept modifications for the time being or ignore their necessity at his peril. It is in such limits that man's reason normally acts. He follows most commonly some interest or set of interests; he tramples down or through or ignores or pushes aside all truth of life and existence, truth of ethics, truth of beauty, truth of reason, truth of spirit which conflicts with his chosen opinions and interests; if he recognises these foreign elements, it is nominally, not in practice, or else with a distortion, a glossing which nullifies their consequences, perverts their spirit or whittles down their significance. It is this subjection to the interests, needs, instincts, passions, prejudices, traditional ideas and opinions of the ordinary mind[1] which constitutes the irrationality of human existence.

But even the man who is capable of governing his life by ideas, who recognises, that is to say, that it ought to express clearly conceived truths and principles of his being or of all being and tries to find out or to know from others what these are, is not often capable of the highest, the free and disinterested use of his rational mind. As others are subject to the tyranny of their interests, prejudices, instincts or passions, so he is subjected to the tyranny of ideas. Indeed, he turns these ideas into interests, obscures them with his prejudices and passions and is unable to think freely about them, unable to distinguish their limits or the relation to them of other, different and opposite ideas and the equal right of these also to existence. Thus, as we constantly see, individuals, masses of men, whole generations are carried away by certain ethical, religious, aesthetic, political ideas or a set of

---

[1] The ordinary mind in man is not truly the thinking mind proper, it is a life-mind, a vital mind as we may call it, which has learned to think and even to reason but for its own ends and on its own lines, not on those of a true mind of knowledge.

ideas, espouse them with passion, pursue them as interests, seek
to make them a system and lasting rule of life and are swept
away in the drive of their action and do not really use the free
and disinterested reason for the right knowledge of existence
and for its right and sane government. The ideas are to a certain
extent fulfilled, they triumph for a time, but their very success
brings disappointment and disillusionment. This happens, first,
because they can only succeed by compromises and pacts with
the inferior, irrational life of man which diminish their validity
and tarnish their light and glory. Often indeed their triumph is
convicted of unreality, and doubt and disillusionment fall on
the faith and enthusiasm which brought victory to their side.
But even were it not so, the ideas themselves are partial and
insufficient; not only have they a very partial triumph, but if their
success were complete, it would still disappoint, because they are
not the whole truth of life and therefore cannot securely govern
and perfect life. Life escapes from the formulas and systems
which our reason labours to impose on it; it proclaims itself too
complex, too full of infinite potentialities to be tyrannised over
by the arbitrary intellect of man.

This is the cause why all human systems have failed in the
end; for they have never been anything but a partial and confused
application of reason to life. Moreover, even where they have
been most clear and rational, these systems have pretended that
their ideas were the whole truth of life and tried so to apply
them. This they could not be, and life in the end has broken or
undermined them and passed on to its own large incalculable
movement. Mankind, thus using its reason as an aid and justification for its interests and passions, thus obeying the drive
of a partial, a mixed and imperfect rationality towards action,
thus striving to govern the complex totalities of life by partial
truths, has stumbled on from experiment to experiment, always
believing that it is about to grasp the crown, always finding that
it has fulfilled as yet little or nothing of what it has to accomplish.
Compelled by nature to apply reason to life, yet possessing only
a partial rationality limited in itself and confused by the siege
of the lower members, it could do nothing else. For the limited

imperfect human reason has no self-sufficient light of its own; it is obliged to proceed by observation, by experiment, by action, through errors and stumblings to a larger experience.

But behind all this continuity of failure there has persisted a faith that the reason of man would end in triumphing over its difficulties, that it would purify and enlarge itself, become sufficient to its work and at last subject rebellious life to its control. For, apart from the stumbling action of the world, there has been a labour of the individual thinker in man and this has achieved a higher quality and risen to a loftier and clearer atmosphere above the general human thought-levels. Here there has been the work of a reason that seeks always after knowledge and strives patiently to find out truth for itself, without bias, without the interference of distorting interests, to study everything, to analyse everything, to know the principle and process of everything. Philosophy, Science, learning, the reasoned arts, all the agelong labour of the critical reason in man have been the result of this effort. In the modern era under the impulsion of Science this effort assumed enormous proportions and claimed for a time to examine successfully and lay down finally the true principle and the sufficient rule of process not only for all the activities of Nature, but for all the activities of man. It has done great things, but it has not been in the end a success. The human mind is beginning to perceive that it has left the heart of almost every problem untouched and illumined only outsides and a certain range of processes. There has been a great and ordered classification and mechanisation, a great discovery and practical result of increasing knowledge, but only on the physical surface of things. Vast abysses of Truth lie below in which are concealed the real springs, the mysterious powers and secretly decisive influences of existence. It is a question whether the intellectual reason will ever be able to give us an adequate account of these deeper and greater things or subject them to the intelligent will as it has succeeded in explaining and canalising, though still imperfectly, yet with much show of triumphant result, the forces of physical Nature. But these other powers are much larger, subtler, deeper down, more hidden, elusive and variable than those of physical Nature.

The whole difficulty of the reason in trying to govern our existence is that because of its own inherent limitations it is unable to deal with life in its complexity or in its integral movements; it is compelled to break it up into parts, to make more or less artificial classifications, to build systems with limited data which are contradicted, upset or have to be continually modified by other data, to work out a selection of regulated potentialities which is broken down by the bursting of a new wave of yet unregulated potentialities. It would almost appear even that there are two worlds, the world of ideas proper to the intellect and the world of life which escapes from the full control of the reason, and that to bridge adequately the gulf between these two domains is beyond the power and province of the reason and the intelligent will. It would seem that these can only create either a series of more or less empirical compromises or else a series of arbitrary and practically inapplicable or only partially applicable systems. The reason of man struggling with life becomes either an empiric or a doctrinaire.

Reason can indeed make itself a mere servant of life; it can limit itself to the work the average normal man demands from it, content to furnish means and justifications for the interests, passions, prejudices of man and clothe them with a misleading garb of rationality or at most supply them with their own secure and enlightened order or with rules of caution and self-restraint sufficient to prevent their more egregious stumbles and most unpleasant consequences. But this is obviously to abdicate its throne or its highest office and to betray the hope with which man set forth on his journey. It may again determine to found itself securely on the facts of life, disinterestedly indeed, that is to say, with a dispassionate critical observation of its principles and processes, but with a prudent resolve not to venture too much forward into the unknown or elevate itself far beyond the immediate realities of our apparent or phenomenal existence. But here again it abdicates; either it becomes a mere critic and observer or else, so far as it tries to lay down laws, it does so within very narrow limits of immediate potentiality and it renounces man's drift towards higher possibilities, his saving gift of idealism. In this limited use of the reason subjected to the rule of an immediate, an apparent vital and physical practicality man cannot rest long satisfied. For his nature pushes him towards the heights; it demands a constant effort of self-transcendence and the impulsion towards things unachieved and even immediately impossible.

On the other hand, when it attempts a higher action reason separates itself from life. Its very attempt at a disinterested and dispassionate knowledge carries it to an elevation where it loses hold of that other knowledge which our instincts and impulses carry within themselves and which, however imperfect, obscure and limited, is still a hidden action of the universal Knowledge-Will inherent in existence that creates and directs all things according to their nature. True, even Science and Philosophy are never entirely dispassionate and disinterested. They fall into subjection to the tyranny of their own ideas, their partial systems, their hasty generalisations and by the innate drive of man towards practice they seek to impose these upon the life. But even so they enter into a world either of abstract ideas or of ideals or of rigid laws from which the complexity of life escapes. The idealist, the thinker, the philosopher, the poet and artist, even the moralist, all those who live much in ideas, when they come to grapple at close quarters with practical life, seem to find themselves something at a loss and are constantly defeated in their endeavour to govern life by their ideas. They exercise a powerful influence, but it is indirectly, more by throwing their ideas into Life which does with them what the secret Will in it chooses than by a direct and successfully ordered action. Not that the pure empiric, the practical man really succeeds any better by his direct action; for that too is taken by the secret Will in life and turned to quite other ends than the practical man had intended. On the contrary, ideals and idealists are necessary; ideals are the savour and sap of life, idealists the most powerful diviners and assistants of its purposes. But reduce your ideal to a system and it at once begins to fail; apply your general laws and fixed ideas systematically as the doctrinaire would do, and Life very soon breaks through or writhes out of their hold or transforms your system, even while it nominally exists, into something the originator would not recognise and would repudiate perhaps as the very contradiction of the principles which he sought to eternise.

The root of the difficulty is this that at the very basis of all our life and existence, internal and external, there is something on which the intellect can never lay a controlling hold, the Absolute, the Infinite. Behind everything in life there is an Absolute, which that thing is seeking after in its own way; everything finite is striving to express an infinite which it feels to be its real truth. Moreover, it is not only each class, each type, each tendency in Nature that is thus impelled to strive after its own secret truth in its own way, but each individual brings in his own variations. Thus there is not only an Absolute, an Infinite in itself which governs its own expression in many forms and tendencies, but there is also a principle of infinite potentiality and variation quite baffling to the reasoning intelligence; for the reason deals successfully only with the settled and the finite. In man this difficulty reaches its acme. For not only is mankind unlimited in potentiality; not only is each of its powers and tendencies seeking after its own absolute in its own way and therefore naturally restless under any rigid control by the reason; but in each man their degrees, methods, combinations vary, each man belongs not only to the common humanity, but to the Infinite in himself and is therefore unique. It is because this is the reality of our existence that the intellectual reason and the intelligent will cannot deal with life as its sovereign, even though they may be at present our supreme instruments and may have been in our evolution supremely important and helpful. The reason can govern, but only as a minister, imperfectly, or as a general arbiter and giver of suggestions which are not really supreme commands, or as one channel of the sovereign authority, because that hidden Power acts at present not directly but through many agents and messengers. The real sovereign is another than the reasoning intelligence. Man's impulse to be free, master of Nature in himself and his environment cannot be really fulfilled until his self-consciousness has grown beyond the rational mentality, become aware of the true sovereign and either identified itself with him or entered into constant communion with his supreme will and knowledge.

Chapter XII

The Office and Limitations
of the Reason

IF THE reason is not the sovereign master of our being nor
even intended to be more than an intermediary or minister,
it cannot succeed in giving a perfect law to the other estates
of the realm, although it may impose on them a temporary
and imperfect order as a passage to a higher perfection. The
rational or intellectual man is not the last and highest ideal of
manhood, nor would a rational society be the last and highest
expression of the possibilities of an aggregate human life, —
unless indeed we give to this word, reason, a wider meaning
than it now possesses and include in it the combined wisdom
of all our powers of knowledge, those which stand below and
above the understanding and logical mind as well as this strictly
rational part of our nature. The Spirit that manifests itself in
man and dominates secretly the phases of his development, is
greater and profounder than his intellect and drives towards a
perfection that cannot be shut in by the arbitrary constructions
of the human reason.

Meanwhile, the intellect performs its function; it leads man
to the gates of a greater self-consciousness and places him with
unbandaged eyes on that wide threshold where a more luminous
Angel has to take him by the hand. It takes first the lower powers
of his existence, each absorbed in its own urge, each striving
with a blind self-sufficiency towards the fulfilment of its own
instincts and primary impulses; it teaches them to understand
themselves and to look through the reflecting eyes of the intelligence on the laws of their own action. It enables them to
discern intelligently the high in themselves from the low, the
pure from the impure and out of a crude confusion to arrive at
more and more luminous formulas of their possibilities. It gives

them self-knowledge and is a guide, teacher, purifier, liberator. For it enables them also to look beyond themselves and at each other and to draw upon each other for fresh motives and a richer working. It strengthens and purifies the hedonistic and the aesthetic activities and softens their quarrel with the ethical mind and instinct; it gives them solidity and seriousness, brings them to the support of the practical and dynamic powers and allies them more closely to the strong actualities of life. It sweetens the ethical will by infusing into it psychic, hedonistic and aesthetic elements and ennobles by all these separately or together the practical, dynamic and utilitarian temperament of the human being. At the same time it plays the part of a judge and legislator, seeks to fix rules, provide systems and regularised combinations which shall enable the powers of the human soul to walk by a settled path and act according to a sure law, an ascertained measure and in a balanced rhythm. Here it finds after a time that its legislative action becomes a force for limitation and turns into a bondage and that the regularised system which it has imposed in the interests of order and conservation becomes a cause of petrifaction and the sealing up of the fountains of life. It has to bring in its own saving faculty of doubt. Under the impulse of the intelligence warned by the obscure revolt of the oppressed springs of life, ethics, aesthetics, the social, political, economic rule begin to question themselves and, if this at first brings in again some confusion, disorder and uncertainty, yet it awakens new movements of imagination, insight, self-knowledge and self-realisation by which old systems and formulas are transformed or disappear, new experiments are made and in the end larger potentialities and combinations are brought into play. By this double action of the intelligence, affirming and imposing what it has seen and again in due season questioning what has been accomplished in order to make a new affirmation, fixing a rule and order and liberating from rule and order, the progress of the race is assured, however uncertain may seem its steps and stages.

But the action of the intelligence is not only turned downward and outward upon our subjective and external life to understand it and determine the law and order of its present movement and its future potentialities. It has also an upward and inward eye and a more luminous functioning by which it accepts divinations from the hidden eternities. It is opened in this power of vision to a Truth above it from which it derives, however imperfectly and as from behind a veil, an indirect knowledge of the universal principles of our existence and its possibilities; it receives and turns what it can seize of them into intellectual forms and these provide us with large governing ideas by which our efforts can be shaped and around which they can be concentrated or massed; it defines the ideals which we seek to accomplish. It provides us with the great ideas that are forces (*idées forces*), ideas which in their own strength impose themselves upon our life and compel it into their moulds. Only the forms we give these ideas are intellectual; they themselves descend from a plane of truth of being where knowledge and force are one, the idea and the power of self-fulfilment in the idea are inseparable. Unfortunately, when translated into the forms of our intelligence which acts only by a separating and combining analysis and synthesis and into the effort of our life which advances by a sort of experimental and empirical seeking, these powers become disparate and conflicting ideals which we have all the difficulty in the world to bring into any kind of satisfactory harmony. Such are the primary principles of liberty and order, good, beauty and truth, the ideal of power and the ideal of love, individualism and collectivism, self-denial and self-fulfilment and a hundred others. In each sphere of human life, in each part of our being and our action the intellect presents us with the opposition of a number of such master ideas and such conflicting principles. It finds each to be a truth to which something essential in our being responds, — in our higher nature a law, in our lower nature an instinct. It seeks to fulfil each in turn, builds a system of action round it and goes from one to the other and back again to what it has left. Or it tries to combine them but is contented with none of the combinations it has made because none brings about their perfect reconciliation or their satisfied oneness. That indeed belongs to a larger and higher consciousness, not yet attained by mankind, where these opposites are ever harmonised and even unified because in their origin they are eternally one. But still every enlarged attempt of the intelligence thus dealing with our inner and outer life increases the width and wealth of our nature, opens it to larger possibilities of self-knowledge and self-realisation and brings us nearer to our awakening into that greater consciousness.

The individual and social progress of man has been thus a double movement of self-illumination and self-harmonising with the intelligence and the intelligent will as the intermediaries between his soul and its works. He has had to bring out numberless possibilities of self-understanding, self-mastery, self-formation out of his first crude life of instincts and impulses; he has been constantly impelled to convert that lower animal or half-animal existence with its imperfect self-conscience into the stuff of intelligent being, instincts into ideas, impulses into ordered movements of an intelligent will. But as he has to proceed out of ignorance into knowledge by a slow labour of self-recognition and mastery of his surroundings and his material and as his intelligence is incapable of seizing comprehensively the whole of himself in knowledge, unable to work out comprehensively the mass of his possibilities in action, he has had to proceed piecemeal, by partial experiments, by creation of different types, by a constant swinging backward and forward between the various possibilities before him and the different elements he has to harmonise.

It is not only that he has to contrive continually some new harmony between the various elements of his being, physical, vitalistic, practical and dynamic, aesthetic, emotional and hedonistic, ethical, intellectual, but each of them again has to arrive at some order of its own disparate materials. In his ethics he is divided by different moral tendencies, justice and charity, self-help and altruism, self-increase and self-abnegation, the tendencies of strength and the tendencies of love, the moral rule of activism and the moral rule of quietism. His emotions are necessary to his development and their indulgence essential

to the outflowering of his rich humanity; yet is he constantly
called upon to coerce and deny them, nor is there any sure rule
to guide him in the perplexity of this twofold need. His hedonistic impulse is called many ways by different fields, objects,
ideals of self-satisfaction. His aesthetic enjoyment, his aesthetic
creation forms for itself under the stress of the intelligence different laws and forms; each seeks to impose itself as the best
and the standard, yet each, if its claim were allowed, would by
its unjust victory impoverish and imprison his faculty and his
felicity in its exercise. His politics and society are a series of
adventures and experiments among various possibilities of autocracy, monarchism, military aristocracy, mercantile oligarchy,
open or veiled plutocracy, pseudo-democracy of various kinds,
bourgeois or proletarian, individualistic or collectivist or bu-
reaucratic, socialism awaiting him, anarchism looming beyond
it; and all these correspond to some truth of his social being,
some need of his complex social nature, some instinct or force
in it which demands that form for its effectuation. Mankind
works out these difficulties under the stress of the spirit within it
by throwing out a constant variation of types, types of character
and temperament, types of practical activity, aesthetic creation,
polity, society, ethical order, intellectual system, which vary from
the pure to the mixed, from the simple harmony to the complex;
each and all of these are so many experiments of individual
and collective self-formation in the light of a progressive and
increasing knowledge. That knowledge is governed by a number
of conflicting ideas and ideals around which these experiments
group themselves: each of them is gradually pushed as far as
possible in its purity and again mixed and combined as much
as possible with others so that there may be a more complex
form and an enriched action. Each type has to be broken in
turn to yield place to new types and each combination has to
give way to the possibility of a new combination. Through it
all there is growing an accumulating stock of self-experience
and self-actualisation of which the ordinary man accepts some
current formulation conventionally as if it were an absolute law
and truth, — often enough he even thinks it to be that, — but

which the more developed human being seeks always either to break or to enlarge and make more profound or subtle in order to increase or make room for an increase of human capacity, perfectibility, happiness.

This view of human life and of the process of our development, to which subjectivism readily leads us, gives us a truer vision of the place of the intellect in the human movement. We have seen that the intellect has a double working, dispassionate and interested, self-centred or subservient to movements not its own. The one is a disinterested pursuit of truth for the sake of Truth and of knowledge for the sake of Knowledge without any ulterior motive, with every consideration put away except the rule of keeping the eye on the object, on the fact under enquiry and finding out its truth, its process, its law. The other is coloured by the passion for practice, the desire to govern life by the truth discovered or the fascination of an idea which we labour to establish as the sovereign law of our life and action. We have seen indeed that this is the superiority of reason over the other faculties of man that it is not confined to a separate absorbed action of its own, but plays upon all the others, discovers their law and truth, makes its discoveries serviceable to them and even in pursuing its own bent and end serves also their ends and arrives at a catholic utility. Man in fact does not live for knowledge alone; life in its widest sense is his principal preoccupation and he seeks knowledge for its utility to life much more than for the pure pleasure of acquiring knowledge. But it is precisely in this putting of knowledge at the service of life that the human intellect falls into that confusion and imperfection which pursues all human action. So long as we pursue knowledge for its own sake, there is nothing to be said: the reason is performing its natural function; it is exercising securely its highest right. In the work of the philosopher, the scientist, the savant labouring to add something to the stock of our ascertainable knowledge, there is as perfect a purity and satisfaction as in that of the poet and artist creating forms of beauty for the aesthetic delight of the race. Whatever individual error and limitation there may be, does not matter; for the collective and progressive knowledge of the race has gained the truth that has been discovered and may be trusted in time to get rid of the error. It is when it tries to apply ideas to life that the human intellect stumbles and finds itself at fault.

Ordinarily, this is because in concerning itself with action the intelligence of man becomes at once partial and passionate and makes itself the servant of something other than the pure truth. But even if the intellect keeps itself as impartial and disinterested as possible, — and altogether impartial, altogether disinterested the human intellect cannot be unless it is content to arrive at an entire divorce from practice or a sort of large but ineffective tolerantism, eclecticism or sceptical curiosity, — still the truths it discovers or the ideas it promulgates become, the moment they are applied to life, the plaything of forces over which the reason has little control. Science pursuing its cold and even way has made discoveries which have served on one side a practical humanitarianism, on the other supplied monstrous weapons to egoism and mutual destruction; it has made possible a gigantic efficiency of organisation which has been used on one side for the economic and social amelioration of the nations and on the other for turning each into a colossal battering-ram of aggression, ruin and slaughter. It has given rise on the one side to a large rationalistic and altruistic humanitarianism, on the other it has justified a godless egoism, vitalism, vulgar will to power and success. It has drawn mankind together and given it a new hope and at the same time crushed it with the burden of a monstrous commercialism. Nor is this due, as is so often asserted, to its divorce from religion or to any lack of idealism. Idealistic philosophy has been equally at the service of the powers of good and evil and provided an intellectual conviction both for reaction and for progress. Organised religion itself has often enough in the past hounded men to crime and massacre and justified obscurantism and oppression.

The truth is that upon which we are now insisting, that reason is in its nature an imperfect light with a large but still restricted mission and that once it applies itself to life and action it becomes subject to what it studies and the servant and counsellor of the forces in whose obscure and ill-understood struggle it intervenes. It can in its nature be used and has always been used to justify any idea, theory of life, system of society or government, ideal of individual or collective action to which the will of man attaches itself for the moment or through the centuries. In philosophy it gives equally good reasons for monism and pluralism or for any halting-place between them, for the belief in Being or for the belief in Becoming, for optimism and pessimism, for activism and quietism. It can justify the most mystic religionism and the most positive atheism, get rid of God or see nothing else. In aesthetics it supplies the basis equally for classicism and romanticism, for an idealistic, religious or mystic theory of art or for the most earthy realism. It can with equal power base austerely a strict and narrow moralism or prove triumphantly the thesis of the antinomian. It has been the sufficient and convincing prophet of every kind of autocracy or oligarchy and of every species of democracy; it supplies excellent and satisfying reasons for competitive individualism and equally excellent and satisfying reasons for communism or against communism and for State socialism or for one variety of socialism against another. It can place itself with equal effectivity at the service of utilitarianism, economism, hedonism, aestheticism, sensualism, ethicism, idealism or any other essential need or activity of man and build around it a philosophy, a political and social system, a theory of conduct and life. Ask it not to lean to one idea alone, but to make an eclectic combination or a synthetic harmony and it will satisfy you; only, there being any number of possible combinations or harmonies, it will equally well justify the one or the other and set up or throw down any one of them according as the spirit in man is attracted to or withdraws from it. For it is really that which decides and the reason is only a brilliant servant and minister of this veiled and secret sovereign.

This truth is hidden from the rationalist because he is supported by two constant articles of faith, first that his own reason is right and the reason of others who differ from him is wrong, and secondly that whatever may be the present deficiencies of the human intellect, the collective human reason will eventually arrive at purity and be able to found human thought and life securely on a clear rational basis entirely satisfying to the intelligence. His first article of faith is no doubt the common expression of our egoism and arrogant fallibility, but it is also something more; it expresses this truth that it is the legitimate function of the reason to justify to man his action and his hope and the faith that is in him and to give him that idea and knowledge, however restricted, and that dynamic conviction, however narrow and intolerant, which he needs in order that he may live, act and grow in the highest light available to him. The reason cannot grasp all truth in its embrace because truth is too infinite for it; but still it does grasp the something of it which we immediately need, and its insufficiency does not detract from the value of its work, but is rather the measure of its value. For man is not intended to grasp the whole truth of his being at once, but to move towards it through a succession of experiences and a constant, though not by any means a perfectly continuous self-enlargement. The first business of reason then is to justify and enlighten to him his various experiences and to give him faith and conviction in holding on to his self-enlargings. It justifies to him now this, now that, the experience of the moment, the receding light of the past, the half-seen vision of the future. Its inconstancy, its divisibility against itself, its power of sustaining opposite views are the whole secret of its value. It would not do indeed for it to support too conflicting views in the same individual, except at moments of awakening and transition, but in the collective body of men and in the successions of Time that is its whole business. For so man moves towards the infinity of the Truth by the experience of its variety; so his reason helps him to build, change, destroy what he has built and prepare a new construction, in a word, to progress, grow, enlarge himself in his self-knowledge and world-knowledge and their works.

The second article of faith of the believer in reason is also an error and yet contains a truth. The reason cannot arrive at any final truth because it can neither get to the root of things nor embrace the totality of their secrets; it deals with the finite, the separate, the limited aggregate, and has no measure for the all and the infinite. Nor can reason found a perfect life for man or a perfect society. A purely rational human life would be a life baulked and deprived of its most powerful dynamic sources; it would be a substitution of the minister for the sovereign. A purely rational society could not come into being and, if it could be born, either could not live or would sterilise and petrify human existence. The root powers of human life, its intimate causes are below, irrational, and they are above, suprarational. But this is true that by constant enlargement, purification, openness the reason of man is bound to arrive at an intelligent sense even of that which is hidden from it, a power of passive, yet sympathetic reflection of the Light that surpasses it. Its limit is reached, its function is finished when it can say to man, "There is a Soul, a Self, a God in the world and in man who works concealed and all is his self-concealing and gradual self-unfolding. His minister I have been, slowly to unseal your eyes, remove the thick integuments of your vision until there is only my own luminous veil between you and him. Remove that and make the soul of man one in fact and nature with this Divine; then you will know yourself, discover the highest and widest law of your being, become the possessors or at least the receivers and instruments of a higher will and knowledge than mine and lay hold at last on the true secret and the whole sense of a human and yet divine living."

Chapter XIII

Reason and Religion

IT WOULD seem then that reason is an insufficient, often an inefficient, even a stumbling and at its best a very partially enlightened guide for humanity in that great endeavour which is the real heart of human progress and the inner justification of our existence as souls, minds and bodies upon the earth. For that endeavour is not only the effort to survive and make a place for ourselves on the earth as the animals do, not only having made to keep it and develop its best vital and egoistic or communal use for the efficiency and enjoyment of the individual, the family or the collective ego, substantially as is done by the animal families and colonies, in bee-hive or ant-hill for example, though in the larger, many-sided way of reasoning animals; it is also, and much more characteristically of our human as distinguished from our animal element, the endeavour to arrive at a harmonised inner and outer perfection, and, as we find in the end, at its highest height, to culminate in the discovery of the divine Reality behind our existence and the complete and ideal Person within us and the shaping of human life in that image. But if that is the truth, then neither the Hellenic ideal of an all-round philosophic, aesthetic, moral and physical culture governed by the enlightened reason of man and led by the wisest minds of a free society, nor the modern ideal of an efficient culture and successful economic civilisation governed by the collective reason and organised knowledge of mankind can be either the highest or the widest goal of social development.

The Hellenic ideal was roughly expressed in the old Latin maxim, a sound mind in a sound body. And by a sound body the ancients meant a healthy and beautiful body well-fitted for the rational use and enjoyment of life. And by a sound mind they meant a clear and balanced reason and an enlightened and well-trained mentality, — trained in the sense of ancient, not of modern education. It was not to be packed with all available information and ideas, cast in the mould of science and a rational utility and so prepared for the efficient performance of social and civic needs and duties, for a professional avocation or for an intellectual pursuit; rather it was to be cultured in all its human capacities intellectual, moral, aesthetic, trained to use them rightly and to range freely, intelligently and flexibly in all questions and in all practical matters of philosophy, science, art, politics and social living. The ancient Greek mind was philosophic, aesthetic and political; the modern mind has been scientific, economic and utilitarian. The ancient ideal laid stress on soundness and beauty and sought to build up a fine and rational human life; the modern lays very little or no stress on beauty, prefers rational and practical soundness, useful adaptation, just mechanism and seeks to build up a well-ordered, well-informed and efficient human life. Both take it that man is partly a mental, partly a physical being with the mentalised physical life for his field and reason for his highest attribute and his highest possibility. But if we follow to the end the new vistas opened by the most advanced tendencies of a subjective age, we shall be led back to a still more ancient truth and ideal that overtops both the Hellenic and the modern levels. For we shall then seize the truth that man is a developing spirit trying here to find and fulfil itself in the forms of mind, life and body; and we shall perceive luminously growing before us the greater ideal of a deeply conscious self-illumined, self-possessing, self-mastering soul in a pure and perfect mind and body. The wider field it seeks will be, not the mentalised physical life with which man has started, but a new spiritualised life inward and outward, by which the perfected internal figures itself in a perfected external living. Beyond man's long intelligent effort towards a perfected culture and a rational society there opens the old religious and spiritual ideal, the hope of the kingdom of heaven within us and the city of God upon earth.

But if the soul is the true sovereign and if its spiritual self-finding, its progressive largest widest integral fulfilment by the power of the spirit are to be accepted as the ultimate secret of our

evolution, then since certainly the instinctive being of man below
reason is not the means of attaining that high end and since we
find that reason also is an insufficient light and power, there
must be a superior range of being with its own proper powers,
— liberated soul-faculties, a spiritual will and knowledge higher
than the reason and intelligent will, — by which alone an entire conscious self-fulfilment can become possible to the human
being. We must remember that our aim of self-fulfilment is an
integral unfolding of the Divine within us, a complete evolution
of the hidden divinity in the individual soul and the collective
life. Otherwise we may simply come back to an old idea of
individual and social living which had its greatness, but did not
provide all the conditions of our perfection. That was the idea of
a spiritualised typal society. It proceeded upon the supposition
that each man has his own peculiar nature which is born from
and reflects one element of the divine nature. The character of
each individual, his ethical type, his training, his social occupa-
tion, his spiritual possibility must be formed or developed within
the conditions of that peculiar element; the perfection he seeks
in this life must be according to its law. The theory of ancient
Indian culture — its practice, as is the way of human practice,
did not always correspond to the theory — worked upon this
supposition. It divided man in society into the fourfold order
— an at once spiritual, psychic, ethical and economic order —
of the Brahmin, Kshatriya, Vaishya and Shudra, — practically,
the spiritual and intellectual man, the dynamic man of will, the
vital, hedonistic and economic man, the material man; the whole
society organised in these four constituent classes represented the
complete image of the creative and active Godhead.

A different division of the typal society is quite possible. But
whatever the arrangement or division, the typal principle cannot
be the foundation of an ideal human society. Even according to
the Indian theory it does not belong either to the periods of
man's highest attainment or to the eras of his lowest possibility;
it is neither the principle of his ideal age, his age of the perfected
Truth, Satyayuga, Kritayuga, in which he lives according to some
high and profound realisation of his divine possibility, nor of his

iron age, the Kaliyuga, in which he collapses towards the life of the instincts, impulses and desires with the reason degraded into a servant of this nether life of man. This too precise order is rather the appropriate principle of the intermediate ages of his cycle in which he attempts to maintain some imperfect form of his true law, his *dharma*, by will-power and force of character in the Treta, by law, arrangement and fixed convention in the Dwapara.[1] The type is not the integral man, it is the fixing and emphasising of the generally prominent part of his active nature. But each man contains in himself the whole divine potentiality and therefore the Shudra cannot be rigidly confined within his Shudrahood, nor the Brahmin in his Brahminhood, but each contains within himself the potentialities and the need of perfection of his other elements of a divine manhood. In the Kali age these potentialities may act in a state of crude disorder, the anarchy of our being which covers our confused attempt at a new order. In the intermediate ages the principle of order may take refuge in a limited perfection, suppressing some elements to perfect others. But the law of the Satya age is the large development of the whole truth of our being in the realisation of a spontaneous and self-supported spiritual harmony. That can only be realised by the evolution, in the measure of which our human capacity in its enlarging cycles becomes capable of it, of the spiritual ranges of our being and the unmasking of their inherent light and power, their knowledge and their divine capacities.

We shall better understand what may be this higher being and those higher faculties, if we look again at the dealings of the reason with the trend towards the absolute in our other faculties, in the divergent principles of our complex existence. Let us study especially its dealings with the suprarational in them and the infrarational, the two extremes between which our intelligence is some sort of mediator. The spiritual or suprarational is always turned at its heights towards the Absolute; in its extension, living

---

[1] Therefore it is said that Vishnu is the King in the Treta, but in the Dwapara the arranger and codifier of the knowledge and the law.

in the luminous infinite, its special power is to realise the infinite in the finite, the eternal unity in all divisions and differences. Our spiritual evolution ascends therefore through the relative to the absolute, through the finite to the infinite, through all divisions to oneness. Man in his spiritual realisation begins to find and seize hold on the satisfying intensities of the absolute in the relative, feels the large and serene presence of the infinite in the finite, discovers the reconciling law of a perfect unity in all divisions and differences. The spiritual will in his outer as in his inner life and formulation must be to effect a great reconciliation between the secret and eternal reality and the finite appearances of a world which seeks to express and in expressing seems to deny it. Our highest faculties then will be those which make this possible because they have in them the intimate light and power and joy by which these things can be grasped in direct knowledge and experience, realised and made normally and permanently effective in will, communicated to our whole nature. The infrarational, on the other hand, has its origin and basis in the obscure infinite of the Inconscient; it wells up in instincts and impulses, which are really the crude and more or less haphazard intuitions of a subconscient physical, vital, emotional and sensational mind and will in us. Its struggle is towards definition, towards self-creation, towards finding some finite order of its obscure knowledge and tendencies. But it has also the instinct and force of the infinite from which it proceeds; it contains obscure, limited and violent velleities that move it to grasp at the intensities of the absolute and pull them down or some touch of them into its finite action: but because it proceeds by ignorance and not by knowledge, it cannot truly succeed in this more vehement endeavour. The life of the reason and intelligent will stands between that upper and this nether power. On one side it takes up and enlightens the life of the instincts and impulses and helps it to find on a higher plane the finite order for which it gropes. On the other side it looks up towards the absolute, looks out towards the infinite, looks in towards the One, but without being able to grasp and hold their realities; for it is able only to consider them with a sort of derivative and remote understanding, because it moves in the relative and, itself limited and definite, it can act only by definition, division and limitation. These three powers of being, the suprarational, rational and infrarational are present, but with an infinitely varying prominence in all our activities.

The limitations of the reason become very strikingly, very characteristically, very nakedly apparent when it is confronted with that great order of psychological truths and experiences which we have hitherto kept in the background — the religious being of man and his religious life. Here is a realm at which the intellectual reason gazes with the bewildered mind of a foreigner who hears a language of which the words and the spirit are unintelligible to him and sees everywhere forms of life and principles of thought and action which are absolutely strange to his experience. He may try to learn this speech and understand this strange and alien life; but it is with pain and difficulty, and he cannot succeed unless he has, so to speak, unlearned himself and become one in spirit and nature with the natives of this celestial empire. Till then his efforts to understand and interpret them in his own language and according to his own notions end at the worst in a gross misunderstanding and deformation. The attempts of the positive critical reason to dissect the phenomena of the religious life sound to men of spiritual experience like the prattle of a child who is trying to shape into the mould of his own habitual notions the life of adults or the blunders of an ignorant mind which thinks fit to criticise patronisingly or adversely the labours of a profound thinker or a great scientist. At the best even this futile labour can extract, can account for only the externals of the things it attempts to explain; the spirit is missed, the inner matter is left out, and as a result of that capital omission even the account of the externals is left without real truth and has only an apparent correctness.

The unaided intellectual reason faced with the phenomena of the religious life is naturally apt to adopt one of two attitudes, both of them shallow in the extreme, hastily presumptuous and erroneous. Either it views the whole thing as a mass of superstition, a mystical nonsense, a farrago of ignorant barbaric survivals, — that was the extreme spirit of the rationalist now happily, though not dead, yet much weakened and almost moribund, — or it patronises religion, tries to explain its origins, to get rid of it by the process of explaining it away; or it labours gently or forcefully to reject or correct its superstitions, crudities, absurdities, to purify it into an abstract nothingness or persuade it to purify itself in the light of the reasoning intelligence; or it allows it a role, leaves it perhaps for the edification of the ignorant, admits its value as a moralising influence or its utility to the State for keeping the lower classes in order, even perhaps tries to invent that strange chimera, a rational religion.

The former attitude has on its positive side played a powerful part in the history of human thought, has even been of a considerable utility in its own way — we shall have to note briefly hereafter how and why — to human progress and in the end even to religion; but its intolerant negations are an arrogant falsity, as the human mind has now sufficiently begun to perceive. Its mistake is like that of a foreigner who thinks everything in an alien country absurd and inferior because these things are not his own ways of acting and thinking and cannot be cut out by his own measures or suited to his own standards. So the thoroughgoing rationalist asks the religious spirit, if it is to stand, to satisfy the material reason and even to give physical proof of its truths, while the very essence of religion is the discovery of the immaterial Spirit and the play of a supraphysical consciousness. So too he tries to judge religion by his idea of its externalities, just as an ignorant and obstreperous foreigner might try to judge a civilisation by the dress, outward colour of life and some of the most external peculiarities in the social manners of the inhabitants. That in this he errs in company with certain of the so-called religious themselves, may be his excuse, but cannot be the justification of his ignorance. The more moderate attitude of the rational mind has also played its part in the history of human thought. Its attempts to explain religion have resulted in the compilation of an immense mass of amazingly ingenious perversions, such as certain pseudo-scientific attempts to form a comparative Science of Religion. It has built up in the approved modern style immense façades of theory with stray bricks of misunderstood facts for their material. Its mild condonations of religion have led to superficial phases of thought which have passed quickly away and left no trace behind them. Its efforts at the creation of a rational religion, perfectly well-intentioned, but helpless and unconvincing, have had no appreciable effect and have failed like a dispersing cloud, *chinnābhram iva naśyati*.

The deepest heart, the inmost essence of religion, apart from its outward machinery of creed, cult, ceremony and symbol, is the search for God and the finding of God. Its aspiration is to discover the Infinite, the Absolute, the One, the Divine, who is all these things and yet no abstraction but a Being. Its work is a sincere living out of the true and intimate relations between man and God, relations of unity, relations of difference, relations of an illuminated knowledge, an ecstatic love and delight, an absolute surrender and service, a casting of every part of our existence out of its normal status into an uprush of man towards the Divine and a descent of the Divine into man. All this has nothing to do with the realm of reason or its normal activities; its aim, its sphere, its process is suprarational. The knowledge of God is not to be gained by weighing the feeble arguments of reason for or against his existence: it is to be gained only by a self-transcending and absolute consecration, aspiration and experience. Nor does that experience proceed by anything like rational scientific experiment or rational philosophic thinking. Even in those parts of religious discipline which seem most to resemble scientific experiment, the method is a verification of things which exceed the reason and its timid scope. Even in those parts of religious knowledge which seem most to resemble intellectual operations, the illuminating faculties are not imagination, logic and rational judgment, but revelations, inspirations, intuitions, intuitive discernments that leap down to us from a plane of suprarational light. The love of God is an infinite and absolute feeling which does not admit of any rational limitation and does not use a language of rational worship and adoration; the delight in God is that peace and bliss which passes all understanding. The surrender to God is the surrender of the whole being to a suprarational light, will, power and love and his service takes no account of the compromises with life which the practical reason of man uses as the best part of its method in the ordinary conduct of mundane existence. Wherever religion really finds itself, wherever it opens itself to its own spirit, — there is plenty of that sort of religious practice which is halting, imperfect, half-sincere, only half-sure of itself and in which reason can get in a word, — its way is absolute and its fruits are ineffable.

Reason has indeed a part to play in relation to this highest field of our religious being and experience, but that part is quite secondary and subordinate. It cannot lay down the law for the religious life, it cannot determine in its own right the system of divine knowledge; it cannot school and lesson the divine love and delight; it cannot set bounds to spiritual experience or lay its yoke upon the action of the spiritual man. Its sole legitimate sphere is to explain as best it can, in its own language and to the rational and intellectual parts of man, the truths, the experiences, the laws of our suprarational and spiritual existence. That has been the work of spiritual philosophy in the East and — much more crudely and imperfectly done — of theology in the West, a work of great importance at moments like the present when the intellect of mankind after a long wandering is again turning towards the search for the Divine. Here there must inevitably enter a part of those operations proper to the intellect, logical reasoning, inferences from the data given by rational experience, analogies drawn from our knowledge of the apparent facts of existence, appeals even to the physical truths of science, all the apparatus of the intelligent mind in its ordinary workings. But this is the weakest part of spiritual philosophy. It convinces the rational mind only where the intellect is already predisposed to belief, and even if it convinces, it cannot give the true knowledge. Reason is safest when it is content to take the profound truths and experiences of the spiritual being and the spiritual life, just as they are given to it, and throw them into such form, order and language as will make them the most intelligible or the least unintelligible to the reasoning mind. Even then it is not quite safe, for it is apt to harden the order into an intellectual system and to present the form as if it were the essence. And, at best, it has to use a language which is not the very tongue of the suprarational truth but its inadequate translation and, since it is not the ordinary tongue either of the rational intelligence, it is open to non-understanding or misunderstanding by the ordinary reason of mankind. It is well-known to the experience of the spiritual seeker that even the highest philosophising cannot give a true inner knowledge, is not the spiritual light, does not open the gates of experience. All it can do is to address the consciousness of man through his intellect and, when it has done, to say, "I have tried to give you the truth in a form and system which will make it intelligible and possible to you; if you are intellectually convinced or attracted, you can now seek the real knowledge, but you must seek it by other means which are beyond my province."

But there is another level of the religious life in which reason might seem justified in interfering more independently and entitled to assume a superior role. For as there is the suprarational life in which religious aspiration finds entirely what it seeks, so too there is also the infrarational life of the instincts, impulses, sensations, crude emotions, vital activities from which all human aspiration takes its beginning. These too feel the touch of the religious sense in man, share its needs and experience, desire its satisfactions. Religion includes this satisfaction also in its scope, and in what is usually called religion it seems even to be the greater part, sometimes to an external view almost the whole; for the supreme purity of spiritual experience does not appear or is glimpsed only through this mixed and turbid current. Much impurity, ignorance, superstition, many doubtful elements must form as the result of this contact and union of our highest tendencies with our lower ignorant nature. Here it would seem that reason has its legitimate part; here surely it can intervene to enlighten, purify, rationalise the play of the instincts and impulses. It would seem that a religious reformation, a movement to substitute a "pure" and rational religion for one that is largely infrarational and impure, would be a distinct advance in the religious development of humanity. To a certain extent this may be, but, owing to the peculiar nature of the religious being, its entire urge towards the suprarational, not without serious qualifications, nor can the rational mind do anything here that is of a high positive value.

Religious forms and systems become effete and corrupt and have to be destroyed, or they lose much of their inner sense and become clouded in knowledge and injurious in practice, and in destroying what is effete or in negating aberrations reason has played an important part in religious history. But in its endeavour to get rid of the superstition and ignorance which have attached themselves to religious forms and symbols, intellectual reason unenlightened by spiritual knowledge tends to deny and, so far as it can, to destroy the truth and the experience which was contained in them. Reformations which give too much to reason and are too negative and protestant, usually create religions which lack in wealth of spirituality and fullness of religious emotion; they are not opulent in their contents; their form and too often their spirit is impoverished, bare and cold. Nor are they really rational; for they live not by their reasoning and dogma, which to the rational mind is as irrational as that of the creeds they replace, still less by their negations, but by their positive quantum of faith and fervour which is suprarational in its whole aim and has too its infrarational elements. If these seem less gross to the ordinary mind than those of less self-questioning creeds, it is often because they are more timid in venturing into the realm of suprarational experience. The life of the instincts and impulses on its religious side cannot be satisfyingly purified by reason, but rather by being sublimated, by being lifted up into the illuminations of the spirit. The natural line of religious development proceeds always by illumination; and religious reformation acts best when either it reilluminates rather than destroys old forms or, where destruction is necessary, replaces them by richer and not by poorer forms, and in any case when it purifies by suprarational illumination, not by rational enlightenment. A purely rational religion could only be a cold and bare Deism, and such attempts have always failed to achieve vitality and permanence; for they act contrary to the *dharma*, the natural law and spirit of religion. If reason is to play any decisive part, it must be an intuitive rather than an intellectual reason, touched always by spiritual intensity and insight. For it must be remembered that the infrarational also has behind it a secret Truth which does not fall within the domain of the Reason and is not wholly amenable to its judgments. The heart has its knowledge, the life has its intuitive spirit within it, its intimations, divinations, outbreaks and upflamings of a Secret Energy, a divine or at least semi-divine aspiration and outreaching which the eye of intuition alone can fathom and only intuitive speech or symbol can shape or utter. To root out these things from religion or to purge religion of any elements necessary for its completeness because the forms are defective or obscure, without having the power to illuminate them from within or the patience to wait for their illumination from above or without replacing them by more luminous symbols, is not to purify but to pauperise.

But the relations of the spirit and the reason need not be, as they too often are in our practice, hostile or without any point of contact. Religion itself need not adopt for its principle the formula "I believe because it is impossible" or Pascal's "I believe because it is absurd." What is impossible or absurd to the unaided reason, becomes real and right to the reason lifted beyond itself by the power of the spirit and irradiated by its light. For then it is dominated by the intuitive mind which is our means of passage to a yet higher principle of knowledge. The widest spirituality does not exclude or discourage any essential human activity or faculty, but works rather to lift all of them up out of their imperfection and groping ignorance, transforms them by its touch and makes them the instruments of the light, power and joy of the divine being and the divine nature.

Chapter XIV

The Suprarational Beauty

RELIGION is the seeking after the spiritual, the supra-rational and therefore in this sphere the intellectual reason may well be an insufficient help and find itself, not only at the end but from the beginning, out of its province and condemned to tread either diffidently or else with a stumbling presumptuousness in the realm of a power and a light higher than its own. But in the other spheres of human consciousness and human activity it may be thought that it has the right to the sovereign place, since these move on the lower plane of the rational and the finite or belong to that border-land where the rational and the infrarational meet and the impulses and the instincts of man stand in need above all of the light and the control of the reason. In its own sphere of finite knowledge, science, philosophy, the useful arts, its right, one would think, must be indisputable. But this does not turn out in the end to be true. Its province may be larger, its powers more ample, its action more justly self-confident, but in the end everywhere it finds itself standing between the two other powers of our being and fulfilling in greater or less degree the same function of an intermediary. On one side it is an enlightener — not always the chief enlightener — and the corrector of our life-impulses and first mental seekings, on the other it is only one minister of the veiled Spirit and a preparer of the paths for the coming of its rule.

This is especially evident in the two realms which in the ordinary scale of our powers stand nearest to the reason and on either side of it, the aesthetic and the ethical being, the search for Beauty and the search for Good. Man's seeking after beauty reaches its most intense and satisfying expression in the great creative arts, poetry, painting, sculpture, architecture, but in its full extension there is no activity of his nature or his life from which it need or ought to be excluded, — provided we understand beauty both in its widest and its truest sense. A complete and universal appreciation of beauty and the making entirely beautiful our whole life and being must surely be a necessary character of the perfect individual and the perfect society. But in its origin this seeking for beauty is not rational; it springs from the roots of our life, it is an instinct and an impulse, an instinct of aesthetic satisfaction and an impulse of aesthetic creation and enjoyment. Starting from the infrarational parts of our being, this instinct and impulse begin with much imperfection and impurity and with great crudities both in creation and in appreciation. It is here that the reason comes in to distinguish, to enlighten, to correct, to point out the deficiencies and the crudities, to lay down laws of aesthetics and to purify our appreciation and our creation by improved taste and right knowledge. While we are thus striving to learn and correct ourselves, it may seem to be the true law-giver both for the artist and the admirer and, though not the creator of our aesthetic instinct and impulse, yet the creator in us of an aesthetic conscience and its vigilant judge and guide. That which was an obscure and erratic activity, it makes self-conscious and rationally discriminative in its work and enjoyment.

But again this is true only in restricted bounds or, if anywhere entirely true, then only on a middle plane of our aesthetic seeking and activity. Where the greatest and most powerful creation of beauty is accomplished and its appreciation and enjoyment rise to the highest pitch, the rational is always surpassed and left behind. The creation of beauty in poetry and art does not fall within the sovereignty or even within the sphere of the reason. The intellect is not the poet, the artist, the creator within us; creation comes by a suprarational influx of light and power which must work always, if it is to do its best, by vision and inspiration. It may use the intellect for certain of its operations, but in proportion as it subjects itself to the intellect, it loses in power and force of vision and diminishes the splendour and truth of the beauty it creates. The intellect may take hold of the influx, moderate and repress the divine enthusiasm of creation and force it to obey the prudence of its dictates, but in doing so it brings down the work to its own inferior level, and the lowering is in proportion to the intellectual interference. For by itself the intelligence can only achieve talent, though it may be a high and even, if sufficiently helped from above, a surpassing talent. Genius, the true creator, is always suprarational in its nature and its instrumentation even when it seems to be doing the work of the reason; it is most itself, most exalted in its work, most sustained in the power, depth, height and beauty of its achievement when it is least touched by, least mixed with any control of the mere intellectuality and least often drops from its heights of vision and inspiration into reliance upon the always mechanical process of intellectual construction. Art-creation which accepts the canons of the reason and works within the limits laid down by it, may be great, beautiful and powerful; for genius can preserve its power even when it labours in shackles and refuses to put forth all its resources: but when it proceeds by means of the intellect, it constructs, but does not create. It may construct well and with a good and faultless workmanship, but its success is formal and not of the spirit, a success of technique and not the embodiment of the imperishable truth of beauty seized in its inner reality, its divine delight, its appeal to a supreme source of ecstasy, Ananda.

There have been periods of artistic creation, ages of reason, in which the rational and intellectual tendency has prevailed in poetry and art; there have even been nations which in their great formative periods of art and literature have set up reason and a meticulous taste as the sovereign powers of their aesthetic activity. At their best these periods have achieved work of a certain greatness, but predominantly of an intellectual greatness and perfection of technique rather than achievements of a supreme inspired and revealing beauty; indeed their very aim has been not the discovery of the deeper truth of beauty, but truth of ideas and truth of reason, a critical rather than a true creative aim. Their leading object has been an intellectual criticism of life and nature elevated by a consummate poetical rhythm and diction rather than a revelation of God and man and life and nature in inspired forms of artistic beauty. But great art is not satisfied with representing the intellectual truth of things, which is always their superficial or exterior truth; it seeks for a deeper and original truth which escapes the eye of the mere sense or the mere reason, the soul in them, the unseen reality which is not that of their form and process but of their spirit. This it seizes and expresses by form and idea, but a significant form, which is not merely a faithful and just or a harmonious reproduction of outward Nature, and a revelatory idea, not the idea which is merely correct, elegantly right or fully satisfying to the reason and taste. Always the truth it seeks is first and foremost the truth of beauty, — not, again, the formal beauty alone or the beauty of proportion and right process which is what the sense and the reason seek, but the soul of beauty which is hidden from the ordinary eye and the ordinary mind and revealed in its fullness only to the unsealed vision of the poet and artist in man who can seize the secret significances of the universal poet and artist, the divine creator who dwells as their soul and spirit in the forms he has created.

The art-creation which lays a supreme stress on reason and taste and on perfection and purity of a technique constructed in obedience to the canons of reason and taste, claimed for itself the name of classical art; but the claim, like the too trenchant distinction on which it rests, is of doubtful validity. The spirit of the real, the great classical art and poetry is to bring out what is universal and subordinate individual expression to universal truth and beauty, just as the spirit of romantic art and poetry is to bring out what is striking and individual and this it often does so powerfully or with so vivid an emphasis as to throw into the background of its creation the universal, on which yet all true art romantic or classical builds and fills in its forms. In truth, all great art has carried in it both a classical and a romantic as well as a realistic element, — understanding realism in the sense of the prominent bringing out of the external truth of things, not the perverse inverted romanticism of the "real" which brings into exaggerated prominence the ugly, common or morbid and puts that forward as the whole truth of life. The type of art to which a great creative work belongs is determined by the prominence it gives to one element and the subdual of the others into subordination to its reigning spirit. But classical art also works by a large vision and inspiration, not by the process of the intellect. The lower kind of classical art and literature, — if classical it be and not rather, as it often is, pseudo-classical, intellectually imitative of the external form and process of the classical, — may achieve work of considerable, though a much lesser power, but of an essentially inferior scope and nature; for to that inferiority it is self-condemned by its principle of intellectual construction. Almost always it speedily degenerates into the formal or academic, empty of real beauty, void of life and power, imprisoned in its slavery to form and imagining that when a certain form has been followed, certain canons of construction satisfied, certain rhetorical rules or technical principles obeyed, all has been achieved. It ceases to be art and becomes a cold and mechanical workmanship.

This predominance given to reason and taste first and foremost, sometimes even almost alone, in the creation and appreciation of beauty arises from a temper of mind which is critical rather than creative; and in regard to creation its theory falls into a capital error. All artistic work in order to be perfect must indeed have in the very act of creation the guidance of an inner power of discrimination constantly selecting and rejecting in accordance with a principle of truth and beauty which remains always faithful to a harmony, a proportion, an intimate relation of the form to the idea; there is at the same time an exact fidelity of the idea to the spirit, nature and inner body of the thing of beauty which has been revealed to the soul and the mind, its *svarūpa* and *svabhāva*. Therefore this discriminating inner sense rejects all that is foreign, superfluous, otiose, all that is a mere diversion distractive and deformative, excessive or defective, while it selects and finds sovereignly all that can bring out the full truth, the utter beauty, the inmost power. But this discrimination is not that of the critical intellect, nor is the harmony, proportion, relation it observes that which can be fixed by any set law of the critical reason; it exists in the very nature and truth of the thing itself, the creation itself, in its secret inner law of beauty and harmony which can be seized by vision, not by intellectual analysis. The discrimination which works in the creator is therefore not an intellectual self-criticism or an obedience to rules imposed on him from outside by any intellectual canons, but itself creative, intuitive, a part of the vision, involved in and inseparable from the act of creation. It comes as part of that influx of power and light from above which by its divine enthusiasm lifts the faculties into their intense suprarational working. When it fails, when it is betrayed by the lower executive instruments rational or infrarational, — and this happens when these cease to be passive and insist on obtruding their own demands or vagaries, — the work is flawed and a subsequent act of self-criticism becomes necessary. But in correcting his work the artist who attempts to do it by rule and intellectual process, uses a false or at any rate an inferior method and cannot do his best. He ought rather to call to his aid the intuitive critical vision and embody it in a fresh act of inspired creation or re-creation after bringing himself back by its means into harmony with the light and law of his original creative initiation. The critical intellect has no direct or independent part in the means of the inspired creator of beauty.

In the appreciation of beauty it has a part, but it is not even there the supreme judge or law-giver. The business of the intellect is to analyse the elements, parts, external processes, apparent principles of that which it studies and explain their relations and workings; in doing this it instructs and enlightens the lower mentality which has, if left to itself, the habit of doing things or seeing what is done and taking all for granted without proper observation and fruitful understanding. But as with truth of religion, so with the highest and deepest truth of beauty, the intellectual reason cannot seize its inner sense and reality, not even the inner truth of its apparent principles and processes, unless it is aided by a higher insight not its own. As it cannot give a method, process or rule by which beauty can or ought to be created, so also it cannot give to the appreciation of beauty that deeper insight which it needs; it can only help to remove the dullness and vagueness of the habitual perceptions and conceptions of the lower mind which prevent it from seeing beauty or which give it false and crude aesthetic habits: it does this by giving to the mind an external idea and rule of the elements of the thing it has to perceive and appreciate. What is farther needed is the awakening of a certain vision, an insight and an intuitive response in the soul. Reason which studies always from outside, cannot give this inner and more intimate contact; it has to aid itself by a more direct insight springing from the soul itself and to call at every step on the intuitive mind to fill up the gap of its own deficiencies.

We see this in the history of the development of literary and artistic criticism. In its earliest stages the appreciation of beauty is instinctive, natural, inborn, a response of the aesthetic sensitiveness of the soul which does not attempt to give any account of itself to the thinking intelligence. When the rational intelligence applies itself to this task, it is not satisfied with recording faithfully the nature of the response and the thing it has felt, but it attempts to analyse, to lay down what is necessary in order to create a just aesthetic gratification, it prepares a grammar of technique, an artistic law and canon of construction, a sort of mechanical rule of process for the creation of beauty, a fixed code or Shastra. This brings in the long reign of academic criticism superficial, technical, artificial, governed by the false idea that technique, of which alone critical reason can give an entirely adequate account, is the most important part of creation and that to every art there can correspond an exhaustive science which will tell us how the thing is done and give us the whole secret and process of its doing. A time comes when the creator of beauty revolts and declares the charter of his own freedom, generally in the shape of a new law or principle of creation, and this freedom once vindicated begins to widen itself and to carry with it the critical reason out of all its familiar bounds. A more developed appreciation emerges which begins to seek for new principles of criticism, to search for the soul of the work itself and explain the form in relation to the soul or to study the creator himself or the spirit, nature and ideas of the age he lived in and so to arrive at a right understanding of his work. The intellect has begun to see that its highest business is not to lay down laws for the creator of beauty, but to help us to understand himself and his work, not only its form and elements but the mind from which it sprang and the impressions its effects create in the mind that receives. Here criticism is on its right road, but on a road to a consummation in which the rational understanding is overpassed and a higher faculty opens, suprarational in its origin and nature.

For the conscious appreciation of beauty reaches its height of enlightenment and enjoyment not by analysis of the beauty enjoyed or even by a right and intelligent understanding of it, — these things are only a preliminary clarifying of our first un-enlightened sense of the beautiful, — but by an exaltation of the soul in which it opens itself entirely to the light and power and joy of the creation. The soul of beauty in us identifies itself with the soul of beauty in the thing created and feels in appreciation the same divine intoxication and uplifting which the artist felt in creation. Criticism reaches its highest point when it becomes the record, account, right description of this response; it must become itself inspired, intuitive, revealing. In other words, the action of the intuitive mind must complete the action of the rational intelligence and it may even wholly replace it and do more powerfully the peculiar and proper work of the intellect itself; it may explain more intimately to us the secret of the form, the strands of the process, the inner cause, essence, mechanism of the defects and limitations of the work as well as of its qualities. For the intuitive intelligence when it has been sufficiently trained and developed, can take up always the work of the intellect and do it with a power and light and insight greater and surer than the power and light of the intellectual judgment in its widest scope. There is an intuitive discrimination which is more keen and precise in its sight than the reasoning intelligence.

What has been said of great creative art, that being the form in which normally our highest and intensest aesthetic satisfaction is achieved, applies to all beauty, beauty in Nature, beauty in life as well as beauty in art. We find that in the end the place of reason and the limits of its achievement are precisely of the same kind in regard to beauty as in regard to religion. It helps to enlighten and purify the aesthetic instincts and impulses, but it cannot give them their highest satisfaction or guide them to a complete insight. It shapes and fulfils to a certain extent the aesthetic intelligence, but it cannot justly pretend to give the definitive law for the creation of beauty or for the appreciation and enjoyment of beauty. It can only lead the aesthetic instinct, impulse, intelligence towards a greatest possible conscious satisfaction, but not to it; it has in the end to hand them over to a higher faculty which is in direct touch with the suprarational and in its nature and workings exceeds the intellect.

And for the same reason, because that which we are seeking through beauty is in the end that which we are seeking through religion, the Absolute, the Divine. The search for beauty is only in its beginning a satisfaction in the beauty of form, the beauty which appeals to the physical senses and the vital impressions, impulsions, desires. It is only in the middle a satisfaction in the beauty of the ideas seized, the emotions aroused, the perception of perfect process and harmonious combination. Behind them the soul of beauty in us desires the contact, the revelation, the uplifting delight of an absolute beauty in all things which it feels to be present, but which neither the senses and instincts by themselves can give, though they may be its channels, — for it is suprasensuous, — nor the reason and intelligence, though they too are a channel, — for it is suprarational, supra-intellectual, — but to which through all these veils the soul itself seeks to arrive. When it can get the touch of this universal, absolute beauty, this soul of beauty, this sense of its revelation in any slightest or greatest thing, the beauty of a flower, a form, the beauty and power of a character, an action, an event, a human life, an idea, a stroke of the brush or the chisel or a scintillation of the mind, the colours of a sunset or the grandeur of the tempest, it is then that the sense of beauty in us is really, powerfully, entirely satisfied. It is in truth seeking, as in religion, for the Divine, the All-Beautiful in man, in nature, in life, in thought, in art; for God is Beauty and Delight hidden in the variation of his masks and forms. When, fulfilled in our growing sense and knowledge of beauty and delight in beauty and our power for beauty, we are able to identify ourselves in soul with this Absolute and Divine in all the forms and activities of the world and shape an image of our inner and our outer life in the highest image we can perceive and embody of the All-Beautiful, then the aesthetic being in us who was born for this end, has fulfilled himself and risen to his divine consummation. To find highest beauty is to find God; to reveal, to embody, to create, as we say, highest beauty is to bring out of our souls the living image and power of God.

Chapter XV

The Suprarational Good

WE BEGIN to see, through the principle and law of our religious being, through the principle and law of our aesthetic being, the universality of a principle and law which is that of all being and which we must therefore hold steadily in view in regard to all human activities. It rests on a truth on which the sages have always agreed, though by the intellectual thinker it may be constantly disputed. It is the truth that all active being is a seeking for God, a seeking for some highest self and deepest Reality secret within, behind and above ourselves and things, a seeking for the hidden Divinity: the truth which we glimpse through religion, lies concealed behind all life; it is the great secret of life, that which it is in labour to discover and to make real to its self-knowledge.

The seeking for God is also, subjectively, the seeking for our highest, truest, fullest, largest self. It is the seeking for a Reality which the appearances of life conceal because they only partially express it or because they express it from behind veils and figures, by oppositions and contraries, often by what seem to be perversions and opposites of the Real. It is the seeking for something whose completeness comes only by a concrete and all-occupying sense of the Infinite and Absolute; it can be established in its integrality only by finding a value of the infinite in all finite things and by the attempt — necessary, inevitable, however impossible or paradoxical it may seem to the normal reason — to raise all relativities to their absolutes and to reconcile their differences, oppositions and contraries by elevation and sublimation to some highest term in which all these are unified. Some perfect highest term there is by which all our imperfect lower terms can be justified and their discords harmonised if once we can induce them to be its conscious expressions, to exist not for themselves but for That, as contributory values of that highest

Truth, fractional measures of that highest and largest common measure. A One there is in which all the entangled discords of this multiplicity of separated, conflicting, intertwining, colliding ideas, forces, tendencies, instincts, impulses, aspects, appearances which we call life, can find the unity of their diversity, the harmony of their divergences, the justification of their claims, the correction of their perversions and aberrations, the solution of their problems and disputes. Knowledge seeks for that in order that Life may know its own true meaning and transform itself into the highest and most harmonious possible expression of a divine Reality. All seeks for that, each power feels out for it in its own way: the infrarational gropes for it blindly along the line of its instincts, needs, impulses; the rational lays for it its trap of logic and order, follows out and gathers together its diversities, analyses them in order to synthetise; the suprarational gets behind and above things and into their inmost parts, there to touch and lay hands on the Reality itself in its core and essence and enlighten all its infinite detail from that secret centre.

This truth comes most easily home to us in Religion and in Art, in the cult of the spiritual and in the cult of the beautiful, because there we get away most thoroughly from the unrestful pressure of the outward appearances of life, the urgent siege of its necessities, the deafening clamour of its utilities. There we are not compelled at every turn to make terms with some gross material claim, some vulgar but inevitable necessity of the hour and the moment. We have leisure and breathing-time to seek the Real behind the apparent: we are allowed to turn our eyes either away from the temporary and transient or through the temporal itself to the eternal; we can draw back from the limitations of the immediately practical and re-create our souls by the touch of the ideal and the universal. We begin to shake off our chains, we get rid of life in its aspect of a prison-house with Necessity for our jailer and utility for our constant taskmaster; we are admitted to the liberties of the soul; we enter God's infinite kingdom of beauty and delight or we lay hands on the keys of our absolute self-finding and open ourselves to the possession or the adoration of the Eternal. There lies the immense value of Religion, the immense value of Art and Poetry to the human spirit; it lies in their immediate power for inner truth, for self-enlargement, for liberation.

But in other spheres of life, in the spheres of what by an irony of our ignorance we call especially practical life, — although, if the Divine be our true object of search and realisation, our normal conduct in them and our current idea of them is the very opposite of practical, — we are less ready to recognise the universal truth. We take a long time to admit it even partially in theory, we are seldom ready at all to follow it in practice. And we find this difficulty because there especially, in all our practical life, we are content to be the slaves of an outward Necessity and think ourselves always excused when we admit as the law of our thought, will and action the yoke of immediate and temporary utilities. Yet even there we must arrive eventually at the highest truth. We shall find out in the end that our daily life and our social existence are not things apart, are not another field of existence with another law than the inner and ideal. On the contrary, we shall never find out their true meaning or resolve their harsh and often agonising problems until we learn to see in them a means towards the discovery and the individual and collective expression of our highest and, because our highest, therefore our truest and fullest self, our largest most imperative principle and power of existence. All life is only a lavish and manifold opportunity given us to discover, realise, express the Divine.

It is in our ethical being that this truest truth of practical life, its real and highest practicality becomes most readily apparent. It is true that the rational man has tried to reduce the ethical life like all the rest to a matter of reason, to determine its nature, its law, its practical action by some principle of reason, by some law of reason. He has never really succeeded and he never can really succeed; his appearances of success are mere pretences of the intellect building elegant and empty constructions with words and ideas, mere conventions of logic and vamped-up syntheses, in sum, pretentious failures which break down at the first strenuous touch of reality. Such was that extraordinary system of utilitarian ethics discovered in the nineteenth century — the great century of science and reason and utility — by one of its most positive and systematic minds and now deservedly discredited. Happily, we need now only smile at its shallow pretentious errors, its substitution of a practical, outward and occasional test for the inner, subjective and absolute motive of ethics, its reduction of ethical action to an impossibly scientific and quite impracticable jugglery of moral mathematics, attractive enough to the reasoning and logical mind, quite false and alien to the whole instinct and intuition of the ethical being. Equally false and impracticable are other attempts of the reason to account for and regulate its principle and phenomena, — the hedonistic theory which refers all virtue to the pleasure and satisfaction of the mind in good or the sociological which supposes ethics to be no more than a system of formulas of conduct generated from the social sense and a ruled direction of the social impulses and would regulate its action by that insufficient standard. The ethical being escapes from all these formulas: it is a law to itself and finds its principle in its own eternal nature which is not in its essential character a growth of evolving mind, even though it may seem to be that in its earthly history, but a light from the ideal, a reflection in man of the Divine.

Not that all these errors have not each of them a truth behind their false constructions; for all errors of the human reason are false representations, a wrong building, effective misconstructions of the truth or of a side or a part of the truth. Utility is a fundamental principle of existence and all fundamental principles of existence are in the end one; therefore it is true that the highest good is also the highest utility. It is true also that, not any balance of the greatest good of the greatest number, but simply the good of others and most widely the good of all is one ideal aim of our outgoing ethical practice; it is that which the ethical man would like to effect, if he could only find the way and be always sure what is the real good of all. But this does not help to regulate our ethical practice, nor does it supply us with its inner principle whether of being or of action, but only produces one of the many considerations by which we can feel our way along

the road which is so difficult to travel. Good, not utility, must
be the principle and standard of good; otherwise we fall into
the hands of that dangerous pretender expediency, whose whole
method is alien to the ethical. Moreover, the standard of utility,
the judgment of utility, its spirit, its form, its application must
vary with the individual nature, the habit of mind, the outlook
on the world. Here there can be no reliable general law to which
all can subscribe, no set of large governing principles such as
it is sought to supply to our conduct by a true ethics. Nor can
ethics at all or ever be a matter of calculation. There is only one
safe rule for the ethical man, to stick to his principle of good,
his instinct for good, his vision of good, his intuition of good
and to govern by that his conduct. He may err, but he will be
on his right road in spite of all stumblings, because he will be
faithful to the law of his nature. The saying of the Gita is always
true; better is the law of one's own nature though ill-performed,
dangerous is an alien law however speciously superior it may
seem to our reason. But the law of nature of the ethical being is
the pursuit of good; it can never be the pursuit of utility.

Neither is its law the pursuit of pleasure high or base, nor
self-satisfaction of any kind, however subtle or even spiritual. It
is true, here too, that the highest good is both in its nature and
inner effect the highest bliss. Ananda, delight of being, is the
spring of all existence and that to which it tends and for which
it seeks openly or covertly in all its activities. It is true too that in
virtue growing, in good accomplished there is great pleasure and
that the seeking for it may well be always there as a subconscient
motive to the pursuit of virtue. But for practical purposes this is
a side aspect of the matter; it does not constitute pleasure into a
test or standard of virtue. On the contrary, virtue comes to the
natural man by a struggle with his pleasure-seeking nature and
is often a deliberate embracing of pain, an edification of strength
by suffering. We do not embrace that pain and struggle for the
pleasure of the pain and the pleasure of the struggle; for that
higher strenuous delight, though it is felt by the secret spirit in
us, is not usually or not at first conscious in the conscient normal
part of our being which is the field of the struggle. The action

of the ethical man is not motived by even an inner pleasure, but by a call of his being, the necessity of an ideal, the figure of an absolute standard, a law of the Divine.

In the outward history of our ascent this does not at first appear clearly, does not appear perhaps at all: there the evolution of man in society may seem to be the determining cause of his ethical evolution. For ethics only begins by the demand upon him of something other than his personal preference, vital pleasure or material self-interest; and this demand seems at first to work on him through the necessity of his relations with others, by the exigencies of his social existence. But that this is not the core of the matter, is shown by the fact that the ethical demand does not always square with the social demand, nor the ethical standard always coincide with the social standard. On the contrary, the ethical man is often called upon to reject and do battle with the social demand, to break, to move away from, to reverse the social standard. His relations with others and his relations with himself are both of them the occasions of his ethical growth; but that which determines his ethical being is his relations with God, the urge of the Divine upon him whether concealed in his nature or conscious in his higher self or inner genius. He obeys an inner ideal, not an outer standard; he answers to a divine law in his being, not to a social claim or a collective necessity. The ethical imperative comes not from around, but from within him and above him.

It has been felt and said from of old that the laws of right, the laws of perfect conduct are the laws of the gods, eternal beyond, laws that man is conscious of and summoned to obey. The age of reason has scouted this summary account of the matter as a superstition or a poetical imagination which the nature and history of the world contradict. But still there is a truth in this ancient superstition or imagination which the rational denial of it misses and the rational confirmations of it, whether Kant's categorical imperative or another, do not altogether restore. If man's conscience is a creation of his evolving nature, if his conceptions of ethical law are mutable and depend on his stage of evolution, yet at the root of them there is something constant in all their mutations which lies at the very roots of his own nature and of world-nature. And if Nature in man and the world is in its beginnings infra-ethical as well as infrarational, as it is at its summit supra-ethical as well as suprarational, yet in that infra-ethical there is something which becomes in the human plane of being the ethical, and that supra-ethical is itself a consummation of the ethical and cannot be reached by any who have not trod the long ethical road. Below hides that secret of good in all things which the human being approaches and tries to deliver partially through ethical instinct and ethical idea; above is hidden the eternal Good which exceeds our partial and fragmentary ethical conceptions.

Our ethical impulses and activities begin like all the rest in the infrarational and take their rise from the subconscient. They arise as an instinct of right, an instinct of obedience to an ununderstood law, an instinct of self-giving in labour, an instinct of sacrifice and self-sacrifice, an instinct of love, of self-subordination and of solidarity with others. Man obeys the law at first without any inquiry into the why and the wherefore; he does not seek for it a sanction in the reason. His first thought is that it is a law created by higher powers than himself and his race and he says with the ancient poet that he knows not whence these laws sprang, but only that they are and endure and cannot with impunity be violated. What the instincts and impulses seek after, the reason labours to make us understand, so that the will may come to use the ethical impulses intelligently and turn the instincts into ethical ideas. It corrects man's crude and often erring misprisions of the ethical instinct, separates and purifies his confused associations, shows as best it can the relations of his often clashing moral ideals, tries to arbitrate and compromise between their conflicting claims, arranges a system and many-sided rule of ethical action. And all this is well, a necessary stage of our advance; but in the end these ethical ideas and this intelligent ethical will which it has tried to train to its control, escape from its hold and soar up beyond its province. Always, even when enduring its rein and curb, they have that inborn tendency.

For the ethical being like the rest is a growth and a seeking towards the absolute, the divine, which can only be attained securely in the suprarational. It seeks after an absolute purity, an absolute right, an absolute truth, an absolute strength, an absolute love and self-giving, and it is most satisfied when it can get them in absolute measure, without limit, curb or compromise, divinely, infinitely, in a sort of godhead and transfiguration of the ethical being. The reason is chiefly concerned with what it best understands, the apparent process, the machinery, the outward act, its result and effect, its circumstance, occasion and motive; by these it judges the morality of the action and the morality of the doer. But the developed ethical being knows instinctively that it is an inner something which it seeks and the outward act is only a means of bringing out and manifesting within ourselves by its psychological effects that inner absolute and eternal entity. The value of our actions lies not so much in their apparent nature and outward result as in their help towards the growth of the Divine within us. It is difficult, even impossible to justify upon outward grounds the absolute justice, absolute right, absolute purity, love or selflessness of an action or course of action; for action is always relative, it is mixed and uncertain in its results, perplexed in its occasions. But it is possible to relate the inner being to the eternal and absolute good, to make our sense and will full of it so as to act out of its impulsion or its intuitions and inspirations. That is what the ethical being labours towards and the higher ethical man increasingly attains to in his inner efforts.

In fact ethics is not in its essence a calculation of good and evil in the action or a laboured effort to be blameless according to the standards of the world, — those are only crude appearances, — it is an attempt to grow into the divine nature. Its parts of purity are an aspiration towards the inalienable purity of God's being; its parts of truth and right are a seeking after conscious unity with the law of the divine knowledge and will; its parts of sympathy and charity are a movement towards the infinity and universality of the divine love; its parts of strength and manhood are an edification of the divine strength and power. That is the heart of its meaning. Its high fulfilment comes when the being of the man undergoes this transfiguration; then it is not his actions that standardise his nature but his nature that gives value to his actions; then he is no longer laboriously virtuous, artificially moral, but naturally divine. Actively, too, he is fulfilled and consummated when he is not led or moved either by the infrarational impulses or the rational intelligence and will, but inspired and piloted by the divine knowledge and will made conscious in his nature. And that can only be done, first by communication of the truth of these things through the intuitive mind as it purifies itself progressively from the invasion of egoism, self-interest, desire, passion and all kinds of self-will, finally through the suprarational light and power, no longer communicated but present and in possession of his being. Such was the supreme aim of the ancient sages who had the wisdom which rational man and rational society have rejected because it was too high a truth for the comprehension of the reason and for the powers of the normal limited human will too bold and immense, too infinite an effort.

Therefore it is with the cult of Good, as with the cult of Beauty and the cult of the spiritual. Even in its first instincts it is already an obscure seeking after the divine and absolute; it aims at an absolute satisfaction, it finds its highest light and means in something beyond the reason, it is fulfilled only when it finds God, when it creates in man some image of the divine Reality. Rising from its infrarational beginnings through its intermediate dependence on the reason to a suprarational consummation, the ethical is like the aesthetic and the religious being of man a seeking after the Eternal.

Chapter XVI

The Suprarational Ultimate of Life

IN ALL the higher powers of his life man may be said to be
seeking, blindly enough, for God. To get at the Divine and
Eternal in himself and the world and to harmonise them, to
put his being and his life in tune with the Infinite reveals itself in
these parts of his nature as his concealed aim and his destiny. He
sets out to arrive at his highest and largest and most perfect self,
and the moment he at all touches upon it, this self in him appears
to be one with some great Soul and Self of Truth and Good and
Beauty in the world to which we give the name of God. To get
at this as a spiritual presence is the aim of religion, to grow
into harmony with its eternal nature of right, love, strength and
purity is the aim of ethics, to enjoy and mould ourselves into
the harmony of its eternal beauty and delight is the aim and
consummation of our aesthetic need and nature, to know and
to be according to its eternal principles of truth is the end of
science and philosophy and of all our insistent drive towards
knowledge.

But all this seems to be something above our normal and
usual being; it is something into which we strive to grow, but
it does not seem to be the normal stuff, the natural being or
atmosphere of the individual and the society in their ordinary
consciousness and their daily life. That life is practical and not
idealistic; it is concerned not with good, beauty, spiritual experience, the higher truth, but with interests, physical needs, desires,
vital necessities. This is real to it, all the rest is a little shadowy;
this belongs to its ordinary labour, all the rest to its leisure;
this to the stuff of which it is made, all the rest to its parts of
ornament and dispensable improvement. To all that rest society
gives a place, but its heart is not there. It accepts ethics as a
bond and an influence, but it does not live for ethical good; its
real gods are vital need and utility and the desires of the body. If

it governs its life partly by ethical laws because otherwise vital need, desire, utility in seeking their own satisfaction through many egoistic individuals would clash among themselves and destroy their own aims, it does not feel called upon to make its life entirely ethical. It concerns itself still less with beauty; even if it admits things beautiful as an embellishment and an amusement, a satisfaction and pastime of the eye and ear and mind, nothing moves it imperatively to make its life a thing of beauty. It allows religion a fixed place and portion, on holy days, in the church or temple, at the end of life when age and the approach of death call the attention forcibly away from this life to other life, at fixed times in the week or the day when it thinks it right for a moment to pause in the affairs of the world and remember God: but to make the whole of life a religion, a remembering of God and a seeking after him, is a thing that is not really done even in societies which like the Indian erect spirituality as their aim and principle. It admits philosophy in a still more remote fashion; and if nowadays it eagerly seeks after science, that is because science helps prodigiously the satisfaction of its vital desires, needs and interests: but it does not turn to seek after an entirely scientific life any more than after an entirely ethical life. A more complete effort in any one of these directions it leaves to the individual, to the few, and to individuals of a special type, the saint, the ethical man, the artist, the thinker, the man of religion; it gives them a place, does some homage to them, assigns some room to the things they represent, but for itself it is content to follow mainly after its own inherent principle of vital satisfaction, vital necessity and utility, vital efficiency.

The reason is that here we get to another power of our being which is different from the ethical, aesthetic, rational and religious, — one which, even if we recognise it as lower in the scale, still insists on its own reality and has not only the right to exist but the right to satisfy itself and be fulfilled. It is indeed the primary power, it is the base of our existence upon earth, it is that which the others take as their starting-point and their foundation. This is the life-power in us, the vitalistic, the dynamic nature. Its whole principle and aim is to be, to assert its existence, to increase, to expand, to possess and to enjoy: its native terms are growth of being, pleasure and power. Life itself here is Being at labour in Matter to express itself in terms of conscious force; human life is the human being at labour to impress himself on the material world with the greatest possible force and intensity and extension. His primary insistent aim must be to live and make for himself a place in the world, for himself and his species, secondly, having made it to possess, produce and enjoy with an ever-widening scope, and finally to spread himself over all the earth-life and dominate it; this is and must be his first practical business. That is what the Darwinians have tried to express by their notion of the struggle for life. But the struggle is not merely to last and live, but to increase, enjoy and possess: its method includes and uses not only a principle and instinct of egoism, but a concomitant principle and instinct of association. Human life is moved by two equally powerful impulses, one of individualistic self-assertion, the other of collective self-assertion; it works by strife, but also by mutual assistance and united effort: it uses two diverse convergent forms of action, two motives which seem to be contradictory but are in fact always coexistent, competitive endeavour and cooperative endeavour. It is from this character of the dynamism of life that the whole structure of human society has come into being, and it is upon the sustained and vigorous action of this dynamism that the continuance, energy and growth of all human societies depends. If this life-force in them fails and these motive-powers lose in vigour, then all begins to languish, stagnate and finally move towards disintegration.

The modern European idea of society is founded upon the primary and predominant part played by this vital dynamism in the formation and maintenance of society; for the European, ever since the Teutonic mind and temperament took possession of western Europe, has been fundamentally the practical, dynamic and kinetic man, vitalistic in the very marrow of his thought and being. All else has been the fine flower of his life and culture, this has been its root and stalk, and in modern times this truth of his temperament, always there, has come aggressively to the surface and triumphed over the traditions of Christian piety and Latinistic culture. This triumphant emergence and lead of the vital man and his motives has been the whole significance of the great economic and political civilisation of the nineteenth century. Life in society consists, for the practical human instincts, in three activities, the domestic and social life of man, — social in the sense of his customary relations with others in the community both as an individual and as a member of one family among many, — his economic activities as a producer, wealth-getter and consumer and his political status and action. Society is the organisation of these three things and, fundamentally, it is for the practical human being nothing more. Learning and science, culture, ethics, aesthetics, religion are assigned their place as aids to life, for its guidance and betterment, for its embellishment, for the consolation of its labours, difficulties and sorrows, but they are no part of its very substance, do not figure among its essential objects. Life itself is the only object of living.

The ancients held a different, indeed a diametrically opposite view. Although they recognised the immense importance of the primary activities, in Asia the social most, in Europe the political, — as every society must which at all means to live and flourish, — yet these were not to them primary in the higher sense of the word; they were man's first business, but not his chief business. The ancients regarded this life as an occasion for the development of the rational, the ethical, the aesthetic, the spiritual being. Greece and Rome laid stress on the three first alone, Asia went farther, made these also subordinate and looked upon them as stepping-stones to a spiritual consummation. Greece and Rome were proudest of their art, poetry and philosophy and cherished these things as much as or even more than their political liberty or greatness. Asia too exalted these three powers and valued inordinately her social organisation, but valued much more highly, exalted with a much greater intensity of worship her saints, her religious founders and thinkers, her spiritual heroes. The modern world has been proudest of its economic organisation, its political liberty, order and progress, the mechanism, comfort and ease of its social and domestic life, its science, but science most in its application to practical life, most for its instruments and conveniences, its railways, tele-graphs, steamships and its other thousand and one discoveries, countless inventions and engines which help man to master the physical world. That marks the whole difference in the attitude.

On this a great deal hangs; for if the practical and vitalistic view of life and society is the right one, if society merely or principally exists for the maintenance, comfort, vital happiness and political and economic efficiency of the species, then our idea that life is a seeking for God and for the highest self and that society too must one day make that its principle cannot stand. Modern society, at any rate in its self-conscious aim, is far enough from any such endeavour; whatever may be the splendour of its achievement, it acknowledges only two gods, life and practical reason organised under the name of science. Therefore on this great primary thing, this life-power and its manifestations, we must look with especial care to see what it is in its reality as well as what it is in its appearance. Its appearance is familiar enough; for of that is made the very stuff and present form of our everyday life. Its main ideals are the physical good and vitalistic well-being of the individual and the community, the entire satisfaction of the desire for bodily health, long life, comfort, luxury, wealth, amusement, recreation, a constant and tireless expenditure of the mind and the dynamic life-force in re-munerative work and production and, as the higher flame-spires of this restless and devouring energy, creations and conquests of various kinds, wars, invasions, colonisation, discovery, commer-cial victory, travel, adventure, the full possession and utilisation of the earth. All this life still takes as its cadre the old existing forms, the family, the society, the nation and it has two impulses, individualistic and collective.

The primary impulse of life is individualistic and makes family, social and national life a means for the greater sat-isfaction of the vital individual. In the family the individual seeks for the satisfaction of his vital instinct of possession, as well as for the joy of companionship, and for the fulfilment of his other vital instinct of self-reproduction. His gains are the

possession of wife, servants, house, wealth, estates, the reproduction of much of himself in the body and mind of his progeny
and the prolongation of his activities, gains and possessions
in the life of his children; incidentally he enjoys the vital and
physical pleasures and the more mental pleasures of emotion
and affection to which the domestic life gives scope. In society
he finds a less intimate but a larger expansion of himself and
his instincts. A wider field of companionship, interchange, associated effort and production, errant or gregarious pleasure,
satisfied emotion, stirred sensation and regular amusement are
the advantages which attach him to social existence. In the nation and its constituent parts he finds a means for the play of a
remoter but still larger sense of power and expansion. If he has
the force, he finds there fame, pre-eminence, leadership or at a
lower pitch the sense of an effective action on a small or a large
scale, in a reduced or a magnified field of public action; if he
cannot have this, still he can feel a share of some kind, a true
portion or fictitious image of participation, in the pride, power
and splendour of a great collective activity and vital expansion.
In all this there is primarily at work the individualist principle of
the vital instinct in which the competitive side of that movement
of our nature associates with the cooperative but predominates
over it. Carried to an excess this predominance creates the ideal
of the arriviste, to whom family, society and nation are not so
much a sympathetic field as a ladder to be climbed, a prey to be
devoured, a thing to be conquered and dominated. In extreme
cases the individualist turn isolates itself from the companion
motive, reverts to a primitive anti-social feeling and creates the
nomad, the adventurer, the ranger of wilds, or the pure solitary,
— solitary not from any intellectual or spiritual impulse, but
because society, once an instrument, has become a prison and
a burden, an oppressive cramping of his expansion, a denial of
breathing-space and elbow-room. But these cases grow rarer,
now that the ubiquitous tentacles of modern society take hold
everywhere; soon there will be no place of refuge left for either
the nomad or the solitary, not even perhaps Saharan deserts or
the secure remotenesses of the Himalayas. Even, it may be, the

refuge of an inner seclusion may be taken from us by a collectivist society intent to make its pragmatic, economic, dynamic most of every individual "cell" of the organism.

For this growing collectivist or cooperative tendency embodies the second instinct of the vital or practical being in man. It shows itself first in the family ideal by which the individual subordinates himself and finds his vital satisfaction and practical account, not in his own predominant individuality, but in the life of a larger vital ego. This ideal played a great part in the old aristocratic views of life; it was there in the ancient Indian idea of the *kula* and the *kuladharma*, and in later India it was at the root of the joint-family system which made the strong economic base of mediaeval Hinduism. It has taken its grossest Vaishya form in the ideal of the British domestic Philistine, the idea of the human individual born here to follow a trade or profession, to marry and procreate a family, to earn his living, to succeed reasonably if not to amass an efficient or ostentatious wealth, to enjoy for a space and then die, thus having done the whole business for which he came into the body and performed all his essential duty in life, — for this apparently was the end unto which man with all his divine possibilities was born! But whatever form it may take, however this grossness may be refined or toned down, whatever ethical or religious conceptions may be superadded, always the family is an essentially practical, vitalistic and economic creation. It is simply a larger vital ego, a more complex vital organism that takes up the individual and englobes him in a more effective competitive and cooperative life unit. The family like the individual accepts and uses society for its field and means of continuance, of vital satisfaction and well-being, of aggrandisement and enjoyment. But this life unit also, this multiple ego can be induced by the cooperative instinct in life to subordinate its egoism to the claims of the society and trained even to sacrifice itself at need on the communal altar. For the society is only a still larger vital competitive and cooperative ego that takes up both the individual and the family into a more complex organism and uses them for the collective satisfaction of its vital needs, claims, interests, aggrandisement, well-being, enjoyment. The individual and family consent to this exploitation for the same reason that induced the individual to take on himself the yoke of the family, because they find their account in this wider vital life and have the instinct in it of their own larger growth, security and satisfaction. The society, still more than the family, is essentially economic in its aims and in its very nature. That accounts for the predominantly economic and materialistic character of modern ideas of Socialism; for these ideas are the full rationalistic flowering of this instinct of collective life. But since the society is one competitive unit among many of its kind, and since its first relations with the others are always potentially hostile, even at the best competitive and not cooperative, and have to be organised in that view, a political character is necessarily added to the social life, even predominates for a time over the economic and we have the nation or State. If we give their due value to these fundamental characteristics and motives of collective existence, it will seem natural enough that the development of the collective and cooperative idea of society should have culminated in a huge, often a monstrous overgrowth of the vitalistic, economic and political ideal of life, society and civilisation.

What account are the higher parts of man's being, those finer powers in him that more openly tend to the growth of his divine nature, to make with this vital instinct or with its gigantic modern developments? Obviously, their first impulse must be to take hold of them and dominate and transform all this crude life into their own image; but when they discover that here is a power apart, as persistent as themselves, that it seeks a satisfaction *per se* and accepts their impress to a certain extent, but not altogether and, as it were, unwillingly, partially, unsatisfactorily, — what then? We often find that ethics and religion especially, when they find themselves in a constant conflict with the vital instincts, the dynamic life-power in man, proceed to an attitude of almost complete hostility and seek to damn them in idea and repress them in fact. To the vital instinct for wealth and well-being they oppose the ideal of a chill and austere poverty; to the vital instinct for pleasure the ideal not only of self-denial, but of absolute mortification; to the vital instinct for health and ease the ascetic's contempt, disgust and neglect of the body; to the vital instinct for incessant action and creation the ideal of calm and inaction, passivity, contemplation; to the vital instinct for power, expansion, domination, rule, conquest the ideal of humility, self-abasement, submission, meek harmlessness, docility in suffering; to the vital instinct of sex on which depends the continuance of the species, the ideal of an unreproductive chastity and celibacy; to the social and family instinct the anti-social ideal of the ascetic, the monk, the solitary, the world-shunning saint. Commencing with discipline and subordination they proceed to complete mortification, which means when translated the putting to death of the vital instincts, and declare that life itself is an illusion to be shed from the soul or a kingdom of the flesh, the world and the devil, — accepting thus the claim of the unenlightened and undisciplined life itself that it is not, was never meant to be, can never become the kingdom of God, a high manifestation of the Spirit.

Up to a certain point this recoil has its uses and may easily even, by *tapasyā*, by the law of energy increasing through compression, develop for a time a new vigour in the life of the society, as happened in India in the early Buddhist centuries. But beyond a certain point it tends, not really to kill, for that is impossible, but to discourage along with the vital instincts the indispensable life-energy of which they are the play and renders them in the end inert, feeble, narrow, unelastic, incapable of energetic reaction to force and circumstance. That was the final result in India of the agelong pressure of Buddhism and its supplanter and successor, Illusionism. No society wholly or too persistently and pervadingly dominated by this denial of the life dynamism can flourish and put forth its possibilities of growth and perfection. For from dynamic it becomes static and from the static position it proceeds to stagnation and degeneration. Even the higher being of man, which finds its account in a vigorous life dynamism, both as a fund of force to be transmuted into its own loftier energies and as a potent channel of connection with the outer life, suffers in the end by this failure and contraction. The ancient Indian ideal recognised this truth and divided life into four essential and indispensable divisions, *artha, kāma, dharma, mokṣa*, vital interests, satisfaction of desires of all kinds, ethics and religion, and liberation or spirituality, and it insisted on the practice and development of all. Still it tended not only to put the last forward as the goal of all the rest, which it is, but to put it at the end of life and its habitat in another world of our being, rather than here in life as a supreme status and formative power on the physical plane. But this rules out the idea of the kingdom of God on earth, the perfectibility of society and of man in society, the evolution of a new and diviner race, and without one or other of these no universal ideal can be complete. It provides a temporary and occasional, but not an inherent justification for life; it holds out no illumining fulfilment either for its individual or its collective impulse.

Let us then look at this vital instinct and life dynamism in its own being and not merely as an occasion for ethical or religious development and see whether it is really rebellious in its very nature to the Divine. We can see at once that what we have described is the first stage of the vital being, the infrarational, the instinctive; this is the crude character of its first native development and persists even when it is trained by the growing application to it of the enlightening reason. Evidently it is in this natural form a thing of the earth, gross, earthy, full even of hideous uglinesses and brute blunders and jarring discords; but so also is the infrarational stage in ethics, in aesthetics, in religion. It is true too that it presents a much more enormous difficulty than these others, more fundamentally and obstinately resists elevation, because it is the very province of the infrarational, a first formulation of consciousness out of the Inconscient, nearest to it in the scale of being. But still it has too, properly looked at, its rich elements of power, beauty, nobility, good, sacrifice, worship, divinity; here too are high-reaching gods, masked but still resplendent. Until recently, and even now, reason, in the garb no longer of philosophy, but of science, has increasingly proposed to take up all this physical and vital life and perfect it by the sole power of rationalism, by a knowledge of the laws of Nature, of sociology and physiology and biology and health, by collectivism, by State education, by a new psychological education and a number of other kindred means. All this is well in its own way and in its limits, but it is not enough and can never come to a truly satisfying success. The ancient attempt of reason in the form of a high idealistic, rational, aesthetic, ethical and religious culture achieved only an imperfect discipline of the vital man and his instincts, sometimes only a polishing, a gloss, a clothing and mannerising of the original uncouth savage. The modern attempt of reason in the form of a broad and thorough rational, utilitarian and efficient instruction and organisation of man and his life is not succeeding any better for all its insistent but always illusory promise of more perfect results in the future. These endeavours cannot indeed be truly successful if our theory of life is right and if this great mass of vital energism contains in itself the imprisoned suprarational, if it has, as it then must have, the instinctive reaching out for something divine, absolute and infinite which is concealed in its blind strivings. Here too reason must be overpassed or surpass itself and become a passage to the Divine.

The first mark of the suprarational, when it intervenes to take up any portion of our being, is the growth of absolute ideals; and since life is Being and Force and the divine state of being is unity and the Divine in force is God as Power taking possession, the absolute vital ideals must be of that nature. Nowhere are they wanting. If we take the domestic and social life of man, we find hints of them there in several forms; but we need only note, however imperfect and dim the present shapes, the strivings of love at its own self-finding, its reachings towards its absolute — the absolute love of man and woman, the absolute maternal or paternal, filial or fraternal love, the love of friends, the love of comrades, love of country, love of humanity. These ideals of which the poets have sung so persistently, are not a mere glamour and illusion, however the egoisms and discords of our instinctive, infrarational way of living may seem to contradict them. Always crossed by imperfection or opposite vital movements, they are still divine possibilities and can be made a first means of our growth into a spiritual unity of being with being. Certain religious disciplines have understood this truth, have taken up these relations boldly and applied them to our soul's communion with God; and by a converse process they can, lifted out of their present social and physical formulas, become for us, not the poor earthly things they are now, but deep and beautiful and wonderful movements of God in man fulfilling himself in life. All the economic development of life itself takes on at its end the appearance of an attempt to get rid of the animal squalor and bareness which is what obligatory poverty really means, and to give to man the divine ease and leisure of the gods. It is pursued in a wrong way, no doubt, and with many ugly circumstances, but still the ideal is darkly there. Politics itself, that apparent game of strife and deceit and charlatanism, can be a large field of absolute idealisms. What of patriotism, — never mind the often ugly instincts from which it starts and which it still obstinately preserves, — but in its aspects of worship, self-giving, discipline, self-sacrifice? The great political ideals of man, monarchy, aristocracy, democracy, apart from the selfishnesses they serve and the rational and practical justifications with which they arm themselves, have had for their soul an ideal, some half-seen truth of the absolute and have carried with them a worship, a loyalty, a loss of self in the idea which have made men ready to suffer and die for them. War and strife themselves have been schools of heroism; they have preserved the heroic in man, they have created the *kṣatriyās tyaktajīvitāḥ* of the Sanskrit epic phrase, the men of power and courage who have abandoned their bodily life for a cause; for without heroism man cannot grow into the Godhead; courage, energy and strength are among the very first principles of the divine nature in action. All this great vital, political, economic life of man with its two powers of competition and cooperation is stumbling blindly forward towards some realisation of power and unity, — in two divine directions, therefore. For the Divine in life is Power possessed of self-mastery, but also of mastery of His world, and man and mankind too move towards conquest of their world, their environment. And again the Divine in fulfilment here is and must be oneness, and the ideal of human unity however dim and far off is coming slowly into sight. The competitive nation-units are feeling, at times, however feebly as yet, the call to cast themselves into a greater unified cooperative life of the human race.

No doubt all is still moving, however touched by dim lights from above, on a lower half rational half infrarational level, clumsily, coarsely, in ignorance of itself and as yet with little nobility of motive. All is being worked out very crudely by the confused clash of life-forces and the guidance of ideas that are half-lights of the intellect, and the means proposed are too mechanical and the aims too material; they miss the truth that the outer life-result can only endure if it is founded on inner realities. But so life in the past has moved always and must at first move. For life organises itself at first round the ego-motive and the instinct of ego-expansion is the earliest means by which men have come into contact with each other; the struggle for possession has been the first crude means towards union, the aggressive assertion of the smaller self the first step towards a growth into the larger self. All has been therefore a half-ordered confusion of the struggle for life corrected by the need and instinct of association, a struggle of individuals, clans, tribes, parties, nations, ideas, civilisations, cultures, ideals, religions, each affirming itself, each compelled into contact, association, strife with the others. For while Nature imposes the ego as a veil behind which she labours out the individual manifestation of the spirit, she also puts a compulsion on it to grow in being until it can at last expand or merge into a larger self in which it meets, harmonises with itself, comprehends in its own consciousness, becomes one with the rest of existence. To assist in this growth Life-Nature throws up in itself ego-enlarging, ego-exceeding, even ego-destroying instincts and movements which combat and correct the smaller self-affirming instincts and movements, — she enforces on her human instrument impulses of love, sympathy, self-denial, self-effacement, self-sacrifice, altruism, the drive towards universality in mind and heart and life, glimmerings of an obscure unanimism that has not yet found thoroughly its own true light and motive-power. Because of this obscurity these powers, unable to affirm their own absolute, to take the lead or dominate, obliged to compromise with the demands of the ego, even to become themselves a form of egoism, are impotent also to bring harmony and transformation to life. Instead of peace they seem to bring rather a sword; for they increase the number and tension of conflict of the unreconciled forces, ideas, impulses of which the individual human consciousness and the life of the collectivity are the arena. The ideal and practical reason of man labours to find amidst all this the right law of life and action; it strives by a rule of moderation and accommodation, by selection and rejection or by the dominance of some chosen ideas or powers to reduce things to harmony, to do consciously what Nature through natural selection and instinct has achieved in her animal kinds, an automatically ordered and settled form and norm of their existence. But the order, the structure arrived at by the reason is always partial, precarious and temporary. It is disturbed by a pull from below and a pull from above. For these powers that life throws up to help towards the growth into a larger self, a wider being, are already reflections of something that is beyond reason, seeds of the spiritual, the absolute. There is the pressure on human life of an Infinite which will not allow it to rest too long in any formulation, — not at least until it has delivered out of itself that which shall be its own self-exceeding and self-fulfilment.

This process of life through a first obscure and confused effort of self-finding is the inevitable result of its beginnings; for life has begun from an involution of the spiritual truth of things in what seems to be its opposite. Spiritual experience tells us that there is a Reality which supports and pervades all things as the Cosmic Self and Spirit, can be discovered by the individual even here in the terrestrial embodiment as his own self and spirit, and is, at its summits and in its essence, an infinite and eternal self-existent Being, Consciousness and Bliss of existence. But what we seem to see as the source and beginning of the material universe is just the contrary — it wears to us the aspect of a Void, an infinite of Non-Existence, an indeterminate Inconscient, an insensitive blissless Zero out of which everything has yet to come. When it begins to move, evolve, create, it puts on the appearance of an inconscient Energy which delivers existence out of the Void in the form of an infinitesimal fragmentation, the electron — or perhaps some still more impalpable minute unit, a not yet discovered, hardly discoverable infinitesimal, — then the atom, the molecule, and out of this fragmentation builds up a formed and concrete universe in the void of its Infinite. Yet we see that this unconscious Energy does at every step the works of a vast and minute Intelligence fixing and combining every possible device to prepare, manage and work out the paradox and miracle of Matter and the awakening of a life and a spirit in Matter; existence grows out of the Void, consciousness emerges and increases out of the Inconscient, an ascending urge towards pleasure, happiness, delight, divine bliss and ecstasy is inexplicably born out of an insensitive Nihil. These phenomena already betray the truth, which we discover when we grow aware in our depths, that the Inconscient is only a mask and within it is the Upanishad's "Conscient in unconscious things". In the beginning, says the Veda, was the ocean of inconscience and out of it That One arose into birth by his greatness, — by the might of his self-manifesting Energy.

But the Inconscient, if a mask, is an effective mask of the Spirit; it imposes on the evolving life and soul the law of a difficult emergence. Life and consciousness, no less than Matter, obey in their first appearance the law of fragmentation. Life organises itself physically round the plasm, the cell, psychologically round the small separative fragmentary ego. Consciousness itself has to concentrate its small beginnings in a poor surface formation and hide behind the veil of this limited surface existence the depths and infinities of its own being. It has to grow slowly in an external formulation till it is ready to break the crust between this petty outer figure of ourselves, which we think to be the whole, and the concealed self within us. Even the spiritual being seems to obey this law of fragmentation and manifest as a unit in the whole a spark of itself that evolves into an individual psyche. It is this little ego, this fragmented consciousness, this concealed

soul-spark on which is imposed the task of meeting and striving
with the forces of the universe, entering into contact with all that
seems to it not itself, increasing under the pressure of inner and
outer Nature till it can become one with all existence. It has to
grow into self-knowledge and world-knowledge, to get within
itself and discover that it is a spiritual being, to get outside of
itself and discover its larger truth as the cosmic Individual, to
get beyond itself and know and live in some supreme Being,
Consciousness and Bliss of existence. For this immense task it
is equipped only with the instruments of its original Ignorance.
Its limited being is the cause of all the difficulty, discord, struggle, division that mars life. The limitation of its consciousness,
unable to dominate or assimilate the contacts of the universal
Energy, is the cause of all its suffering, pain and sorrow. Its
limited power of consciousness formulated in an ignorant will
unable to grasp or follow the right law of its life and action is
the cause of all its error, wrongdoing and evil. There is no other
true cause; for all apparent causes are themselves circumstance
and result of this original sin of the being. Only when it rises
and widens out of this limited separative consciousness into the
oneness of the liberated Spirit, can it escape from these results
of its growth out of the Inconscience.

If we see this as the truth behind Life, we can understand at
once why it has had to follow its present curve of ignorant self-
formulation. But also we see what through it all it is obscurely
seeking, trying to grasp and form, feeling out for in its own
higher impulses and deepest motives, and why these are in it
—useless, perturbing and chimerical if it were only an animal
product of inconscient Nature,—these urgings towards self-
discovery, mastery, unity, freedom from its lower self, spiritual
release. Evolving out of its first involved condition in Matter and
in plant life, effecting a first imperfect organised consciousness
in the animal it arrives in man, the mental being, at the possibility of a new, a conscious evolution which will bring it to its
goal and at a certain stage of his development it wakes in him
the overmastering impulse to pass on from mental to spiritual
being. Life cannot arrive at its secret ultimates by following its

first infrarational motive forces of instinct and desire; for all here is a groping and seeking without finding, a field of brief satisfactions stamped with the Inconscient's seal of insufficiency and impermanence. But neither can human reason give it what it searches after; for reason can only establish half-lights and a provisional order. Therefore with man as he is the upward urge in life cannot rest satisfied always; its evolutionary impulse cannot stop short at this transitional term, this half-achievement. It has to aim at a higher scale of consciousness, deliver out of life and mind something that is still latent and inchoate.

The ultimates of life are spiritual and only in the full light of the liberated self and spirit can it achieve them. That full light is not intellect or reason, but a knowledge by inner unity and identity which is the native self-light of the fully developed spiritual consciousness and, preparing that, on the way to it, a knowledge by intimate inner contact with the truth of things and beings which is intuitive and born of a secret oneness. Life seeks for self-knowledge; it is only by the light of the spirit that it can find it. It seeks for a luminous guidance and mastery of its own movements; it is only when it finds within itself this inner self and spirit and by it or in obedience to it governs its own steps that it can have the illumined will it needs and the unerring leadership. For it is so only that the blind certitudes of the instincts and the speculative hypotheses and theories and the experimental and inferential certitudes of reason can be replaced by the seeing spiritual certitudes. Life seeks the fulfilment of its instincts of love and sympathy, its yearnings after accord and union; but these are crossed by opposing instincts and it is only the spiritual consciousness with its realised abiding oneness that can abolish these oppositions. Life seeks for full growth of being, but it can attain to it only when the limited being has found in itself its own inmost soul of existence and around it its own widest self of cosmic consciousness by which it can feel the world and all being in itself and as itself. Life seeks for power; it is only the power of the spirit and the power of this conscious oneness that can give it mastery of its self and its world. It seeks for pleasure, happiness, bliss; but the infrarational forms of these things are stricken with imperfection, fragmentariness, impermanence and the impact of their opposites. Moreover infrarational life still bears some stamp of the Inconscient in an underlying insensitiveness, a dullness of fibre, a weakness of vibratory response, — it cannot attain to true happiness or bliss and what it can obtain of pleasure it cannot support for long or bear or keep any extreme intensity of these things. Only the spirit has the secret of an unmixed and abiding happiness or ecstasy, is capable of a firm tenseness of vibrant response to it, can achieve and justify a spiritual pleasure or joy of life as one form of the infinite and universal delight of being. Life seeks a harmonious fulfilment of all its powers, now divided and in conflict, all its possibilities, parts, members; it is only in the consciousness of the one self and spirit that that is found, for there they arrive at their full truth and their perfect agreement in the light of the integral Self-existence.

There is then a suprarational ultimate of Life no less than a suprarational Truth, Good and Beauty. The endeavour to reach it is the spiritual meaning of this seeking and striving Life-nature.

Chapter XVII

Religion as the Law of Life

SINCE the infinite, the absolute and transcendent, the universal, the One is the secret summit of existence and to reach the spiritual consciousness and the Divine the ultimate goal and aim of our being and therefore of the whole development of the individual and the collectivity in all its parts and all its activities, reason cannot be the last and highest guide; culture, as it is understood ordinarily, cannot be the directing light or find out the regulating and harmonising principle of all our life and action. For reason stops short of the Divine and only compromises with the problems of life, and culture in order to attain the Transcendent and Infinite must become spiritual culture, something much more than an intellectual, aesthetic, ethical and practical training. Where then are we to find the directing light and the regulating and harmonising principle? The first answer which will suggest itself, the answer constantly given by the Asiatic mind, is that we shall find it directly and immediately in religion. And this seems a reasonable and at first sight a satisfying solution; for religion is that instinct, idea, activity, discipline in man which aims directly at the Divine, while all the rest seem to aim at it only indirectly and reach it with difficulty after much wandering and stumbling in the pursuit of the outward and imperfect appearances of things. To make all life religion and to govern all activities by the religious idea would seem to be the right way to the development of the ideal individual and ideal society and the lifting of the whole life of man into the Divine.

A certain pre-eminence of religion, the overshadowing or at least the colouring of life, an overtopping of all the other instincts and fundamental ideas by the religious instinct and the religious idea is, we may note, not peculiar to Asiatic civilisations, but has always been more or less the normal state of the human mind and of human societies, or if not quite that, yet a notable and prominent part of their complex tendencies, except in certain comparatively brief periods of their history, in one of which we find ourselves today and are half turning indeed to emerge from it but have not yet emerged. We must suppose then that in this leading, this predominant part assigned to religion by the normal human collectivity there is some great need and truth of our natural being to which we must always after however long an infidelity return. On the other hand, we must recognise the fact that in a time of great activity, of high aspiration, of deep sowing, of rich fruit-bearing, such as the modern age with all its faults and errors has been, a time especially when humanity got rid of much that was cruel, evil, ignorant, dark, odious, not by the power of religion, but by the power of the awakened intelligence and of human idealism and sympathy, this predominance of religion has been violently attacked and rejected by that portion of humanity which was for that time the standard-bearer of thought and progress, Europe after the Renascence, modern Europe.

This revolt in its extreme form tried to destroy religion altogether, boasted indeed of having killed the religious instinct in man, — a vain and ignorant boast, as we now see, for the religious instinct in man is most of all the one instinct in him that cannot be killed, it only changes its form. In its more moderate movements the revolt put religion aside into a corner of the soul by itself and banished its intermiscence in the intellectual, aesthetic, practical life and even in the ethical; and it did this on the ground that the intermiscence of religion in science, thought, politics, society, life in general had been and must be a force for retardation, superstition, oppressive ignorance. The religionist may say that this accusation was an error and an atheistic perversity, or he may say that a religious retardation, a pious ignorance, a contented static condition or even an orderly stagnation full of holy thoughts of the Beyond is much better than a continuous endeavour after greater knowledge, greater mastery, more happiness, joy, light upon this transient earth. But the catholic thinker cannot accept such a plea; he is obliged to see that so long as man has not realised the divine and the ideal in his life, — and it may well be even when he has realised it, since the divine is the infinite, — progress and not unmoving status is the necessary and desirable law of his life, — not indeed any breathless rush after novelties, but a constant motion towards a greater and greater truth of the spirit, the thought and the life not only in the individual, but in the collectivity, in the communal endeavour, in the turn, ideals, temperament, make of the society, in its strivings towards perfection. And he is obliged too to see that the indictment against religion, not in its conclusion, but in its premiss had something, had even much to justify it, — not that religion in itself must be, but that historically and as a matter of fact the accredited religions and their hierarchs and exponents have too often been a force for retardation, have too often thrown their weight on the side of darkness, oppression and ignorance, and that it has needed a denial, a revolt of the oppressed human mind and heart to correct these errors and set religion right. And why should this have been if religion is the true and sufficient guide and regulator of all human activities and the whole of human life?

We need not follow the rationalistic or atheistic mind through all its aggressive indictment of religion. We need not for instance lay a too excessive stress on the superstitions, aberrations, violences, crimes even, which Churches and cults and creeds have favoured, admitted, sanctioned, supported or exploited for their own benefit, the mere hostile enumeration of which might lead one to echo the cry of the atheistic Roman poet, "To such a mass of ills could religion persuade mankind." As well might one cite the crimes and errors which have been committed in the name of liberty or of order as a sufficient condemnation of the ideal of liberty or the ideal of social order. But we have to note the fact that such a thing was possible and to find its explanation. We cannot ignore for instance the blood-stained and fiery track which formal external Christianity has left furrowed across the mediaeval history of Europe almost from the days of Constantine, its first hour of secular triumph, down to very recent times, or the sanguinary comment which such an institution as the Inquisition affords on the claim of religion to be the directing light and regulating power in ethics and society, or religious wars and wide-spread State persecutions on its claim to guide the political life of mankind. But we must observe the root of this evil, which is not in true religion itself, but in its infrarational parts, not in spiritual faith and aspiration, but in our ignorant human confusion of religion with a particular creed, sect, cult, religious society or Church. So strong is the human tendency to this error that even the old tolerant Paganism slew Socrates in the name of religion and morality, feebly persecuted non-national faiths like the cult of Isis or the cult of Mithra and more vigorously what it conceived to be the subversive and anti-social religion of the early Christians; and even in still more fundamentally tolerant Hinduism with all its spiritual broadness and enlightenment it led at one time to the milder mutual hatred and occasional though brief-lived persecution of Buddhist, Jain, Shaiva, Vaishnava.

The whole root of the historic insufficiency of religion as a guide and control of human society lies there. Churches and creeds have, for example, stood violently in the way of philosophy and science, burned a Giordano Bruno, imprisoned a Galileo, and so generally misconducted themselves in this matter that philosophy and science had in self-defence to turn upon Religion and rend her to pieces in order to get a free field for their legitimate development; and this because men in the passion and darkness of their vital nature had chosen to think that religion was bound up with certain fixed intellectual conceptions about God and the world which could not stand scrutiny, and therefore scrutiny had to be put down by fire and sword; scientific and philosophical truth had to be denied in order that religious error might survive. We see too that a narrow religious spirit often oppresses and impoverishes the joy and beauty of life, either from an intolerant asceticism or, as the Puritans attempted it, because they could not see that religious austerity is not the whole of religion, though it may be an important side of it, is not the sole ethico-religious approach to God, since love, charity, gentleness, tolerance, kindliness are also and even more divine, and they forgot or never knew that God is love and beauty as well as purity. In politics religion has often thrown itself on the side of power and resisted the coming of larger political ideals, because it was itself, in the form of a Church, supported by power and because it confused religion with the Church, or because it stood for a false theocracy, forgetting that true theocracy is the kingdom of God in man and not the kingdom of a Pope, a priesthood or a sacerdotal class. So too it has often supported a rigid and outworn social system, because it thought its own life bound up with social forms with which it happened to have been associated during a long portion of its own history and erroneously concluded that even a necessary change there would be a violation of religion and a danger to its existence. As if so mighty and inward a power as the religious spirit in man could be destroyed by anything so small as the change of a social form or so outward as a social readjustment! This error in its many shapes has been the great weakness of religion as practised in the past and the opportunity and justification for the revolt of the intelligence, the aesthetic sense, the social and political idealism, even the ethical spirit of the human being against what should have been its own highest tendency and law.

Here then lies one secret of the divergence between the ancient and the modern, the Eastern and Western ideal, and here also one clue to their reconciliation. Both rest upon a certain strong justification and their quarrel is due to a misunderstanding. It is true in a sense that religion should be the dominant thing in life, its light and law, but religion as it should be and is in its inner nature, its fundamental law of being, a seeking after God, the cult of spirituality, the opening of the deepest life of the soul to the indwelling Godhead, the eternal Omnipresence. On the other hand, it is true that religion when it identifies itself only with a creed, a cult, a Church, a system of ceremonial forms, may well become a retarding force and there may therefore arise a necessity for the human spirit to reject its control over the varied activities of life. There are two aspects of religion, true religion and religionism. True religion is spiritual religion, that which seeks to live in the spirit, in what is beyond the intellect, beyond the aesthetic and ethical and practical being of man, and to inform and govern these members of our being by the higher light and law of the spirit. Religionism, on the contrary, entrenches itself in some narrow pietistic exaltation of the lower members or lays exclusive stress on intellectual dogmas, forms and ceremonies, on some fixed and rigid moral code, on some religio-political or religio-social system. Not that these things are altogether negligible or that they must be unworthy or unnecessary or that a spiritual religion need disdain the aid of forms, ceremonies, creeds or systems. On the contrary, they are needed by man because the lower members have to be exalted and raised before they can be fully spiritualised, before they can directly feel the spirit and obey its law. An intellectual formula is often needed by the thinking and reasoning mind, a form or ceremony by the aesthetic temperament or other parts of the infrarational being, a set moral code by man's vital nature in their turn towards the inner life. But these things are aids and supports, not the essence; precisely because they belong to the rational and infrarational parts, they can be nothing more and, if too blindly insisted on, may even hamper the suprarational light. Such as they are, they have to be offered to man and used by him, but not to be imposed on him as his sole law by a forced and inflexible domination. In the use of them toleration and free permission of variation is the first rule which should be observed. The spiritual essence of religion is alone the one thing supremely needful, the thing to which we have always to hold and subordinate to it every other element or motive.

But here comes in an ambiguity which brings in a deeper source of divergence. For by spirituality religion seems often to mean something remote from earthly life, different from it, hostile to it. It seems to condemn the pursuit of earthly aims as a trend opposed to the turn to a spiritual life and the hopes of man on earth as an illusion or a vanity incompatible with the hope of man in heaven. The spirit then becomes something aloof which man can only reach by throwing away the life of his lower members. Either he must abandon this nether life after a certain point, when it has served its purpose, or must persistently discourage, mortify and kill it. If that be the true sense of religion, then obviously religion has no positive message for human society in the proper field of social effort, hope and aspiration or for the individual in any of the lower members of his being. For each principle of our nature seeks naturally for perfection in its own sphere and, if it is to obey a higher power, it must be because that power gives it a greater perfection and a fuller satisfaction even in its own field. But if perfectibility is denied to it and therefore the aspiration to perfection taken away by the spiritual urge, then it must either lose faith in itself and the power to pursue the natural expansion of its energies and activities or it must reject the call of the spirit in order to follow its own bend and law, *dharma*. This quarrel between earth and heaven, between the spirit and its members becomes still more sterilising if spirituality takes the form of a religion of sorrow and suffering and austere mortification and the gospel of the vanity of things; in its exaggeration it leads to such nightmares of the soul as that terrible gloom and hopelessness of the Middle Ages in their worst moment when the one hope of mankind seemed to be in the approaching and expected end of the world, an inevitable and desirable Pralaya. But even in less pronounced and intolerant forms of this pessimistic attitude with regard to the world, it becomes a force for the discouragement of life and cannot, therefore, be a true law and guide for life. All pessimism is to that extent a denial of the Spirit, of its fullness and power, an impatience with the ways of God in the world, an insufficient faith in the divine Wisdom and Will that created the world and for ever guide it. It admits a wrong notion about that supreme Wisdom and Power and therefore cannot itself be the supreme wisdom and power of the spirit to which the world can look for guidance and for the uplifting of its whole life towards the Divine.

The Western recoil from religion, that minimising of its claim and insistence by which Europe progressed from the mediaeval religious attitude through the Renascence and the Reformation to the modern rationalistic attitude, that making of the ordinary earthly life our one preoccupation, that labour to fulfil ourselves by the law of the lower members, divorced from all spiritual seeking, was an opposite error, the contrary ignorant extreme, the blind swing of the pendulum from a wrong affirmation to a wrong negation. It is an error because perfection cannot be found in such a limitation and restriction; for it denies the complete law of human existence, its deepest urge, its most secret impulse. Only by the light and power of the highest can the lower be perfectly guided, uplifted and accomplished. The lower life of man is in form undivine, though in it there is the secret of the divine, and it can only be divinised by finding the higher law and the spiritual illumination. On the other hand, the impatience which condemns or despairs of life or discourages its growth because it is at present undivine and is not in harmony with the spiritual life, is an equal ignorance, *andham tamaḥ*. The world-shunning monk, the mere ascetic may indeed well find by this turn his own individual and peculiar salvation, the spiritual recompense of his renunciation and Tapasya, as the materialist may find by his own exclusive method the appropriate rewards of his energy and concentrated seeking; but neither can be the true guide of mankind and its law-giver. The monastic attitude implies a fear, an aversion, a distrust of life and its aspirations, and one cannot wisely guide that with which one is entirely out of sympathy, that which one wishes to minimise and discourage. The sheer ascetic spirit, if it directed life and human society, could only prepare it to be a means for denying itself and getting away from its own motives. An ascetic guidance might tolerate the lower activities, but only with a view to persuade them in the end to minimise and finally cease from their own action. But a spirituality which draws back from life to envelop it without being dominated by it does not labour under this disability. The spiritual man who can guide human life towards its perfection is typified in the ancient Indian idea of the Rishi, one who has lived fully the life of man and found the word of the supra-intellectual, supramental, spiritual truth. He has risen above these lower limitations and can view all things from above, but also he is in sympathy with their effort and can view them from within; he has the complete inner knowledge and the higher surpassing knowledge. Therefore he can guide the world humanly as God guides it divinely, because like the Divine he is in the life of the world and yet above it.

In spirituality, then, understood in this sense, we must seek for the directing light and the harmonising law, and in religion only in proportion as it identifies itself with this spirituality. So long as it falls short of this, it is one human activity and power among others, and, even if it be considered the most important and the most powerful, it cannot wholly guide the others. If it seeks always to fix them into the limits of a creed, an unchangeable law, a particular system, it must be prepared to see them revolting from its control; for although they may accept this impress for a time and greatly profit by it, in the end they must move by the law of their being towards a freer activity and an untrammelled movement. Spirituality respects the freedom of the human soul, because it is itself fulfilled by freedom; and the deepest meaning of freedom is the power to expand and grow towards perfection by the law of one's own nature, *dharma*. This liberty it will give to all the fundamental parts of our being. It will give that freedom to philosophy and science which ancient Indian religion gave, — freedom even to deny the spirit, if they will, — as a result of which philosophy and science never felt in ancient India any necessity of divorcing themselves from religion, but grew rather into it and under its light. It will give the same freedom to man's seeking for political and social perfection and to all his other powers and aspirations. Only it will be vigilant to illuminate them so that they may grow into the light and law of the spirit, not by suppression and restriction, but by a self-searching, self-controlled expansion and a many-sided finding of their greatest, highest and deepest potentialities. For all these are potentialities of the spirit.

Chapter XVIII

The Infrarational Age of the Cycle

IN SPIRITUALITY then would lie our ultimate, our only hope for the perfection whether of the individual or of the communal man; not the spirit which for its separate satisfaction turns away from the earth and her works, but that greater spirit which surpasses and yet accepts and fulfils them. A spirituality that would take up into itself man's rationalism, aestheticism, ethicism, vitalism, corporeality, his aspiration towards knowledge, his attraction towards beauty, his need of love, his urge towards perfection, his demand for power and fullness of life and being, a spirituality that would reveal to these ill-accorded forces their divine sense and the conditions of their godhead, reconcile them all to each other, illumine to the vision of each the way which they now tread in half-lights and shadows, in blindness or with a deflected sight, is a power which even man's too self-sufficient reason can accept or may at least be brought one day to accept as sovereign and to see in it its own supreme light, its own infinite source. For that reveals itself surely in the end as the logical ultimate process, the inevitable development and consummation of all for which man is individually and socially striving. A satisfying evolution of the nascent spirituality still raw and inchoate in the race is the possibility to which an age of subjectivism is a first glimmer of awakening or towards which it shows a first profound potentiality of return. A deeper, wider, greater, more spiritualised subjective understanding of the individual and communal self and its life and a growing reliance on the spiritual light and the spiritual means for the final solution of its problems are the only way to a true social perfection. The free rule, that is to say, the predominant lead, control and influence of the developed spiritual man — not the half-spiritualised priest, saint or prophet or the raw religionist — is our hope for a divine guidance of the race. A spiritualised society can alone bring about a reign of individual harmony and communal happiness; or, in words which, though liable to abuse by the reason and the passions, are still the most expressive we can find, a new kind of theocracy, the kingdom of God upon earth, a theocracy which shall be the government of mankind by the Divine in the hearts and minds of men.

Certainly, this will not come about easily, or, as men have always vainly hoped from each great new turn and revolution of politics and society, by a sudden and at once entirely satisfying change and magical transformation. The advance, however it comes about, will be indeed of the nature of a miracle, as are all such profound changes and immense developments; for they have the appearance of a kind of realised impossibility. But God works all his miracles by an evolution of secret possibilities which have been long prepared, at least in their elements, and in the end by a rapid bringing of all to a head, a throwing together of the elements so that in their fusion they produce a new form and name of things and reveal a new spirit. Often the decisive turn is preceded by an apparent emphasising and raising to their extreme of things which seem the very denial, the most uncompromising opposite of the new principle and the new creation. Such an evolution of the elements of a spiritualised society is that which a subjective age makes at least possible, and if at the same time it raises to the last height of active power things which seem the very denial of such a potentiality, that need be no index of a practical impossibility of the new birth, but on the contrary may be the sign of its approach or at the lowest a strong attempt at achievement. Certainly, the whole effort of a subjective age may go wrong; but this happens oftenest when by the insufficiency of its materials, a great crudeness of its starting-point and a hasty shallowness or narrow intensity of its inlook into itself and things it is foredoomed to a fundamental error of self-knowledge. It becomes less likely when the spirit of the age is full of freedom, variety and a many-sided seeking, a persistent effort after knowledge and perfection in all the domains of human activity; that can well convert itself into an intense and yet flexible straining after the infinite and the divine on many sides and in many aspects. In such circumstances, though a full advance may possibly not be made, a great step forward can be predicted.

We have seen that there are necessarily three stages of the social evolution or, generally, of the human evolution in both individual and society. Our evolution starts with an infrarational stage in which men have not yet learned to refer their life and action in its principles and its forms to the judgment of the clarified intelligence; for they still act principally out of their instincts, impulses, spontaneous ideas, vital intuitions or obey a customary response to desire, need and circumstance, — it is these things that are canalised or crystallised in their social institutions. Man proceeds by various stages out of these beginnings towards a rational age in which his intelligent will more or less developed becomes the judge, arbiter and presiding motive of his thought, feeling and action, the moulder, destroyer and re-creator of his leading ideas, aims and intuitions. Finally, if our analysis and forecast are correct, the human evolution must move through a subjective towards a suprarational or spiritual age in which he will develop progressively a greater spiritual, supra-intellectual and intuitive, perhaps in the end a more than intuitive, a gnostic consciousness. He will be able to perceive a higher divine end, a divine sanction, a divine light of guidance for all he seeks to be, think, feel and do, and able, too, more and more to obey and live in this larger light and power. That will not be done by any rule of infrarational religious impulse and ecstasy, such as characterised or rather darkly illumined the obscure confusion and brute violence of the Middle Ages, but by a higher spiritual living for which the clarities of the reason are a necessary preparation and into which they too will be taken up, transformed, brought to their invisible source.

These stages or periods are much more inevitable in the psychological evolution of mankind than the Stone and other Ages marked out by Science in his instrumental culture, for they depend not on outward means or accidents, but on the very nature of his being. But we must not suppose that they are naturally exclusive and absolute in their nature, or complete in their tendency or fulfilment when they come, or rigidly marked off from each other in their action or their time. For they not only arise out of each other, but may be partially developed in each other and they may come to coexist in different parts of the earth at the same time. But, especially, since man as a whole is always a complex being, even man savage or degenerate, he cannot be any of these things exclusively or absolutely, — so long as he has not exceeded himself, has not developed into the superman, has not, that is to say, spiritualised and divinised his whole being. At his animal worst he is still some kind of thinking or reflecting animal: even the infrarational man cannot be utterly infrarational, but must have or tend to have some kind of play more or less evolved or involved of the reason and a more or less crude suprarational element, a more or less disguised working of the spirit. At his lucid mental best, he is still not a pure mental being, a pure intelligence; even the most perfect intellectual is not and cannot be wholly or merely rational, — there are vital urgings that he cannot exclude, visits or touches of a light from above that are not less suprarational because he does not recognise their source. No god, but at his highest a human being touched with a ray of the divine influence, man's very spirituality, however dominant, must have, while he is still this imperfectly evolved human, its rational and infrarational tendencies and elements. And as with the psychological life of individuals, so must it be with the ages of his communal existence; these may be marked off from each other by the predominant play of one element, its force may overpower the others or take them into itself or make some compromise, but an exclusive play seems to be neither intended nor possible.

Thus an infrarational period of human and social development need not be without its elements, its strong elements of reason and of spirituality. Even the savage, whether he be primitive or degenerate man, has some coherent idea of this world and the beyond, a theory of life and a religion. To us with our more advanced rationality his theory of life may seem incoherent, because we have lost its point of view and its principle of mental associations. But it is still an act of reason, and within its limits he is capable of a sufficient play of thought both ideative and practical, as well as a clear ethical idea and motive, some aesthetic notions and an understood order of society poor and barbarous to our view, but well enough contrived and put together to serve the simplicity of its objects. Or again we may not realise the element of reason in a primitive theory of life or of spirituality in a barbaric religion, because it appears to us to be made up of symbols and forms to which a superstitious value is attached by these undeveloped minds. But this is because the reason at this stage has an imperfect and limited action and the element of spirituality is crude or undeveloped and not yet self-conscious; in order to hold firmly their workings and make them real and concrete to his mind and spirit primitive man has to give them shape in symbols and forms to which he clings with a barbaric awe and reverence, because they alone can embody for him his method of self-guidance in life. For the dominant thing in him is his infrarational life of instinct, vital intuition and impulse, mechanical custom and tradition, and it is that to which the rest of him has to give some kind of primary order and first glimmerings of light. The unrefined reason and unenlightened spirit in him cannot work for their own ends; they are bond-slaves of his infrarational nature.

At a higher stage of development or of a return towards a fuller evolution, — for the actual savage in humanity is perhaps not the original primitive man, but a relapse and reversion towards primitiveness, — the infrarational stage of society may arrive at a very lofty order of civilisation. It may have great intuitions of the meaning or general intention of life, admirable ideas of the arrangement of life, a harmonious, well-adapted, durable and serviceable social system, an imposing religion which will not be without its profundities, but in which symbol and ceremonial will form the largest portion and for the mass of man will be almost the whole of religion. In this stage pure reason and pure spirituality will not govern the society or move large bodies of men, but will be represented, if at all, by individuals at first few, but growing in number as these two powers increase in their purity and vigour and attract more and more votaries.

This may well lead to an age, if the development of reason is strongest, of great individual thinkers who seize on some idea of life and its origins and laws and erect that into a philosophy, of critical minds standing isolated above the mass who judge life, not yet with a luminous largeness, a minute flexibility of understanding or a clear and comprehensive profundity, but still with power of intelligence, insight, acuteness, perhaps even a preeminent social thinker here and there who, taking advantage of some crisis or disturbance, is able to get the society to modify or reconstruct itself on the basis of some clearly rational and intelligent principle. Such an age seems to be represented by the traditions of the beginnings of Greek civilisation, or rather the beginnings of its mobile and progressive period. Or if spirituality predominates, there will be great mystics capable of delving into the profound and still occult psychological possibilities of our nature who will divine and realise the truth of the self and spirit in man and, even though they keep these things secret and imparted only to a small number of initiates, may yet succeed in deepening with them the crude forms of the popular life. Even such a development is obscurely indicated in the old traditions of the mysteries. In prehistoric India we see it take a peculiar and unique turn which determined the whole future trend of the society and made Indian civilisation a thing apart and of its own kind in the history of the human race. But these things are only a first beginning of light in the midst of a humanity which is still infrarational as well as infra-spiritual and, even when it undergoes the influence of these precursors, responds only obscurely to their inspirations and without any clearly intelligent or awakened spiritual reception of what they impart or impose. It still turns everything into infrarational form and disfiguring tradition and lives spiritually by ill-understood ceremonial and disguising symbol. It feels obscurely the higher things, tries to live them in its own stumbling way, but it does not yet understand; it cannot lay hold either on the intellectual form or the spiritual heart of their significance.

As reason and spirituality develop, they begin to become a larger and more diffused force, less intense perhaps, but wider

and more effective on the mass. The mystics become the sowers
of the seed of an immense spiritual development in which whole
classes of society and even men from all classes seek the light, as
happened in India in the age of the Upanishads. The solitary individual thinkers are replaced by a great number of writers, poets,
thinkers, rhetoricians, sophists, scientific inquirers, who pour
out a profuse flood of acute speculation and inquiry stimulating
the thought-habit and creating even in the mass a generalised
activity of the intelligence, — as happened in Greece in the age
of the sophists. The spiritual development, arising uncurbed by
reason in an infrarational society, has often a tendency to outrun
at first the rational and intellectual movement. For the greatest
illuminating force of the infrarational man, as he develops, is
an inferior intuition, an instinctively intuitional sight arising
out of the force of life in him, and the transition from this
to an intensity of inner life and the growth of a deeper spiritual
intuition which outleaps the intellect and seems to dispense with
it, is an easy passage in the individual man. But for humanity
at large this movement cannot last; the mind and intellect must
develop to their fullness so that the spirituality of the race may
rise securely upward upon a broad basis of the developed lower
nature in man, the intelligent mental being. Therefore we see
that the reason in its growth either does away with the distinct
spiritual tendency for a time, as in ancient Greece, or accepts it
but spins out around its first data and activities a vast web of
the workings of the intelligence, so that, as in India, the early
mystic seer is replaced by the philosopher-mystic, the religious
thinker and even the philosopher pure and simple.

For a time the new growth and impulse may seem to take
possession of a whole community as in Athens or in old Aryan
India. But these early dawns cannot endure in their purity, so
long as the race is not ready. There is a crystallisation, a lessening
of the first impetus, a new growth of infrarational forms in
which the thought or the spirituality is overgrown with inferior
accretions or it is imbedded in the form and may even die in it,
while the tradition of the living knowledge, the loftier life and
activity remains the property of the higher classes or a highest

class. The multitude remains infrarational in its habit of mind, though perhaps it may still keep in capacity an enlivened intelligence or a profound or subtle spiritual receptiveness as its gain from the past. So long as the hour of the rational age has not arrived, the irrational period of society cannot be left behind; and that arrival can only be when not a class or a few but the multitude has learned to think, to exercise its intelligence actively — it matters not at first however imperfectly — upon their life, their needs, their rights, their duties, their aspirations as human beings. Until then we have as the highest possible development a mixed society, infrarational in the mass, but saved for civilisation by a higher class whose business it is to seek after the reason and the spirit, to keep the gains of mankind in these fields, to add to them, to enlighten and raise with them as much as possible the life of the whole.

At this point we see that Nature in her human mass tends to move forward slowly on her various lines of active mind and life towards a greater application of reason and spirituality which shall at last bring near the possibility of a rational and, eventually, a spiritual age of mankind. Her difficulties proceed from two sides. First, while she originally developed thought and reason and spirituality by exceptional individuals, now she develops them in the mass by exceptional communities or nations, — at least in the relative sense of a nation governed, led and progressively formed and educated by its intellectually or spiritually cultured class or classes. But the exceptional nation touched on its higher levels by a developed reason or spirituality or both, as were Greece and later Rome in ancient Europe, India, China and Persia in ancient Asia, is surrounded or neighboured by enormous masses of the old infrarational humanity and endangered by this menacing proximity; for until a developed science comes in to redress the balance, the barbarian has always a greater physical force and unexhausted native power of aggression than the cultured peoples. At this stage the light and power of civilisation always collapses in the end before the attack of the outer darkness. Then ascending Nature has to train the conquerors more or less slowly, with long difficulty and much loss and delay to develop among themselves what their incursion has temporarily destroyed or impaired. In the end humanity gains by the process; a greater mass of the nations is brought in, a larger and more living force of progress is applied, a starting-point is reached from which it can move to richer and more varied gains. But a certain loss is always the price of this advance.

But even within the communities themselves reason and spirituality at this stage are always hampered and endangered by existing in a milieu and atmosphere not their own. The élite, the classes in charge of these powers, are obliged to throw them into forms which the mass of human ignorance they lead and rule will accept, and both reason and spirituality tend to be stifled by these forms, to get stereotyped, fossilised, void of life, bound up from their natural play. Secondly, since they are after all part of the mass, these higher enlightened elements are themselves much under the influence of their infrarational parts and do not, except in individuals, arrive at the entirely free play of the reason or the free light of the spirit. Thirdly, there is always the danger of these elements gravitating downward to the ignorance below or even collapsing into it. Nature guards herself by various devices for maintaining the tradition of intellectual and spiritual activity in the favoured classes; here she makes it a point of honour for them to preserve and promote the national culture, there she establishes a preservative system of education and discipline. And in order that these things may not degenerate into mere traditionalism, she brings in a series of intellectual or spiritual movements which by their shock revivify the failing life and help to bring about a broadening and an enlarging and to drive the dominant reason or spirituality deeper down into the infrarational mass. Each movement indeed tends to petrify after a shorter or longer activity, but a fresh shock, a new wave arrives in time to save and regenerate. Finally, she reaches the point when, all immediate danger of relapse overcome, she can proceed to her next decisive advance in the cycle of social evolution. This must take the form of an attempt to universalise first of all the habit of reason and the application of the intelligence and intelligent will to life. Thus is instituted the rational age of human society, the great endeavour to bring the power of the reason and intelligence to bear on all that we are and do and to organise in their light and by their guiding force the entire existence of the race.

Chapter XIX

The Curve of the Rational Age

THE PRESENT age of mankind may be characterised from this point of view of a graded psychological evolution of the race as a more and more rapidly accelerated attempt to discover and work out the right principle and secure foundations of a rational system of society. It has been an age of progress; but progress is of two kinds, adaptive, with a secure basis in an unalterable social principle and constant change only in the circumstances and machinery of its application to suit fresh ideas and fresh needs, or else radical, with no long-secure basis, but instead a constant root questioning of the practical foundations and even the central principle of the established society. The modern age has resolved itself into a constant series of radical progressions.

This series seems to follow always a typical course, first a luminous seed-time and a period of enthusiastic effort and battle, next a partial victory and achievement and a brief era of possession, then disillusionment and the birth of a new idea and endeavour. A principle of society is put forward by the thinker, seizes on the general mind and becomes a social gospel; brought immediately or by rapid stages into practice, it dethrones the preceding principle and takes its place as the foundation of the community's social or political life. This victory won, men live for a time in the enthusiasm or, when the enthusiasm sinks, in the habit of their great achievement. After a little they begin to feel less at ease with the first results and are moved to adapt, to alter constantly, to develop more or less restlessly the new system, — for it is the very nature of the reason to observe, to be open to novel ideas, to respond quickly to new needs and possibilities and not to repose always in the unquestioning acceptance of every habit and old association. Still men do not yet think of questioning their social principle or imagine that it will ever need alteration, but are intent only to perfect its forms and make its application more thorough, its execution more sincere and effective. A time, however, arrives when the reason becomes dissatisfied and sees that it is only erecting a mass of new conventions and that there has been no satisfying change; there has been a shifting of stresses, but the society is not appreciably nearer to perfection. The opposition of the few thinkers who have already, perhaps almost from the first, started to question the sufficiency of the social principle, makes itself felt and is accepted by increasing numbers; there is a movement of revolt and the society starts on the familiar round to a new radical progression, a new revolution, the reign of a more advanced social principle.

This process has to continue until the reason can find a principle of society or else a combination and adjustment of several principles which will satisfy it. The question is whether it will ever be satisfied or can ever rest from questioning the foundation of established things, — unless indeed it sinks back into a sleep of tradition and convention or else goes forward by a great awakening to the reign of a higher spirit than its own and opens into a suprarational or spiritual age of mankind. If we may judge from the modern movement, the progress of the reason as a social renovator and creator, if not interrupted in its course, would be destined to pass through three successive stages which are the very logic of its growth, the first individualistic and increasingly democratic with liberty for its principle, the second socialistic, in the end perhaps a governmental communism with equality and the State for its principle, the third — if that ever gets beyond the stage of theory — anarchistic in the higher sense of that much-abused word, either a loose voluntary cooperation or a free communalism with brotherhood or comradeship and not government for its principle. It is in the transition to its third and consummating stage, if or whenever that comes, that the power and sufficiency of the reason will be tested; it will then be seen whether the reason can really be the master of our nature, solve the problems of our interrelated and conflicting egoisms and bring about within itself a perfect principle of society or must give way to a higher guide. For till this third stage has its trial, it is Force that in the last resort really governs. Reason only gives to Force the plan of its action and a system to administer.

We have already seen that it is individualism which opens the way to the age of reason and that individualism gets its impulse and its chance of development because it follows upon an age of dominant conventionalism. It is not that in the pre-individualistic, pre-rational ages there were no thinkers upon society and the communal life of man; but they did not think in the characteristic method of the logical reason, critical, all-observing, all-questioning, and did not proceed on the constructive side by the carefully mechanising methods of the highly rationalised intelligence when it passes from the reasoned perception of a truth to the endeavour after its pure, perfect and universal orderly application. Their thought and their building of life were much less logical than spontaneously intelligent, organic and intuitive. Always they looked upon life as it was and sought to know its secret by keen discernment, intuition and insight; symbols embodying the actual and ideal truth of life and being, types setting them in an arrangement and psychological order, institutions giving them a material fixity in their effectuation by life, this was the form in which they shaped their attempt to understand and mentalise life, to govern life by mind, but mind in its spontaneously intuitive or its reflectively seeing movements before they have been fixed into the geometrical patterns of the logical intelligence.

But reason seeks to understand and interpret life by one kind of symbol only, the idea; it generalises the facts of life according to its own strongly cut ideative conceptions so that it may be able to master and arrange them, and having hold of an idea it looks for its largest general application. And in order that these ideas may not be a mere abstraction divorced from the realised or realisable truth of things, it has to be constantly comparing them with facts. It has to be always questioning facts so that it may find the ideas by which they can be more and more adequately explained, ordered and managed, and it has always to be questioning ideas in order, first, to see whether they square with actual facts and, secondly, whether there are not new facts to suit which they must be modified or enlarged or which can be evolved out of them. For reason lives not only in actual facts, but in possibilities, not only in realised truths, but in ideal truths; and the ideal truth once seen, the impulse of the idealising intelligence is to see too whether it cannot be turned into a fact, cannot be immediately or rapidly realised in life. It is by this inherent characteristic that the age of reason must always be an age of progress.

So long as the old method of mentalising life served its purpose, there was no necessity for men in the mass to think out their way of life by the aid of the reason. But the old method ceased to serve its purpose as soon as the symbols, types, institutions it created became conventions so imprisoning truth that there was no longer a force of insight sufficient to deliver the hidden reality from its artificial coatings. Man may for a time, for a long time even, live by the mere tradition of things whose reality he has lost, but not permanently; the necessity of questioning all his conventions and traditions arises, and by that necessity reason gets her first real chance of an entire self-development. Reason can accept no tradition merely for the sake of its antiquity or its past greatness: it has to ask, first, whether the tradition contains at all any still living truth and, secondly, whether it contains the best truth available to man for the government of his life. Reason can accept no convention merely because men are agreed upon it: it has to ask whether they are right in their agreement, whether it is not an inert and false acquiescence. Reason cannot accept any institution merely because it serves some purpose of life: it has to ask whether there are not greater and better purposes which can be best served by new institutions. There arises the necessity of a universal questioning, and from that necessity arises the idea that society can only be perfected by the universal application of the rational intelligence to the whole of life, to its principle as to its details, to its machinery and to the powers that drive the machine.

This reason which is to be universally applied, cannot be the reason of a ruling class; for in the present imperfection of the human race that always means in practice the fettering and misapplication of reason degraded into a servant of power to maintain the privileges of the ruling class and justify the existing order. It cannot be the reason of a few pre-eminent thinkers; for, if the mass is infrarational, the application of their ideas becomes in practice disfigured, ineffective, incomplete, speedily altered into mere form and convention. It must be the reason of each and all seeking for a basis of agreement. Hence arises the principle of individualistic democracy, that the reason and will of every individual in the society must be allowed to count equally with the reason and will of every other in determining its government, in selecting the essential basis and in arranging the detailed ordering of the common life. This must be, not because the reason of one man is as good as the reason of any other, but because otherwise we get back inevitably to the rule of a predominant class which, however modified by being obliged to consider to some extent the opinion of the ruled, must exhibit always the irrational vice of reason subordinated to the purposes of power and not flexibly used for its own proper and ideal ends. Secondly, each individual must be allowed to govern his life according to the dictates of his own reason and will so far as that can be done without impinging on the same right in others. This is a necessary corollary of the primary principle on which the age of reason founds its initial movement. It is sufficient for the first purposes of the rational age that each man should be supposed to have sufficient intelligence to understand views which are presented and explained to him, to consider the opinions of his fellows and to form in consultation with them his own judgment. His individual judgment so formed and by one device or another made effective is the share he contributes to the building of the total common judgment by which society must be ruled, his little brick in appearance insignificant and yet indispensable to the imposing whole. And it is sufficient also for the first ideal of the rational age that this common judgment should be effectively organised only for the indispensable common ends of the society, while in all else men must be left free to govern their own life according to their own reason and will and find freely its best possible natural adjustment with the lives of others. In this way by the practice of the free use of reason men can grow into rational beings and learn to live by common agreement a liberal, a vigorous, a natural and yet rationalised existence.

In practice it is found that these ideas will not hold for a long time. For the ordinary man is not yet a rational being; emerging from a long infrarational past, he is not naturally able to form a reasonable judgment, but thinks either according to his own interests, impulses and prejudices or else according to the ideas of others more active in intelligence or swift in action who are able by some means to establish an influence over his mind. Secondly, he does not yet use his reason in order to come to an agreement with his fellows, but rather to enforce his own opinions by struggle and conflict with the opinions of others. Exceptionally he may utilise his reason for the pursuit of truth, but normally it serves for the justification of his impulses, prejudices and interests, and it is these that determine or at least quite discolour and disfigure his ideals, even when he has learned at all to have ideals. Finally, he does not use his freedom to arrive at a rational adjustment of his life with the life of others; his natural tendency is to enforce the aims of his life even at the expense of or, as it is euphemistically put, in competition with the life of others. There comes thus to be a wide gulf between the ideal and the first results of its practice. There is here a disparity between fact and idea that must lead to inevitable disillusionment and failure.

The individualistic democratic ideal brings us at first in actual practice to the more and more precarious rule of a dominant class in the name of democracy over the ignorant, numerous and less fortunate mass. Secondly, since the ideal of freedom and equality is abroad and cannot any longer be stifled, it must lead to the increasing effort of the exploited masses to assert their down-trodden right and to turn, if they can, this pseudo-democratic falsehood into the real democratic truth; therefore, to a war of classes. Thirdly, it develops inevitably as part of its process a perpetual strife of parties, at first few and simple in composition, but afterwards as at the present time an impotent and sterilising chaos of names, labels, programmes, war-cries. All lift the banner of conflicting ideas or ideals, but all are really fighting out under that flag a battle of conflicting interests. Finally, individualistic democratic freedom results fatally in an increasing stress of competition which replaces the ordered tyrannies of the infrarational periods of humanity by a sort of ordered conflict. And this conflict ends in the survival not of the spiritually, rationally or physically fittest, but of the most fortunate and vitally successful. It is evident enough that, whatever else it may be, this is not a rational order of society; it is not at all the perfection which the individualistic reason of man had contemplated as its ideal or set out to accomplish.

The natural remedy for the first defects of the individualistic theory in practice would seem to be education; for if man is not by nature, we may hope at least that he can be made by education and training something like a rational being. Universal education, therefore, is the inevitable second step of the democratic movement in its attempt to rationalise human society. But a rational education means necessarily three things, first, to teach men how to observe and know rightly the facts on which they have to form a judgment; secondly, to train them to think fruitfully and soundly; thirdly, to fit them to use their knowledge and their thought effectively for their own and the common good. Capacity of observation and knowledge, capacity of intelligence and judgment, capacity of action and high character are required for the citizenship of a rational order of society; a general deficiency in any of these difficult requisites is a sure source of failure. Unfortunately, — even if we suppose that any training made available to the millions can ever be of this rare character, — the actual education given in the most advanced countries has not had the least relation to these necessities. And just as the first defects and failures of democracy have given occasion to the enemy to blaspheme and to vaunt the superiority or even the quite imaginary perfection of the ideal past, so also the first defects of its great remedy, education, have led many superior minds to deny the efficacy of education and its power to transform the human mind and driven them to condemn the democratic ideal as an exploded fiction.

Democracy and its panacea of education and freedom have certainly done something for the race. To begin with, the people are, for the first time in the historical period of history, erect, active and alive, and where there is life, there is always a hope of better things. Again, some kind of knowledge and with it some kind of active intelligence based on knowledge and strengthened by the habit of being called on to judge and decide between conflicting issues and opinions in all sorts of matters have been much more generalised than was formerly possible. Men are being progressively trained to use their minds, to apply intelligence to life, and that is a great gain. If they have not yet learned to think for themselves or to think soundly, clearly and rightly, they are at least more able now to choose with some kind of initial intelligence, however imperfect as yet it may be, the thought they shall accept and the rule they shall follow. Equal educational equipment and equal opportunity of life have by no means been acquired; but there is a much greater equalisation than was at all possible in former states of society. But here a new and enormous defect has revealed itself which is proving fatal to the social idea which engendered it. For given even perfect equality of educational and other opportunity, — and that does not yet really exist and cannot in the individualistic state of society, — to what purpose or in what manner is the opportunity likely to be used? Man, the half infrarational being, demands three things for his satisfaction, power, if he can have it, but at any rate the use and reward of his faculties and the enjoyment of his desires. In the old societies the possibility of these could be secured by him to a certain extent according to his birth, his fixed status and the use of his capacity within the limits of his hereditary status. That basis once removed and no proper substitute provided, the same ends can only be secured by success in a scramble for the one power left, the power of wealth. Accordingly, instead of a harmoniously ordered society there has been developed a huge organised competitive system, a frantically rapid and one-sided development of industrialism and, under the garb of democracy, an increasing plutocratic tendency that shocks by its ostentatious grossness and the magnitudes of its gulfs and distances. These have been the last results of the individualistic ideal and its democratic machinery, the initial bankruptcies of the rational age.

The first natural result has been the transition of the rational mind from democratic individualism to democratic socialism. Socialism, labouring under the disadvantageous accident of its birth in a revolt against capitalism, an uprising against the rule of the successful bourgeois and the plutocrat, has been compelled to work itself out by a war of classes. And, worse still, it has started from an industrialised social system and itself taken on at the beginning a purely industrial and economic appearance. These are accidents that disfigure its true nature. Its true nature, its real justification is the attempt of the human reason to carry on the rational ordering of society to its fulfilment, its will to get rid of this great parasitical excrescence of unbridled competition, this giant obstacle to any decent ideal or practice of human living. Socialism sets out to replace a system of organised economic battle by an organised order and peace. This can no longer be done on the old lines, an artificial or inherited inequality brought about by the denial of equal opportunity and justified by the affirmation of that injustice and its result as an eternal law of society and of Nature. That is a falsehood which the reason of man will no longer permit. Neither can it be done, it seems, on the basis of individual liberty; for that has broken down in the practice. Socialism therefore must do away with the democratic basis of individual liberty, even if it professes to respect it or to be marching towards a more rational freedom. It shifts at first the fundamental emphasis to other ideas and fruits of the democratic ideal, and it leads by this transference of stress to a radical change in the basic principle of a rational society. Equality, not a political only, but a perfect social equality, is to be the basis. There is to be equality of opportunity for all, but also equality of status for all, for without the last the first cannot be secured; even if it were established, it could not endure. This equality again is impossible if personal, or at least inherited right in property is to exist, and therefore socialism abolishes — except at best on a small scale — the right of personal property as it is now understood and makes war on the hereditary principle. Who then is to possess the property? It can only be the community as a whole. And who is to administer it? Again, the community as a whole. In order to justify this idea, the socialistic principle has practically to deny the existence of the individual or his right to exist except as a member of the society and for its sake. He belongs entirely to the society, not only his property, but himself, his labour, his capacities, the education it gives him and its results, his mind, his knowledge, his individual life, his family life, the life of his children. Moreover, since his individual reason cannot be trusted to work out naturally a right and rational adjustment of his life with the life of others, it is for the reason of the whole community to arrange that too for him. Not the reasoning minds and wills of the individuals, but the collective reasoning mind and will of the community has to govern. It is this which will determine not only the principles and all the details of the economic and political order, but the whole life of the community and of the individual as a working, thinking, feeling cell of this life, the development of his capacities, his actions, the use of the knowledge he has acquired, the whole ordering of his vital, his ethical, his intelligent being. For so only can the collective reason and intelligent will of the race overcome the egoism of individualistic life and bring about a perfect principle and rational order of society in a harmonious world.

It is true that this inevitable character of socialism is denied or minimised by the more democratic socialists; for the socialistic mind still bears the impress of the old democratic ideas and cherishes hopes that betray it often into strange illogicalities. It assures us that it will combine some kind of individual freedom, a limited but all the more true and rational freedom, with the rigours of the collectivist idea. But it is evidently these rigours to which things must tend if the collectivist idea is to prevail and not to stop short and falter in the middle of its course. If it proves itself thus wanting in logic and courage, it may very

well be that it will speedily or in the end be destroyed by the
foreign element it tolerates and perish without having sounded
its own possibilities. It will pass perhaps, unless guided by a
rational wisdom which the human mind in government has not
yet shown, after exceeding even the competitive individualistic
society in its cumbrous incompetence.[1] But even at its best the
collectivist idea contains several fallacies inconsistent with the
real facts of human life and nature. And just as the idea of
individualistic democracy found itself before long in difficulties
on that account because of the disparity between life's facts and
the mind's idea, difficulties that have led up to its discredit and
approaching overthrow, the idea of collectivist democracy too
may well find itself before long in difficulties that must lead to
its discredit and eventual replacement by a third stage of the
inevitable progression. Liberty protected by a State in which all
are politically equal, was the idea that individualistic democracy
attempted to elaborate. Equality, social and political equality
enforced through a perfect and careful order by a State which
is the organised will of the whole community, is the idea on
which socialistic democracy stakes its future. If that too fails
to make good, the rational and democratic Idea may fall back
upon a third form of society founding an essential rather than
formal liberty and equality upon fraternal comradeship in a free
community, the ideal of intellectual as of spiritual Anarchism.[2]

    In fact the claim to equality like the thirst for liberty is

[1] These hesitations of social democracy, its uneasy mental poise between two opposing
principles, socialistic regimentation and democratic liberty, may be the root cause of the
failure of socialism to make good in so many countries even when it had every chance
on its side and its replacement by the more vigorous and ruthlessly logical forces of
Communism and Fascism. On the other hand, in the northernmost countries of Europe
a temporising, reformist, practical Socialism compromising between the right regulation
of the communal life and the freedom of the individual has to some extent made good;
but it is still doubtful whether it will be allowed to go to the end of its road. If it has that
chance, it is still to be seen whether the drive of the idea and the force it carries in it for
complete self-effectuation will not prevail in the end over the spirit of compromise.

[2] In the theory of communism State socialism is only a passage; a free classless Stateless
communal life is the eventual ideal. But it is not likely that the living State machine once
in power with all that are interested in its maintenance would let go its prey or allow
itself to be abolished without a struggle.

individualistic in its origin, — it is not native or indispensable to the essence of the collectivist ideal. It is the individual who demands liberty for himself, a free movement for his mind, life, will, action; the collectivist trend and the State idea have rather the opposite tendency, they are self-compelled to take up more and more the compulsory management and control of the mind, life, will, action of the community — and the individual's as part of it — until personal liberty is pressed out of existence. But similarly it is the individual who demands for himself equality with all others; when a class demands, it is still the individual multiplied claiming for himself and all who are of his own grade, political or economic status an equal place, privilege or opportunity with those who have acquired or inherited a superiority of status. The social Reason conceded first the claim to liberty, but in practice (whatever might have been the theory) it admitted only so much equality — equality before the law, a helpful but not too effective political equality of the vote — as was necessary to ensure a reasonable freedom for all. Afterwards when the injustices and irrationalities of an unequalised competitive freedom, the enormity of the gulfs it created, became apparent, the social Reason shifted its ground and tried to arrive at a more complete communal justice on the basis of a political, economic, educational and social equality as complete as might be; it has laboured to make a plain level on which all can stand together. Liberty in this change has had to undergo the former fate of equality; for only so much liberty — perhaps or for a time — could survive as can be safely allowed without the competitive individual getting enough room for his self-assertive growth to upset or endanger the equalitarian basis. But in the end the discovery cannot fail to be made that an artificial equality has also its irrationalities, its contradictions of the collective good, its injustices even and its costly violations of the truth of Nature. Equality like individualistic liberty may turn out to be not a panacea but an obstacle in the way of the best management and control of life by the collective reason and will of the community.

But if both equality and liberty disappear from the human scene, there is left only one member of the democratic trinity,

204 The Human Cycle

brotherhood or, as it is now called, comradeship, that has some chance of survival as part of the social basis. This is because it seems to square better with the spirit of collectivism; we see accordingly the idea of it if not the fact still insisted on in the new social systems, even those in which both liberty and equality are discarded as noxious democratic chimeras. But comradeship without liberty and equality can be nothing more than the like association of all — individuals, functional classes, guilds, syndicates, soviets or any other units — in common service to the life of the nation under the absolute control of the collectivist State. The only liberty left at the end would be the "freedom" to serve the community under the rigorous direction of the State authority; the only equality would be an association of all alike in a Spartan or Roman spirit of civic service with perhaps a like status, theoretically equal at least for all functions; the only brotherhood would be the sense of comradeship in devoted dedication to the organised social Self, the State. In fact the democratic trinity, stripped of its godhead, would fade out of existence; the collectivist ideal can very well do without them, for none of them belong to its grain and very substance.

This is indeed already the spirit, the social reason — or rather the social gospel — of the totalitarianism whose swelling tide threatens to engulf all Europe and more than Europe. Totalitarianism of some kind seems indeed to be the natural, almost inevitable destiny, at any rate the extreme and fullest outcome of Socialism or, more generally, of the collectivist idea and impulse. For the essence of Socialism, its justifying ideal, is the governance and strict organisation of the total life of the society as a whole and in detail by its own conscious reason and will for the best good and common interest of all, eliminating exploitation by individual or class, removing internal competition, haphazard confusion and waste, enforcing and perfecting coordination, assuring the best functioning and a sufficient life for all. If a democratic polity and machinery best assure such a working, as was thought at first, it is this that will be chosen and the result will be Social Democracy. That ideal still holds sway in northern Europe and it may there yet have a chance of proving that a successful collectivist rationalisation of society is quite possible. But if a non-democratic polity and machinery are found to serve the purpose better, then there is nothing inherently sacrosanct for the collectivist mind in the democratic ideal; it can be thrown on the rubbish-heap where so many other exploded sanctities have gone. Russian communism so discarded with contempt democratic liberty and attempted for a time to substitute for the democratic machine a new sovietic structure, but it has preserved the ideal of a proletarian equality for all in a classless society. Still its spirit is a rigorous totalitarianism on the basis of the "dictatorship of the proletariate", which amounts in fact to the dictatorship of the Communist party in the name or on behalf of the proletariate. Non-proletarian totalitarianism goes farther and discards democratic equality no less than democratic liberty; it preserves classes — for a time only, it may be, — but as a means of social functioning, not as a scale of superiority or a hierarchic order. Rationalisation is no longer the turn; its place is taken by a revolutionary mysticism which seems to be the present drive of the Time Spirit.

This is a symptom that can have a considerable significance. In Russia the Marxist system of Socialism has been turned almost into a gospel. Originally a rationalistic system worked out by a logical thinker and discoverer and systematiser of ideas, it has been transformed by the peculiar turn of the Russian mind into something like a social religion, a collectivist *mystique*, an inviolable body of doctrines with all denial or departure treated as a punishable heresy, a social cult enforced by the intolerant piety and enthusiasm of a converted people. In Fascist countries the swing away from Rationalism is marked and open; a surface vital subjectivism has taken its place and it is in the name of the national soul and its self-expression and manifestation that the leaders and prophets teach and violently enforce their totalitarian *mystique*. The essential features are the same in Russia and in Fascist countries, so that to the eye of the outsider their deadly quarrel seems to be a blood-feud of kinsmen fighting for the inheritance of their slaughtered parents — Democracy and the Age of Reason. There is the seizure of the life of the community by a dominant individual leader, Führer, Dux, dictator, head of a small active minority, the Nazi, Fascist or Communist party, and supported by a militarised partisan force; there is a rapid crystallisation of the social, economic, political life of the people into a new rigid organisation effectively controlled at every point; there is the compulsory casting of thought, education, expression, action, into a set iron mould, a fixed system of ideas and life-motives, with a fierce and ruthless, often a sanguinary repression of all that denies and differs; there is a total unprecedented compression of the whole communal existence so as to compel a maximum efficiency and a complete unanimity of mind, speech, feeling, life.

If this trend becomes universal, it is the end of the Age of Reason, the suicide or the execution — by decapitation or lethal pressure, *peine forte et dure*, — of the rational and intellectual expansion of the human mental being. Reason cannot do its work, act or rule if the mind of man is denied freedom to think or freedom to realise its thought by action in life. But neither can a subjective age be the outcome; for the growth of subjectivism also cannot proceed without plasticity, without movement of self-search, without room to move, expand, develop, change. The result is likely to be rather the creation of a tenebrous No Man's Land where obscure mysticisms, materialistic, vitalistic or mixed, clash and battle for the mastery of human life. But this consummation is not certain; chaos and confusion still reign and all hangs in the balance. Totalitarian mysticism may not be able to carry out its menace of occupying the globe, may not even endure. Spaces of the earth may be left where a rational idealism can still survive. The terrible compression now exercised on the national mind and life may lead to an explosion from within or, on the other hand, having fulfilled its immediate aim may relax and give way in calmer times to a greater plasticity which will restore to the human mind or soul a more natural line of progress, a freer field for their self-expanding impulse.

In that case the curve of the Age of Reason, now threatened with an abrupt cessation, may prolong and complete itself; the subjective turn of the human mind and life, avoiding a premature plunge into any general external action before it has found itself, may have time and freedom to evolve, to seek out its own truth, its own lines and so become ready to take up the spiral of the human social evolution where the curve of the Age of Reason naturally ends by its own normal evolution and make ready the ways of a deeper spirit.

Chapter XX

The End of the Curve of Reason

THE RATIONAL collectivist idea of society has at first sight a powerful attraction. There is behind it a great truth, that every society represents a collective being and in it and by it the individual lives and he owes to it all that he can give it. More, it is only by a certain relation to the society, a certain harmony with this greater collective self that he can find the complete use for his many developed or developing powers and activities. Since it is a collective being, it must, one would naturally suppose, have a discoverable collective reason and will which should find more and more its right expression and right working if it is given a conscious and effective means of organised self-expression and execution. And this collective will and intelligence, since it is according to the original idea that of all in a perfect equality, might naturally be trusted to seek out and work out its own good where the ruling individual and class would always be liable to misuse their power for quite other ends. The right organisation of social life on a basis of equality and comradeship ought to give each man his proper place in society, his full training and development for the common ends, his due share of work, leisure and reward, the right value of his life in relation to the collective being, society. Moreover it would be a place, share, value regulated by the individual and collective good and not an exaggerated or a depressed value brought to him fortuitously by birth or fortune, purchased by wealth or won by a painful and wasteful struggle. And certainly the external efficiency of the community, the measured, ordered and economical working of its life, its power for production and general well-being must enormously increase, as even the quite imperfect development of collective action in the recent past has shown, in a well-organised and concentrated State.

If it be objected that to bring about this result in its completeness the liberty of the individual will have to be destroyed or reduced to an almost vanishing quantity, it might be answered that the right of the individual to any kind of egoistic freedom as against the State which represents the mind, the will, the good and interest of the whole community, *sarvam brahma*, is a dangerous fiction, a baneful myth. Individual liberty of life and action — even if liberty of thought and speech is for a time conceded, though this too can hardly remain unimpaired when once the socialistic State has laid its grip firmly on the individual, — may well mean in practice an undue freedom given to his infra-rational parts of nature, and is not that precisely the thing in him that has to be thoroughly controlled, if not entirely suppressed, if he is to become a reasonable being leading a reasonable life? This control can be most wisely and effectively carried out by the collective reason and will of the State which is larger, better, more enlightened than the individual's; for it profits, as the average individual cannot do, by all the available wisdom and aspiration in the society. Indeed, the enlightened individual may well come to regard this collective reason and will as his own larger mind, will and conscience and find in a happy obedience to it a strong delivery from his own smaller and less rational self and therefore a more real freedom than any now claimed by his little separate ego. It used already to be argued that the disciplined German obeying the least gesture of the policeman, the State official, the military officer was really the freest, happiest and most moral individual in all Europe and therefore in the whole world. The same reasoning in a heightened form might perhaps be applied to the drilled felicities of Fascist Italy and Nazi Germany. The State, educating and governing the individual, undertakes to intellectualise, ethicise, practicalise and generally perfect him and to see to it that he remains, whether he will or no, always and in all things — strictly on the lines approved by the State — intellectual, ethical, practical and thoroughly perfect.

The pity of it is that this excellent theory, quite as much as the individualist theory that ran before it, is sure to stumble over a discrepancy between its set ideas and the actual facts of human nature; for it ignores the complexity of man's being and all that that complexity means. And especially it ignores the soul of man and its supreme need of freedom, of the control also of his lower members, no doubt, — for that is part of the total freedom towards which he is struggling, — but of a growing self-control, not a mechanical regulation by the mind and will of others. Obedience too is a part of its perfection, — but a free and natural obedience to a true guiding power and not to a mechanised government and rule. The collective being is a fact; all mankind may be regarded as a collective being: but this being is a soul and life, not merely a mind or a body. Each society develops into a sort of sub-soul or group-soul of this humanity and develops also a general temperament, character, type of mind, evolves governing ideas and tendencies that shape its life and its institutions. But the society has no discoverable common reason and will belonging alike to all its members; for the group-soul rather works out its tendencies by a diversity of opinions, a diversity of wills, a diversity of life, and the vitality of the group-life depends largely upon the working of this diversity, its continuity, its richness. Since that is so, government by the organised State must mean always government by a number of individuals, — whether that number be in theory the minority or the majority makes in the end little fundamental difference. For even when it is the majority that nominally governs, in fact it is always the reason and will of a comparatively few effective men — and not really any common reason and will of all — that rules and regulates things with the consent of the half-hypnotised mass.[1] There is no reason to suppose that the immediate socialisation of the State would at all alter, the mass of men not being yet thoroughly rationalised and developed minds, this practical necessity of State government.

---

[1] This truth has come out with a startling force of self-demonstration in Communist Russia and National Socialist Germany, — not to speak of other countries. The vehement reassertion of humanity's need of a King crowned or uncrowned — Dictator, Leader, Duce or Führer — and a ruling and administering oligarchy has been the last outcome of a century and a half of democracy as it has been too the first astonishing result of the supposed rise of the proletariate to power.

In the old infrarational societies, at least in their inception, what governed was not the State, but the group-soul itself evolving its life organised into customary institutions and self-regulations to which all had to conform; for the rulers were only its executors and instruments. This entailed indeed a great subjection of the individual to the society, but it was not felt, because the individualistic idea was yet unborn and such diversities as arose were naturally provided for in one way or another, — in some cases by a remarkable latitude of social variation which government by the State tends more and more to suppress. As State government develops, we have a real suppression or oppression of the minority by the majority or the majority by the minority, of the individual by the collectivity, finally, of all by the relentless mechanism of the State. Democratic liberty tried to minimise this suppression; it left a free play for the individual and restricted as much as might be the role of the State. Collectivism goes exactly to the opposite extreme; it will leave no sufficient elbow-room to the individual free-will, and the more it rationalises the individual by universal education of a highly developed kind, the more this suppression will be felt, — unless indeed all freedom of thought is negated and the minds of all are forced into a single standardised way of thinking.

Man needs freedom of thought and life and action in order that he may grow, otherwise he will remain fixed where he was, a stunted and static being. If his individual mind and reason are ill-developed, he may consent to grow, as does the infrarational mind, in the group-soul, in the herd, in the mass, with that subtle half-conscient general evolution common to all in the lower process of Nature. As he develops individual reason and will, he needs and society must give him room for an increasing play of individual freedom and variation, at least so far as that does not develop itself to the avoidable harm of others and of society as a whole. Given a full development and free play of the individual mind, the need of freedom will grow with the immense variation which this development must bring with it, and if only a free play in thought and reason is allowed, but the free play of the intelligent will in life and action is inhibited by the excessive regulation of the life, then an intolerable contradiction and falsity will be created. Men may bear it for a time in consideration of the great and visible new benefits of order, economic development, means of efficiency and the scientific satisfaction of the reason which the collectivist arrangement of society will bring; but when its benefits become a matter of course and its defects become more and more realised and prominent, dissatisfaction and revolt are sure to set in in the clearest and most vigorous minds of the society and propagate themselves throughout the mass. This intellectual and vital dissatisfaction may very well take under such circumstances the form of anarchistic thought, because that thought appeals precisely to this need of free variation in the internal life and its outward expression which will be the source of revolt, and anarchistic thought must be necessarily subversive of the socialistic order. The State can only combat it by an education adapted to its fixed forms of life, an education that will seek to drill the citizen in a fixed set of ideas, aptitudes, propensities as was done in the old infrarational order of things and by the suppression of freedom of speech and thinking so as to train and compel all to be of one mind, one sentiment, one opinion, one feeling; but this remedy will be in a rational society self-contradictory, ineffective, or if effective, then worse than the evil it seeks to combat. On the other hand, if from the first freedom of thought is denied, that means the end of the Age of Reason and of the ideal of a rational society. Man the mental being disallowed the use — except in a narrow fixed groove — of his mind and mental will, will stop short in his growth and be even as the animal and as the insect a stationary species.

This is the central defect through which a socialistic State is bound to be convicted of insufficiency and condemned to pass away before the growth of a new ideal. Already the pressure of the State organisation on the life of the individual has reached a point at which it is ceasing to be tolerable. If it continues to be what it is now, a government of the life of the individual by the comparatively few and not, as it pretends, by a common will and reason, if, that is to say, it becomes patently undemocratic or remains pseudo-democratic, then it will be this falsity through which anarchistic thought will attack its existence. But the innermost difficulty would not disappear even if the social- istic State became really democratic, really the expression of the free reasoned will of the majority in agreement. Any true development of that kind would be difficult indeed and has the appearance of a chimera: for collectivism pretends to regulate life not only in its few fundamental principles and its main lines, as every organised society must tend to do, but in its details, it aims at a thoroughgoing scientific regulation, and an agreement of the free reasoned will of millions in all the lines and most of the details of life is a contradiction in terms. Whatever the perfection of the organised State, the suppression or oppression of individual freedom by the will of the majority or of a mi- nority would still be there as a cardinal defect vitiating its very principle. And there would be something infinitely worse. For a thoroughgoing scientific regulation of life can only be brought about by a thoroughgoing mechanisation of life. This tendency to mechanisation is the inherent defect of the State idea and its practice. Already that is the defect upon which both intellectual anarchistic thought and the insight of the spiritual thinker have begun to lay stress, and it must immensely increase as the State idea rounds itself into a greater completeness in practice. It is indeed the inherent defect of reason when it turns to govern life and labours by quelling its natural tendencies to put it into some kind of rational order.

Life differs from the mechanical order of the physical uni- verse with which the reason has been able to deal victoriously just because it is mechanical and runs immutably in the groove of fixed cosmic habits. Life, on the contrary, is a mobile, progressive and evolving force, — a force that is the increasing expression of an infinite soul in creatures and, as it progresses, becomes more and more aware of its own subtle variations, needs, di- versities. The progress of Life involves the development and interlocking of an immense number of things that are in conflict with each other and seem often to be absolute oppositions and contraries. To find amid these oppositions some principle or standing-ground of unity, some workable lever of reconciliation

which will make possible a larger and better development on
a basis of harmony and not of conflict and struggle, must be
increasingly the common aim of humanity in its active life-
evolution, if it at all means to rise out of life's more confused,
painful and obscure movement, out of the compromises made
by Nature with the ignorance of the Life-mind and the nescience
of Matter. This can only be truly and satisfactorily done when
the soul discovers itself in its highest and completest spiritual
reality and effects a progressive upward transformation of its
life-values into those of the spirit; for there they will all find their
spiritual truth and in that truth their standing-ground of mutual
recognition and reconciliation. The spiritual is the one truth of
which all others are the veiled aspects, the brilliant disguises or
the dark disfigurements, and in which they can find their own
right form and true relation to each other. This is a work the
reason cannot do. The business of the reason is intermediate:
it is to observe and understand this life by the intelligence and
discover for it the direction in which it is going and the laws
of its self-development on the way. In order that it may do its
office, it is obliged to adopt temporarily fixed view-points none
of which is more than partially true and to create systems none
of which can really stand as the final expression of the integral
truth of things. The integral truth of things is truth not of the
reason but of the spirit.

In the realm of thought that does not matter; for as there
the reason does not drive at practice, it is able with impunity to
allow the most opposite view-points and systems to exist side
by side, to compare them, seek for reconciliations, synthetise
in the most various ways, change constantly, enlarge, elevate;
it is free to act without thinking at every point of immediate
practical consequences. But when the reason seeks to govern life,
it is obliged to fix its view-point, to crystallise its system; every
change becomes or at least seems a thing doubtful, difficult and
perilous, all the consequences of which cannot be foreseen, while
the conflict of view-points, principles, systems leads to strife and
revolution and not to a basis of harmonious development. The
reason mechanises in order to arrive at fixity of conduct and

practice amid the fluidity of things; but while mechanism is a sufficient principle in dealing with physical forces, because it is in harmony with the law or dharma of physical Nature, it can never truly succeed in dealing with conscious life, because there it is contrary to the law of life, its highest dharma. While, then, the attempt at a rational ordering of society is an advance upon the comparative immobility and slow subconscient or half-conscient evolution of infrarational societies and the confusedly mixed movement of semi-rational societies, it can never arrive at perfection by its own methods, because reason is neither the first principle of life, nor can be its last, supreme and sufficient principle.

The question remains whether anarchistic thought supervening upon the collectivistic can any more successfully find a satisfying social principle. For if it gets rid of mechanism, the one practical means of a rationalising organisation of life, on what will it build and with what can it create? It may be contended as against the anarchistic objection that the collectivist period is, if not the last and best, at least a necessary stage in social progress. For the vice of individualism is that in insisting upon the free development and self-expression of the life and the mind or the life-soul in the individual, it tends to exaggerate the egoism of the mental and vital being and prevent the recognition of unity with others on which alone a complete self-development and a harmless freedom can be founded. Collectivism at least insists upon that unity by entirely subordinating the life of the isolated ego to the life of the greater group-ego, and its office may be thus to stamp upon the mentality and life-habits of the individual the necessity of unifying his life with the life of others. Afterwards, when again the individual asserts his freedom, as some day he must, he may have learned to do it on the basis of this unity and not on the basis of his separate egoistic life. This may well be the intention of Nature in human society in its movement towards a collectivist principle of social living. Collectivism may itself in the end realise this aim if it can modify its own dominant principle far enough to allow for a free individual development on the basis of unity and a closely harmonised common existence.

But to do that it must first spiritualise itself and transform the very soul of its inspiring principle: it cannot do it on the basis of the logical reason and a mechanically scientific ordering of life.

Anarchistic thought, although it has not yet found any sure form, cannot but develop in proportion as the pressure of society on the individual increases, since there is something in that pressure which unduly oppresses a necessary element of human perfection. We need not attach much importance to the grosser vitalistic or violent anarchism which seeks forcibly to react against the social principle or claims the right of man to "live his own life" in the egoistic or crudely vitalistic sense. But there is a higher, an intellectual anarchistic thought which in its aim and formula recovers and carries to its furthest logical conclusions a very real truth of nature and of the divine in man. In its revolt against the opposite exaggeration of the social principle, we find it declaring that all government of man by man by the power of compulsion is an evil, a violation, a suppression or deformation of a natural principle of good which would otherwise grow and prevail for the perfection of the human race. Even the social principle in itself is questioned and held liable for a sort of fall in man from a natural to an unnatural and artificial principle of living.

The exaggeration and inherent weakness of this exclusive idea are sufficiently evident. Man does not actually live as an isolated being, nor can he grow by an isolated freedom. He grows by his relations with others and his freedom must exercise itself in a progressive self-harmonising with the freedom of his fellow-beings. The social principle therefore, apart from the forms it has taken, would be perfectly justified, if by nothing else, then by the need of society as a field of relations which afford to the individual his occasion for growing towards a greater perfection. We have indeed the old dogma that man was originally innocent and perfect; the conception of the first ideal state of mankind as a harmonious felicity of free and natural living in which no social law or compulsion existed because none was needed, is as old as the Mahabharata. But even this theory has to recognise a downward lapse of man from his natural perfection. The fall was not brought about by the introduction of the social principle in the arrangement of his life, but rather the social principle and the governmental method of compulsion had to be introduced as a result of the fall. If, on the contrary, we regard the evolution of man not as a fall from perfection but a gradual ascent, a growth out of the infrarational status of his being, it is clear that only by a social compulsion on the vital and physical instincts of his infrarational egoism, a subjection to the needs and laws of the social life, could this growth have been brought about on a large scale. For in their first crudeness the infrarational instincts do not correct themselves quite voluntarily without the pressure of need and compulsion, but only by the erection of a law other than their own which teaches them finally to erect a yet greater law within for their own correction and purification. The principle of social compulsion may not have been always or perhaps ever used quite wisely, — it is a law of man's imperfection, imperfect in itself, and must always be imperfect in its method and result: but in the earlier stages of his evolution it was clearly inevitable, and until man has grown out of the causes of its necessity, he cannot be really ready for the anarchistic principle of living.

But it is at the same time clear that the more the outer law is replaced by an inner law, the nearer man will draw to his true and natural perfection. And the perfect social state must be one in which governmental compulsion is abolished and man is able to live with his fellow-man by free agreement and cooperation. But by what means is he to be made ready for this great and difficult consummation? Intellectual anarchism relies on two powers in the human being of which the first is the enlightenment of his reason; the mind of man, enlightened, will claim freedom for itself, but will equally recognise the same right in others. A just equation will of itself emerge on the ground of a true, self-found and unperverted human nature. This might conceivably be sufficient, although hardly without a considerable change and progress in man's mental powers, if the life of the individual could be lived in a predominant isolation with only a small number of points of necessary contact with the lives of others. Actually, our existence is closely knit with the existences around us and there is a common life, a common work, a common effort and aspiration without which humanity cannot grow to its full height and wideness. To ensure coordination and prevent clash and conflict in this constant contact another power is needed than the enlightened intellect. Anarchistic thought finds this power in a natural human sympathy which, if it is given free play under the right conditions, can be relied upon to ensure natural cooperation: the appeal is to what the American poet calls the love of comrades, to the principle of fraternity, the third and most neglected term of the famous revolutionary formula. A free equality founded upon spontaneous cooperation, not on governmental force and social compulsion, is the highest anarchistic ideal.

This would seem to lead us either towards a free cooperative communism, a unified life where the labour and property of all is there for the benefit of all, or else to what may better be called communalism, the free consent of the individual to live in a society where the just freedom of his individuality will be recognised, but the surplus of his labour and acquisitions will be used or given by him without demur for the common good under a natural cooperative impulse. The severest school of anarchism rejects all compromise with communism. It is difficult to see how a Stateless Communism which is supposed to be the final goal of the Russian ideal, can operate on the large and complex scale necessitated by modern life. And indeed it is not clear how even a free communalism could be established or maintained without some kind of governmental force and social compulsion or how it could fail to fall away in the end either on one side into a rigorous collectivism or on the other to struggle, anarchy and disruption. For the logical mind in building its social idea takes no sufficient account of the infrarational element in man, the vital egoism to which the most active and effective part of his nature is bound: that is his most constant motive and it defeats in the end all the calculations of the idealising reason, undoes its elaborate systems or accepts only the little that it can assimilate to its own need and purpose. If that strong element, that ego-force in him is too much overshadowed, cowed and depressed, too much rationalised, too much denied an outlet, then the life of man becomes artificial, top-heavy, poor in the sap of vitality, mechanical, uncreative. And on the other hand, if it is not suppressed, it tends in the end to assert itself and derange the plans of the rational side of man, because it contains in itself powers whose right satisfaction or whose final way of transformation reason cannot discover.

If Reason were the secret highest law of the universe or if man the mental being were limited by mentality, it might be possible for him by the power of the reason to evolve out of the dominance of infrarational Nature which he inherits from the animal. He could then live securely in his best human self as a perfected rational and sympathetic being, balanced and well-ordered in all parts, the sattwic man of Indian philosophy; that would be his summit of possibility, his consummation. But his nature is rather transitional; the rational being is only a middle term of Nature's evolution. A rational satisfaction cannot give him safety from the pull from below nor deliver him from the attraction from above. If it were not so, the ideal of intellectual Anarchism might be more feasible as well as acceptable as a theory of what human life might be in its reasonable perfection; but, man being what he is, we are compelled in the end to aim higher and go farther.

A spiritual or spiritualised anarchism might appear to come nearer to the real solution or at least touch something of it from afar. As it expresses itself at the present day, there is much in it that is exaggerated and imperfect. Its seers seem often to preach an impossible self-abnegation of the vital life and an asceticism which instead of purifying and transforming the vital being, seeks to suppress and even kill it; life itself is impoverished or dried up by this severe austerity in its very springs. Carried away by a high-reaching spirit of revolt, these prophets denounce civilisation as a failure because of its vitalistic exaggerations, but set up an opposite exaggeration which might well cure civilisation of some of its crying faults and uglinesses, but would deprive us also of many real and valuable gains. But apart from these excesses of a too logical thought and a one-sided impulsion, apart from the inability of any "ism" to express the truth of the spirit which exceeds all such compartments, we seem here to be near to the real way out, to the discovery of the saving motive-force. The solution lies not in the reason, but in the soul of man, in its spiritual tendencies. It is a spiritual, an inner freedom that can alone create a perfect human order. It is a spiritual, a greater than the rational enlightenment that can alone illumine the vital nature of man and impose harmony on its self-seekings, antag-onisms and discords. A deeper brotherhood, a yet unfound law of love is the only sure foundation possible for a perfect social evolution, no other can replace it. But this brotherhood and love will not proceed by the vital instincts or the reason where they can be met, baffled or deflected by opposite reasonings and other discordant instincts. Nor will it found itself in the natural heart of man where there are plenty of other passions to combat it. It is in the soul that it must find its roots; the love which is founded upon a deeper truth of our being, the brotherhood or, let us say, — for this is another feeling than any vital or mental sense of brotherhood, a calmer more durable motive-force, — the spiritual comradeship which is the expression of an inner realisation of oneness. For so only can egoism disappear and the true individualism of the unique godhead in each man found itself on the true communism of the equal godhead in the race; for the Spirit, the inmost self, the universal Godhead in every being is that whose very nature of diverse oneness it is to realise the perfection of its individual life and nature in the existence of all, in the universal life and nature.

This is a solution to which it may be objected that it puts off the consummation of a better human society to a far-off date in the future evolution of the race. For it means that no machinery invented by the reason can perfect either the individual or the collective man; an inner change is needed in human nature, a change too difficult to be ever effected except by the few. This is not certain; but in any case, if this is not the solution, then there is no solution, if this is not the way, then there is no way for the human kind. Then the terrestrial evolution must pass beyond man as it has passed beyond the animal and a greater race must come that will be capable of the spiritual change, a form of life must be born that is nearer to the divine. After all there is no logical necessity for the conclusion that the change cannot begin at all because its perfection is not immediately possible. A decisive turn of mankind to the spiritual ideal, the beginning of a constant ascent and guidance towards the heights may not be altogether impossible, even if the summits are attainable at first only by the pioneer few and far-off to the tread of the race. And that beginning may mean the descent of an influence that will alter at once the whole life of mankind in its orientation and enlarge for ever, as did the development of his reason and more than any development of the reason, its potentialities and all its structure.

Chapter XXI

The Spiritual Aim and Life

A SOCIETY founded upon spirituality will differ in two essential points from the normal human society which begins from and ends with the lower nature. The normal human society starts from the gregarious instinct modified by a diversity and possible antagonism of interests, from an association and clash of egos, from a meeting, combination, conflict of ideas, tendencies and principles; it tries first to patch up an accommodation of converging interests and a treaty of peace between discords, founded on a series of implied contracts, natural or necessary adjustments which become customs of the aggregate life, and to these contracts as they develop it gives the name of social law. By establishing, as against the interests which lead to conflict, the interests which call for association and mutual assistance, it creates or stimulates sympathies and habits of helpfulness that give a psychological support and sanction to its mechanism of law, custom and contract. It justifies the mass of social institutions and habitual ways of being which it thus creates by the greater satisfaction and efficiency of the physical, the vital and the mental life of man, in a word, by the growth and advantages of civilisation. A good many losses have indeed to be written off as against these gains, but those are to be accepted as the price we must pay for civilisation.

The normal society treats man essentially as a physical, vital and mental being. For the life, the mind, the body are the three terms of existence with which it has some competence to deal. It develops a system of mental growth and efficiency, an intellectual, aesthetic and moral culture. It evolves the vital side of human life and creates an ever-growing system of economic efficiency and vital enjoyment, and this system becomes more and more rich, cumbrous and complex as civilisation develops. Depressing by its mental and vital overgrowth the natural vigour of the physical and animal man, it tries to set the balance right by systems of physical culture, a cumbrous science of habits and remedies intended to cure the ills it has created and as much amelioration as it can manage of the artificial forms of living that are necessary to its social system. In the end, however, experience shows that society tends to die by its own development, a sure sign that there is some radical defect in its system, a certain proof that its idea of man and its method of development do not correspond to all the reality of the human being and to the aim of life which that reality imposes.

There is then a radical defect somewhere in the process of human civilisation; but where is its seat and by what issue shall we come out of the perpetual cycle of failure? Our civilised development of life ends in an exhaustion of vitality and a refusal of Nature to lend her support any further to a continued advance upon these lines; our civilised mentality, after disturbing the balance of the human system to its own greater profit, finally discovers that it has exhausted and destroyed that which fed it and loses its power of healthy action and productiveness. It is found that civilisation has created many more problems than it can solve, has multiplied excessive needs and desires the satisfaction of which it has not sufficient vital force to sustain, has developed a jungle of claims and artificial instincts in the midst of which life loses its way and has no longer any sight of its aim. The more advanced minds begin to declare civilisation a failure and society begins to feel that they are right. But the remedy proposed is either a halt or even a retrogression, which means in the end more confusion, stagnation and decay, or a reversion to "Nature" which is impossible or can only come about by a cataclysm and disintegration of society; or even a cure is aimed at by carrying artificial remedies to their acme, by more and more Science, more and more mechanical devices, a more scientific organisation of life, which means that the engine shall replace life, the arbitrary logical reason substitute itself for complex Nature and man be saved by machinery. As well say that to carry a disease to its height is the best way to its cure.

It may be suggested on the contrary and with some chance

of knocking at the right door that the radical defect of all our systems is their deficient development of just that which society has most neglected, the spiritual element, the soul in man which is his true being. Even to have a healthy body, a strong vitality and an active and clarified mind and a field for their action and enjoyment, carries man no more than a certain distance; afterwards he flags and tires for want of a real self-finding, a satisfying aim for his action and progress. These three things do not make the sum of a complete manhood; they are means to an ulterior end and cannot be made for ever an aim in themselves. Add a rich emotional life governed by a well-ordered ethical standard, and still there is the savour of something left out, some supreme good which these things mean, but do not in themselves arrive at, do not discover till they go beyond themselves. Add a religious system and a widespread spirit of belief and piety, and still you have not found the means of social salvation. All these things human society has developed, but none of them has saved it from disillusionment, weariness and decay. The ancient intellectual cultures of Europe ended in disruptive doubt and sceptical impotence, the pieties of Asia in stagnation and decline. Modern society has discovered a new principle of survival, progress, but the aim of that progress it has never discovered, — unless the aim is always more knowledge, more equipment, convenience and comfort, more enjoyment, a greater and still greater complexity of the social economy, a more and more cumbrously opulent life. But these things must lead in the end where the old led, for they are only the same thing on a larger scale; they lead in a circle, that is to say, nowhere: they do not escape from the cycle of birth, growth, decay and death, they do not really find the secret of self-prolongation by constant self-renewal which is the principle of immortality, but only seem for a moment to find it by the illusion of a series of experiments each of which ends in disappointment. That so far has been the nature of modern progress. Only in its new turn inwards, towards a greater subjectivity now only beginning, is there a better hope; for by that turning it may discover that the real truth of man is to be found in his soul. It is not indeed certain that a subjective age will lead us there, but it gives us the possibility, can turn in that direction, if used rightly, the more inward movement.

It will be said that this is an old discovery and that it governed the old societies under the name of religion. But that was only an appearance. The discovery was there, but it was made for the life of the individual only, and even for him it looked beyond the earth for its fulfilment and at earth only as the place of his preparation for a solitary salvation or release from the burden of life. Human society itself never seized on the discovery of the soul as a means for the discovery of the law of its own being or on a knowledge of the soul's true nature and need and its fulfilment as the right way of terrestrial perfection. If we look at the old religions in their social as apart from their individual aspect, we see that the use society made of them was only of their most unspiritual or at any rate of their less spiritual parts. It made use of them to give an august, awful and would-be eternal sanction to its mass of customs and institutions; it made of them a veil of mystery against human questioning and a shield of darkness against the innovator. So far as it saw in religion a means of human salvation and perfection, it laid hands upon it at once to mechanise it, to catch the human soul and bind it on the wheels of a socio-religious machinery, to impose on it in the place of spiritual freedom an imperious yoke and an iron prison. It saddled upon the religious life of man a Church, a priesthood and a mass of ceremonies and set over it a pack of watchdogs under the name of creeds and dogmas, dogmas which one had to accept and obey under pain of condemnation to eternal hell by an eternal judge beyond, just as one had to accept and to obey the laws of society on pain of condemnation to temporal imprisonment or death by a mortal judge below. This false socialisation of religion has been always the chief cause of its failure to regenerate mankind.

For nothing can be more fatal to religion than for its spiritual element to be crushed or formalised out of existence by its outward aids and forms and machinery. The falsehood of the old social use of religion is shown by its effects. History has exhibited more than once the coincidence of the greatest religious fervour and piety with darkest ignorance, with an obscure squalor and long vegetative stagnancy of the mass of human life, with the unquestioned reign of cruelty, injustice and oppression, or with an organisation of the most ordinary, unaspiring and unraised existence hardly relieved by some touches of intellectual or half-spiritual light on the surface, — the end of all this a widespread revolt that turned first of all against the established religion as the key-stone of a regnant falsehood, evil and ignorance. It is another sign when the too scrupulously exact observation of a socio-religious system and its rites and forms, which by the very fact of this misplaced importance begin to lose their sense and true religious value, becomes the law and most prominent aim of religion rather than any spiritual growth of the individual and the race. And a great sign too of this failure is when the individual is obliged to flee from society in order to find room for his spiritual growth; when, finding human life given over to the unregenerated mind, life and body and the place of spiritual freedom occupied by the bonds of form, by Church and Shastra, by some law of the Ignorance, he is obliged to break away from all these to seek for growth into the spirit in the monastery, on the mountain-top, in the cavern, in the desert and the forest. When there is that division between life and the spirit, sentence of condemnation is passed upon human life. Either it is left to circle in its routine or it is decried as worthless and unreal, a vanity of vanities, and loses that confidence in itself and inner faith in the value of its terrestrial aims, *śraddhā*, without which it cannot come to anything. For the spirit of man must strain towards the heights; when it loses its tension of endeavour, the race must become immobile and stagnant or even sink towards darkness and the dust. Even where life rejects the spirit or the spirit rejects life, there may be a self-affirmation of the inner being; there may even be a glorious crop of saints and hermits in a forcing-soil of spirituality, but unless the race, the society, the nation is moved towards the spiritualisation of life or moves forward led by the light of an ideal, the end must be littleness, weakness and stagnation. Or the race has to turn to the intellect for rescue, for some hope or new ideal, and arrive by a circle through an age of rationalism at a fresh effort towards the restatement of spiritual truth and a new attempt to spiritualise human life.

The true and full spiritual aim in society will regard man not as a mind, a life and a body, but as a soul incarnated for a divine fulfilment upon earth, not only in heavens beyond, which after all it need not have left if it had no divine business here in the world of physical, vital and mental nature. It will therefore regard the life, mind and body neither as ends in themselves, sufficient for their own satisfaction, nor as mortal members full of disease which have only to be dropped off for the rescued spirit to flee away into its own pure regions, but as first instruments of the soul, the yet imperfect instruments of an unseized diviner purpose. It will believe in their destiny and help them to believe in themselves, but for that very reason in their highest and not only in their lowest or lower possibilities. Their destiny will be, in its view, to spiritualise themselves so as to grow into visible members of the spirit, lucid means of its manifestation, themselves spiritual, illumined, more and more conscious and perfect. For, accepting the truth of man's soul as a thing entirely divine in its essence, it will accept also the possibility of his whole being becoming divine in spite of Nature's first patent contradictions of this possibility, her darkened denials of this ultimate certitude, and even with these as a necessary earthly starting-point. And as it will regard man the individual, it will regard too man the collectivity as a soul-form of the Infinite, a collective soul myriadly embodied upon earth for a divine fulfilment in its manifold relations and its multitudinous activities. Therefore it will hold sacred all the different parts of man's life which correspond to the parts of his being, all his physical, vital, dynamic, emotional, aesthetic, ethical, intellectual, psychic evolution, and see in them instruments for a growth towards a diviner living. It will regard every human society, nation, people or other organic aggregate from the same standpoint, sub-souls, as it were, means of a complex manifestation and self-fulfilment of the Spirit, the divine Reality, the conscious Infinite in man upon earth. The possible godhead of man because he is inwardly of one being with God will be its one solitary creed and dogma.

But it will not seek to enforce even this one uplifting dogma by any external compulsion upon the lower members of man's natural being; for that is *nigraha*, a repressive contraction of the nature which may lead to an apparent suppression of the evil, but not to a real and healthy growth of the good; it will rather hold up this creed and ideal as a light and inspiration to all his members to grow into the godhead from within themselves, to become freely divine. Neither in the individual nor in the society will it seek to imprison, wall in, repress, impoverish, but to let in the widest air and the highest light. A large liberty will be the law of a spiritual society and the increase of freedom a sign of the growth of human society towards the possibility of true spiritualisation. To spiritualise in this sense a society of slaves, slaves of power, slaves of authority, slaves of custom, slaves of dogma, slaves of all sorts of imposed laws which they live under rather than live by them, slaves internally of their own weakness, ignorance and passions from whose worst effect they seek or need to be protected by another and external slavery, can never be a successful endeavour. They must shake off their fetters first in order to be fit for a higher freedom. Not that man has not to wear many a yoke in his progress upward; but only the yoke which he accepts because it represents, the more perfectly the better, the highest inner law of his nature and its aspiration, will be entirely helpful to him. The rest buy their good results at a heavy cost and may retard as much as or even more than they accelerate his progress.

The spiritual aim will recognise that man as he grows in his being must have as much free space as possible for all its members to grow in their own strength, to find out themselves and their potentialities. In their freedom they will err, because experience comes through many errors, but each has in itself a divine principle and they will find it out, disengage its presence, significance and law as their experience of themselves deepens and increases. Thus true spirituality will not lay a yoke upon science and philosophy or compel them to square their conclusions with any statement of dogmatic religious or even of assured spiritual truth, as some of the old religions attempted, vainly, ignorantly, with an unspiritual obstinacy and arrogance. Each part of man's being has its own dharma which it must follow and will follow in the end, put on it what fetters you please. The dharma of science, thought and philosophy is to seek for truth by the intellect dispassionately, without prepossession and prejudgment, with no other first propositions than the law of thought and observation itself imposes. Science and philosophy are not bound to square their observations and conclusions with any current ideas of religious dogma or ethical rule or aesthetic prejudice. In the end, if left free in their action, they will find the unity of Truth with Good and Beauty and God and give these a greater meaning than any dogmatic religion or any formal ethics or any narrower aesthetic idea can give us. But meanwhile they must be left free even to deny God and good and beauty if they will, if their sincere observation of things so points them. For all these rejections must come round in the end of their circling and return to a larger truth of the things they refuse. Often we find atheism both in individual and society a necessary passage to deeper religious and spiritual truth: one has sometimes to deny God in order to find him; the finding is inevitable at the end of all earnest scepticism and denial.

The same law holds good in Art; the aesthetic being of man rises similarly on its own curve towards its diviner possibilities. The highest aim of the aesthetic being is to find the Divine through beauty; the highest Art is that which by an inspired use of significant and interpretative form unseals the doors of the spirit. But in order that it may come to do this greatest thing largely and sincerely, it must first endeavour to see and depict man and Nature and life for their own sake, in their own characteristic truth and beauty; for behind these first characters lies always the beauty of the Divine in life and man and Nature and it is through their just transformation that what was at first veiled by them has to be revealed. The dogma that Art must be religious or not be at all, is a false dogma, just as is the claim that it must be subservient to ethics or utility or scientific truth or philosophic ideas. Art may make use of these things as elements, but it has its own *svadharma*, essential law, and it will rise to the widest spirituality by following out its own natural lines with no other yoke than the intimate law of its own being.

Even with the lower nature of man, though here we are naturally led to suppose that compulsion is the only remedy, the spiritual aim will seek for a free self-rule and development from within rather than a repression of his dynamic and vital being from without. All experience shows that man must be given a certain freedom to stumble in action as well as to err in knowledge so long as he does not get from within himself his freedom from wrong movement and error; otherwise he cannot grow. Society for its own sake has to coerce the dynamic and vital man, but coercion only chains up the devil and alters at best his form of action into more mitigated and civilised movements; it does not and cannot eliminate him. The real virtue of the dynamic and vital being, the Life Purusha, can only come by his finding a higher law and spirit for his activity within himself; to give him that, to illuminate and transform and not to destroy his impulse is the true spiritual means of regeneration.

Thus spirituality will respect the freedom of the lower members, but it will not leave them to themselves; it will present to them the truth of the spirit in themselves, translated into their own fields of action, presented in a light which illumines all their activities and shows them the highest law of their own freedom. It will not, for instance, escape from scientific materialism by a barren contempt for physical life or a denial of Matter, but pursue rather the sceptical mind into its own affirmations and denials and show it there the Divine. If it cannot do that, it is proved that it is itself unenlightened or deficient, because one-sided, in its light. It will not try to slay the vitality in man by denying life, but will rather reveal to life the divine in itself as the principle of its own transformation. If it cannot do that, it is because it has itself not yet wholly fathomed the meaning of the creation and the secret of the Avatar.

The spiritual aim will seek to fulfil itself therefore in a fullness of life and man's being in the individual and the race which will be the base for the heights of the spirit, — the base becoming in the end of one substance with the peaks. It will not proceed by a scornful neglect of the body, nor by an ascetic starving of the vital being and an utmost bareness or even squalor as the rule of spiritual living, nor by a puritanic denial of art and beauty and the aesthetic joy of life, nor by a neglect of science and philosophy as poor, negligible or misleading intellectual pursuits, — though the temporary utility even of these exaggerations as against the opposite excesses need not be denied; it will be all things to all, but in all it will be at once their highest aim and meaning and the most all-embracing expression of themselves in which all they are and seek for will be fulfilled. It will aim at establishing in society the true inner theocracy, not the false theocracy of a dominant Church or priesthood, but that of the inner Priest, Prophet and King. It will reveal to man the divinity in himself as the Light, Strength, Beauty, Good, Delight, Immortality that dwells within and build up in his outer life also the kingdom of God which is first discovered within us. It will show man the way to seek for the Divine in every way of his being, *sarvabhāvena,*[1] and so find it and live in it, that however — even in all kinds of ways — he lives and acts, he shall live and act in that,[2] in the Divine, in the Spirit, in the eternal Reality of his being.

[1] Gita.
[2] Gita. *Sarvathā vartamāno'pi sa yogī mayi vartate.*

16

Chapter XXII

The Necessity of the Spiritual Transformation

OUR NORMAL conduct of life, whether the individual or the social, is actually governed by the balance between two complementary powers, — first, an implicit will central to the life and inherent in the main power of its action and, secondly, whatever modifying will can come in from the Idea in mind — for man is a mental being — and operate through our as yet imperfect mental instruments to give this life force a conscious orientation and a conscious method. Life normally finds its own centre in our vital and physical being, in its cravings and its needs, in its demand for persistence, growth, expansion, enjoyment, in its reachings after all kinds of power and possession and activity and splendour and largeness. The first self-direction of this Life-Force, its first orderings of method are instinctive and either entirely or very largely subconscient and magnificently automatic: the ease, spontaneity, fine normality, beauty, self-satisfaction, abundant vital energy and power of the subhuman life of Nature up to the animal is due to its entire obedience to this instinctive and automatic urge. It is a vague sense of this truth and of the very different and in this respect inferior character of human life that makes the thinker, when dissatisfied with our present conditions, speak of a life according to Nature as the remedy for all our ills. An attempt to find such a rule in the essential nature of man has inspired many revolutionary conceptions of ethics and society and individual self-development down to the latest of the kind, the strangely inspired vitalistic philosophy of Nietzsche. The common defect of these conceptions is to miss the true character of man and the true law of his being, his Dharma.

Nietzsche's idea that to develop the superman out of our

present very unsatisfactory manhood is our real business, is in itself an absolutely sound teaching. His formulation of our aim, "to become ourselves", "to exceed ourselves", implying, as it does, that man has not yet found all his true self, his true nature by which he can successfully and spontaneously live, could not be bettered. But then the question of questions is there, what is our self, and what is our real nature? What is that which is growing in us, but into which we have not yet grown? It is something divine, is the answer, a divinity Olympian, Apollonian, Dionysiac, which the reasoning and consciously willing animal, man, is labouring more or less obscurely to become. Certainly, it is all that; but in what shall we find the seed of that divinity and what is the poise in which the superman, once self-found, can abide and be secure from lapse into this lower and imperfect manhood? Is it the intellect and will, the double-aspected *buddhi* of the Indian psychological system? But this is at present a thing so perplexed, so divided against itself, so uncertain of everything it gains, up to a certain point indeed magically creative and efficient but, when all has been said and done, in the end so splendidly futile, so at war with and yet so dependent upon and subservient to our lower nature, that even if in it there lies concealed some seed of the entire divinity, it can hardly itself be the seed and at any rate gives us no such secure and divine poise as we are seeking. Therefore we say, not the intellect and will, but that supreme thing in us yet higher than the Reason, the spirit, here concealed behind the coatings of our lower nature, is the secret seed of the divinity and will be, when discovered and delivered, luminous above the mind, the wide ground upon which a divine life of the human being can be with security founded.

When we speak of the superman, we speak evidently of something abnormal or supernormal to our present nature, so much so that the very idea of it becomes easily alarming and repugnant to our normal humanity. The normal human does not desire to be called out from its constant mechanical round to scale what may seem to it impossible heights and it loves still less the prospect of being exceeded, left behind and dominated,

— although the object of a true supermanhood is not exceeding
and domination for its own sake but precisely the opening of our
normal humanity to something now beyond itself that is yet its
own destined perfection. But mark that this thing which we have
called normal humanity, is itself something abnormal in Nature,
something the like and parity of which we look around in vain
to discover; it is a rapid freak, a sudden miracle. Abnormality
in Nature is no objection, no necessary sign of imperfection,
but may well be an effort at a much greater perfection. But
this perfection is not found until the abnormal can find its own
secure normality, the right organisation of its life in its own kind
and power and on its own level. Man is an abnormal who has
not found his own normality, — he may imagine he has, he may
appear to be normal in his own kind, but that normality is only
a sort of provisional order; therefore, though man is infinitely
greater than the plant or the animal, he is not perfect in his own
nature like the plant and the animal. This imperfection is not a
thing to be at all deplored, but rather a privilege and a promise,
for it opens out to us an immense vista of self-development and
self-exceeding. Man at his highest is a half-god who has risen up
out of the animal Nature and is splendidly abnormal in it, but the
thing which he has started out to be, the whole god, is something
so much greater than what he is that it seems to him as abnormal
to himself as he is to the animal. This means a great and arduous
labour of growth before him, but also a splendid crown of his
race and his victory. A kingdom is offered to him beside which
his present triumphs in the realms of mind or over external
Nature will appear only as a rough hint and a poor beginning.

What precisely is the defect from which all his imperfection
springs? We have already indicated it, — that has indeed been
the general aim of the preceding chapters, — but it is necessary
to state it now more succinctly and precisely. We see that at first
sight man seems to be a double nature, an animal nature of the
vital and physical being which lives according to its instincts,
impulses, desires, its automatic orientation and method, and
with that a half-divine nature of the self-conscious intellectual,
ethical, aesthetic, intelligently emotional, intelligently dynamic

being who is capable of finding and understanding the law of his own action and consciously using and bettering it, a reflecting mind that understands Nature, a will that uses, elevates, perfects Nature, a sense that intelligently enjoys Nature. The aim of the animal part of us is to increase vital possession and enjoyment; the aim of the semi-divine part of us is also to grow, possess and enjoy, but first to possess and enjoy intelligently, aesthetically, ethically, by the powers of the mind much more than by the powers of the life and body, and, secondly, to possess and enjoy, not so much the vital and physical except in so far as that is necessary as a foundation and starting-point, a preliminary necessity or condition, a standing-ground and basis, but things intellectual, ethical and aesthetic, and to grow not so much in the outward life, except in so far as that is necessary to the security, ease and dignity of our human existence, but in the true, the good and the beautiful. This is the manhood of man, his unique distinction and abnormality in the norm of this inconscient material Nature.

This means that man has developed a new power of being, — let us call it a new soul-power, with the premiss that we regard the life and the body also as a soul-power, — and the being who has done that is under an inherent obligation not only to look at the world and revalue all in it from this new elevation, but to compel his whole nature to obey this power and in a way reshape itself in its mould, and even to reshape, so far as he can, his environmental life into some image of this greater truth and law. In doing this lies his *svadharma*, his true rule and way of being, the way of his perfection and his real happiness. Failing in this, he fails in the aim of his nature and his being, and has to begin again until he finds the right path and arrives at a successful turning-point, a decisive crisis of transformation. Now this is precisely what man has failed to do. He has effected something, he has passed a certain stage of his journey. He has laid some yoke of the intellectual, ethical, aesthetic rule on his vital and physical parts and made it impossible for himself to be content with or really to be the mere human animal. But more he has not been able to do successfully. The transformation of his life into the image of the true, the good and the beautiful seems as far off as ever; if ever he comes near to some imperfect form of it, — and even then it is only done by a class or by a number of individuals with some reflex action on the life of the mass, — he slides back from it in a general decay of his life, or else stumbles on from it into some bewildering upheaval out of which he comes with new gains indeed but also with serious losses. He has never arrived at any great turning-point, any decisive crisis of transformation.

The main failure, the root of the whole failure indeed, is that he has not been able to shift upward what we have called the implicit will central to his life, the force and assured faith inherent in its main power of action. His central will of life is still situated in his vital and physical being, its drift is towards vital and physical enjoyment, enlightened indeed and checked to a certain extent in its impulses by the higher powers, but enlightened only and very partially, not transformed, — checked, not dominated and uplifted to a higher plane. The higher life is still only a thing superimposed on the lower, a permanent intruder upon our normal existence. The intruder interferes constantly with the normal life, scolds, encourages, discourages, lectures, manipulates, readjusts, lifts up only to let fall, but has no power to transform, alchemise, re-create. Indeed it does not seem itself quite to know where all this effort and uneasy struggle is meant to lead us, — sometimes it thinks, to a quite tolerable human life on earth, the norm of which it can never successfully fix, and sometimes it imagines our journey is to another world whither by a religious life or else an edifying death it will escape out of all this pother and trouble of mortal being. Therefore these two elements live together in a continual, a mutual perplexity, made perpetually uneasy, uncomfortable and ineffectual by each other, somewhat like an ill-assorted wife and husband, always at odds and yet half in love with or at least necessary to each other, unable to beat out a harmony, yet condemned to be joined in an unhappy leash until death separates them. All the uneasiness, dissatisfaction, disillusionment, weariness, melancholy, pessimism of the human mind comes from man's practical failure to solve the riddle and the difficulty of his double nature.

We have said that this failure is due to the fact that this higher power is only a mediator, and that thoroughly to transform the vital and physical life in its image is perhaps not possible, but at any rate not the intention of Nature in us. It may be urged perhaps that after all individuals have succeeded in effecting some figure of transformation, have led entirely ethical or artistic or intellectual lives, even shaped their life by some ideal of the true, the good and the beautiful, and whatever the individual has done, the race too may and should eventually succeed in doing; for the exceptional individual is the future type, the forerunner. But to how much did their success really amount? Either they impoverished the vital and physical life in them in order to give play to one element of their being, lived a one-sided and limited existence, or else they arrived at a compromise by which, while the higher life was given great prominence, the lower was still allowed to graze in its own field under the eye more or less strict or the curb more or less indulgent of the higher power or powers: in itself, in its own instincts and demands it remained unchanged. There was a dominance, but not a transformation.

Life cannot be entirely rational, cannot conform entirely to the ethical or the aesthetic or the scientific and philosophic mentality; mind is not the destined archangel of the transformation. All appearances to the contrary are always a *trompe l'oeil*, an intellectual, aesthetic or ethical illusion. Dominated, repressed life may be, but it reserves its right; and though individuals or a class may establish this domination for a time and impose some simulacrum of it upon the society, Life in the end circumvents the intelligence; it gets strong elements in it — for always there are traitor elements at work — to come over to its side and re-establishes its instincts, recovers its field; or if it fails in this, it has its revenge in its own decay which brings about the decay of the society, the disappointment of the perennial hope. So much so, that there are times when mankind perceives this fact and, renouncing the attempt to dominate the life-instinct, determines to use the intelligence for its service and to give it light in its own field instead of enslaving it to a higher but chimerical ideal.

Such a period was the recent materialistic age, when the intellect of man seemed decided to study thoroughly Life and Matter, to admit only that, to recognise mind only as an instrument of Life and Matter, and to devote all its knowledge to a tremendous expansion of the vital and physical life, its practicality, its efficiency, its comfort and the splendid ordering of its instincts of production, possession and enjoyment. That was the character of the materialistic, commercial, economic age of mankind, a period in which the ethical mind persisted painfully, but with decreasing self-confidence, an increasing self-questioning and a tendency to yield up the fortress of the moral law to the life-instinct, the aesthetic instinct and intelligence flourished as a rather glaring exotic ornament, a sort of rare orchid in the button-hole of the vital man, and reason became the magnificent servant of Life and Matter. The titanic development of the vital Life which followed, is ending as the Titans always end; it lit its own funeral pyre in the conflagration of a world-war, its natural upshot, a struggle between the most "efficient" and "civilised" nations for the possession and enjoyment of the world, of its wealth, its markets, its available spaces, an inflated and plethoric commercial expansion, largeness of imperial size and rule. For that is what the great war signified and was in its real origin, because that was the secret or the open intention of all pre-war diplomacy and international politics; and if a nobler idea was awakened at least for a time, it was only under the scourge of Death and before the terrifying spectre of a gigantic mutual destruction. Even so the awakening was by no means complete, nor everywhere quite sincere, but it was there and it was struggling towards birth even in Germany, once the great protagonist of the vitalistic philosophy of life. In that awakening lay some hope of better things. But for the moment at least the vitalistic aim has once more raised its head in a new form and the hope has dimmed in a darkness and welter in which only the eye of faith can see chaos preparing a new cosmos.

The first result of this imperfect awakening seemed likely to be a return to an older ideal, with a will to use the reason and the ethical mind better and more largely in the ordering of individual, of national and of international life. But such an attempt, though well enough as a first step, cannot be the real and final solution; if our effort ends there, we shall not arrive. The solution lies, we have said, in an awakening to our real, because our highest self and nature, — that hidden self which we are not yet, but have to become and which is not the strong and enlightened vital Will hymned by Nietzsche, but a spiritual self and spiritual nature that will use the mental being which we already are, but the mental being spiritualised, and transform by a spiritual ideality the aim and action of our vital and physical nature. For this is the formula of man in his highest potentiality, and safety lies in tending towards our highest and not in resting content with an inferior potentiality. To follow after the highest in us may seem to be to live dangerously, to use again one of Nietzsche's inspired expressions, but by that danger comes victory and security. To rest in or follow after an inferior potentiality may seem safe, rational, comfortable, easy, but it ends badly, in some futility or in a mere circling, down the abyss or in a stagnant morass. Our right and natural road is towards the summits.

We have then to return to the pursuit of an ancient secret which man, as a race, has seen only obscurely and followed after lamely, has indeed understood only with his surface mind and not in its heart of meaning, — and yet in following it lies his social no less than his individual salvation, — the ideal of the kingdom of God, the secret of the reign of the Spirit over mind and life and body. It is because they have never quite lost hold of this secret, never disowned it in impatience for a lesser victory, that the older Asiatic nations have survived so persistently and can now, as if immortal, raise their faces towards a new dawn; for they have fallen asleep, but they have not perished. It is true that they have for a time failed in life, where the European nations who trusted to the flesh and the intellect have succeeded; but that success, speciously complete but only for a time, has always turned into a catastrophe. Still Asia had failed in life, she had fallen in the dust, and even if the dust in which she was lying was sacred, as the modern poet of Asia has declared, —

though the sacredness may be doubted, — still the dust is not the proper place for man, nor is to lie prostrate in it his right human attitude. Asia temporarily failed not because she followed after things spiritual, as some console themselves by saying, — as if the spirit could be at all a thing of weakness or a cause of weakness, — but because she did not follow after the spirit sufficiently, did not learn how entirely to make it the master of life. Her mind either made a gulf and a division between life and the Spirit or else rested in a compromise between them and accepted as final socio-religious systems founded upon that compromise. So to rest is perilous; for the call of the Spirit more than any other demands that we shall follow it always to the end, and the end is neither a divorce and departure nor a compromise, but a conquest of all by the spirit and that reign of the seekers after perfection which, in the Hindu religious symbol, the last Avatar comes to accomplish.

This truth it is important to note, for mistakes made on the path are often even more instructive than the mistakes made by a turning aside from the path. As it is possible to superimpose the intellectual, ethical or aesthetic life or the sum of their motives upon the vital and physical nature, to be satisfied with a partial domination or a compromise, so it is possible to superimpose the spiritual life or some figure of strength or ascendency of spiritual ideas and motives on the mental, vital and physical nature and either to impoverish the latter, to impoverish the vital and physical existence and even to depress the mental as well in order to give the spiritual an easier domination, or else to make a compromise and leave the lower being to its pasture on condition of its doing frequent homage to the spiritual existence, admitting to a certain extent, greater or less, its influence and formally acknowledging it as the last state and the finality of the human being. This is the most that human society has ever done in the past, and though necessarily that must be a stage of the journey, to rest there is to miss the heart of the matter, the one thing needful. Not a humanity leading its ordinary life, what is now its normal round, touched by spiritual influences, but a humanity aspiring whole-heartedly to a law that is now abnormal to it until its whole life has been elevated into spirituality, is the steep way that lies before man towards his perfection and the transformation that it has to achieve.

The secret of the transformation lies in the transference of our centre of living to a higher consciousness and in a change of our main power of living. This will be a leap or an ascent even more momentous than that which Nature must at one time have made from the vital mind of the animal to the thinking mind still imperfect in our human intelligence. The central will implicit in life must be no longer the vital will in the life and the body, but the spiritual will of which we have now only rare and dim intimations and glimpses. For now it comes to us hardly disclosed, weakened, disguised in the mental Idea; but it is in its own nature supramental and it is its supramental power and truth that we have somehow to discover. The main power of our living must be no longer the inferior vital urge of Nature which is already accomplished in us and can only whirl upon its rounds about the ego-centre, but that spiritual force of which we sometimes hear and speak but have not yet its inmost secret. For that is still retired in our depths and waits for our transcendence of the ego and the discovery of the true individual in whose universality we shall be united with all others. To transfer from the vital being, the instrumental reality in us, to the spirit, the central reality, to elevate to that height our will to be and our power of living is the secret which our nature is seeking to discover. All that we have done hitherto is some half-successful effort to transfer this will and power to the mental plane; our highest endeavour and labour has been to become the mental being and to live in the strength of the idea. But the mental idea in us is always intermediary and instrumental; always it depends on something other than it for its ground of action and therefore although it can follow for a time after its own separate satisfaction, it cannot rest for ever satisfied with that alone. It must either gravitate downwards and outwards towards the vital and physical life or it must elevate itself inwards and upwards towards the spirit.

And that must be why in thought, in art, in conduct, in life we are always divided between two tendencies, one idealistic, the other realistic. The latter very easily seems to us more real, more solidly founded, more in touch with actualities because it relies upon a reality which is patent, sensible and already accomplished; the idealistic easily seems to us something unreal, fantastic, unsubstantial, nebulous, a thing more of thoughts and words than of live actualities, because it is trying to embody a reality not yet accomplished. To a certain extent we are perhaps right; for the ideal, a stranger among the actualities of our physical existence, is in fact a thing unreal until it has either in some way reconciled itself to the imperfections of our outer life or else has found the greater and purer reality for which it is seeking and imposed it on our outer activities; till then it hangs between two worlds and has conquered neither the upper light nor the nether darkness. Submission to the actual by a compromise is easy; discovery of the spiritual truth and the transformation of our actual way of living is difficult: but it is precisely this difficult thing that has to be done, if man is to find and fulfil his true nature. Our idealism is always the most rightly human thing in us, but as a mental idealism it is a thing ineffective. To be effective it has to convert itself into a spiritual realism which shall lay its hands on the higher reality of the spirit and take up for it this lower reality of our sensational, vital and physical nature.

This upward transference of our will to be and our power of life we have, then, to make the very principle of our perfection. That will, that power must choose between the domination of the vital part in us and the domination of the spirit. Nature can rest in the round of vital being, can produce there a sort of perfection, but that is the perfection of an arrested development satisfied with its own limits. This she can manage in the plant and the animal, because the life and the body are there at once the instrument and the aim; they do not look beyond themselves. She cannot do it in man because here she has shot up beyond her physical and vital basis; she has developed in him the mind which is an outflowering of the life towards the light of the Spirit, and the life and the body are now instrumental and no longer their own aim. Therefore the perfection of man cannot consist in pursuing the unillumined round of the physical life. Neither can it be found in the wider rounds of the mental being; for that also is instrumental and tends towards something else beyond it, something whose power indeed works in it, but whose larger truth is superconscient to its present intelligence, supramental. The perfection of man lies in the unfolding of the ever-perfect Spirit.

The lower perfection of Nature in the plant and the animal comes from an instinctive, an automatic, a subconscient obedience in each to the vital truth of its own being. The higher perfection of the spiritual life will come by a spontaneous obedience of spiritualised man to the truth of his own realised being, when he has become himself, when he has found his own real nature. For this spontaneity will not be instinctive and subconscient, it will be intuitive and fully, integrally conscious. It will be a glad obedience to a spontaneous principle of spiritual light, to the force of a unified and integralised highest truth, largest beauty, good, power, joy, love, oneness. The object of this force acting in life will and must be as in all life growth, possession, enjoyment, but a growth which is a divine manifestation, a possession and enjoyment spiritual and of the spirit in things, — an enjoyment that will use, but will not depend on the mental, vital and physical symbols of our living. Therefore this will not be a limited perfection of arrested development dependent on the repetition of the same forms and the same round of actions, any departure from which becomes a peril and a disturbance. It will be an illimitable perfection capable of endless variation in its forms, — for the ways of the Spirit are countless and endless, — but securely the same in all variations, one but multitudinously infinite.

Therefore, too, this perfection cannot come by the mental idea dealing with the Spirit as it deals with life. The idea in mind seizing upon the central will in Spirit and trying to give this higher force a conscious orientation and method in accordance with the ideas of the intellect is too limited, too darkened, too poor a force to work this miracle. Still less can it come if we chain the spirit to some fixed mental idea or system of religious cult, intellectual truth, aesthetic norm, ethical rule, practical action, way of vital and physical life, to a particular arrangement of forms and actions and declare all departure from that a peril and a disturbance or a deviation from spiritual living. That was the mistake made in Asia and the cause of its arrested development and decline; for this is to subject the higher to the lower principle and to bind down the self-disclosing Spirit to a provisional and imperfect compromise with mind and the vital nature. Man's true freedom and perfection will come when the spirit within bursts through the forms of mind and life and, winging above to its own gnostic fiery height of ether, turns upon them from that light and flame to seize them and transform into its own image.

In fact, as we have seen, the mind and the intellect are not the key-power of our existence. For they can only trace out a round of half-truths and uncertainties and revolve in that unsatisfying circle. But concealed in the mind and life, in all the action of the intellectual, the aesthetic, the ethical, the dynamic and practical, the emotional, sensational, vital and physical being, there is a power that sees by identity and intuition and gives to all these things such truth and such certainty and stability as they are able to compass. Obscurely we are now beginning to see something of this behind all our science and philosophy and all our other activities. But so long as this power has to work for the mind and life and not for itself, to work in their forms and not by its own spontaneous light, we cannot make any great use of this discovery, cannot get the native benefit of this inner Daemon. Man's road to spiritual supermanhood will be open when he declares boldly that all he has yet developed, including the intellect of which he is so rightly and yet so vainly proud, are now no longer sufficient for him, and that to uncase, discover, set free this greater Light within shall be henceforward his pervading preoccupation. Then will his philosophy, art, science, ethics, social existence, vital pursuits be no longer an exercise of mind and life, done for themselves, carried in a circle, but a means for the discovery of a greater Truth behind mind and life and for the bringing of its power into our human existence. We shall be on the right road to become ourselves, to find our true law of perfection, to live our true satisfied existence in our real being and divine nature.

Chapter XXIII

Conditions for the Coming
of a Spiritual Age

A CHANGE of this kind, the change from the mental and vital to the spiritual order of life, must necessarily be accomplished in the individual and in a great number of individuals before it can lay any effective hold upon the community. The Spirit in humanity discovers, develops, builds its formations first in the individual man: it is through the progressive and formative individual that it offers the discovery and the chance of a new self-creation to the mind of the race. For the communal mind holds things subconsciently at first or, if consciously, then in a confused chaotic manner: it is only through the individual mind that the mass can arrive at a clear knowledge and creation of the thing it held in its subconscient self. Thinkers, historians, sociologists who belittle the individual and would like to lose him in the mass or think of him chiefly as a cell, an atom, have got hold only of the obscurer side of the truth of Nature's workings in humanity. It is because man is not like the material formations of Nature or like the animal, because she intends in him a more and more conscious evolution, that individuality is so much developed in him and so absolutely important and indispensable. No doubt what comes out in the individual and afterwards moves the mass, must have been there already in the universal Mind and the individual is only an instrument for its manifestation, discovery, development: but he is an indispensable instrument and an instrument not merely of subconscient Nature, not merely of an instinctive urge that moves the mass, but more directly of the Spirit of whom that Nature is itself the instrument and the matrix of his creations. All great changes therefore find their first clear and effective power and their direct shaping force in the mind and spirit of an individual or of a limited number of individuals. The mass follows, but unfortunately in a very imperfect and confused fashion which often or even usually ends in the failure or distortion of the thing created. If it were not so, mankind could have advanced on its way with a victorious rapidity instead of with the lumbering hesitations and soon exhausted rushes that seem to be all of which it has yet been capable.

Therefore if the spiritual change of which we have been speaking is to be effected, it must unite two conditions which have to be simultaneously satisfied but are most difficult to bring together. There must be the individual and the individuals who are able to see, to develop, to re-create themselves in the image of the Spirit and to communicate both their idea and its power to the mass. And there must be at the same time a mass, a society, a communal mind or at the least the constituents of a group-body, the possibility of a group-soul which is capable of receiving and effectively assimilating, ready to follow and effectively arrive, not compelled by its own inherent deficiencies, its defect of preparation to stop on the way or fall back before the decisive change is made. Such a simultaneity has never yet happened, although the appearance of it has sometimes been created by the ardour of a moment. That the combination must happen some day is a certainty, but none can tell how many attempts will have to be made and how many sediments of spiritual experience will have to be accumulated in the subconscient mentality of the communal human being before the soil is ready. For the chances of success are always less powerful in a difficult upward effort affecting the very roots of our nature than the numerous possibilities of failure. The initiator himself may be imperfect, may not have waited to become entirely the thing that he has seen. Even the few who have the apostolate in their charge may not have perfectly assimilated and shaped it in themselves and may hand on the power of the Spirit still farther diminished to the many who will come after them. The society may be intellectually, vitally, ethically, temperamentally unready, with the result that the final acceptance of the spiritual idea by the society may be also the beginning of its debasement and distortion and of the consequent departure or diminution of the Spirit. Any or all of these things may happen, and the result will be, as has so often happened in the past, that even though some progress is made and an important change effected, it will not be the decisive change which can alone re-create humanity in a diviner image.

What then will be that state of society, what that readiness of the common mind of man which will be most favourable to this change, so that even if it cannot at once effectuate itself, it may at least make for its ways a more decisive preparation than has been hitherto possible? For that seems the most important element, since it is that, it is the unpreparedness, the unfitness of the society or of the common mind of man which is always the chief stumbling-block. It is the readiness of this common mind which is of the first importance; for even if the condition of society and the principle and rule that govern society are opposed to the spiritual change, even if these belong almost wholly to the vital, to the external, the economic, the mechanical order, as is certainly the way at present with human masses, yet if the common human mind has begun to admit the ideas proper to the higher order that is in the end to be, and the heart of man has begun to be stirred by aspirations born of these ideas, then there is a hope of some advance in the not distant future. And here the first essential sign must be the growth of the subjective idea of life, — the idea of the soul, the inner being, its powers, its possibilities, its growth, its expression and the creation of a true, beautiful and helpful environment for it as the one thing of first and last importance. The signals must be there that are precursors of a subjective age in humanity's thought and social endeavour.

These ideas are likely first to declare their trend in philosophy, in psychological thinking, in the arts, poetry, painting, sculpture, music, in the main idea of ethics, in the application of subjective principles by thinkers to social questions, even perhaps, though this is a perilous effort, to politics and economics, that hard refractory earthy matter which most resists all but a gross utilitarian treatment. There will be new unexpected departures of science or at least of research, — since to such a turn in its most fruitful seekings the orthodox still deny the name of science. Discoveries will be made that thin the walls between soul and matter; attempts there will be to extend exact knowledge into the psychological and psychic realms with a realisation of the truth that these have laws of their own which are other than the physical, but not the less laws because they escape the external senses and are infinitely plastic and subtle. There will be a labour of religion to reject its past heavy weight of dead matter and revivify its strength in the fountains of the spirit. These are sure signs, if not of the thing to be, at least of a great possibility of it, of an effort that will surely be made, another endeavour perhaps with a larger sweep and a better equipped intelligence capable not only of feeling but of understanding the Truth that is demanding to be heard. Some such signs we can see at the present time although they are only incipient and sporadic and have not yet gone far enough to warrant a confident certitude. It is only when these groping beginnings have found that for which they are seeking, that it can be successfully applied to the remoulding of the life of man. Till then nothing better is likely to be achieved than an inner preparation and, for the rest, radical or revolutionary experiments of a doubtful kind with the details of the vast and cumbrous machinery under which life now groans and labours.

A subjective age may stop very far short of spirituality; for the subjective turn is only a first condition, not the thing itself, not the end of the matter. The search for the Reality, the true self of man, may very easily follow out the natural order described by the Upanishad in the profound apologue of the seekings of Bhrigu, son of Varuna. For first the seeker found the ultimate reality to be Matter and the physical, the material being, the external man our only self and spirit. Next he fixed on life as the Reality and the vital being as the self and spirit; in the third essay he penetrated to Mind and the mental being; only afterwards could he get beyond the superficial subjective through the supramental Truth-Consciousness to the eternal, the blissful, the ever creative Reality of which these are the sheaths.

But humanity may not be as persistent or as plastic as the son of Varuna, the search may stop short anywhere. Only if it is intended that he shall now at last arrive and discover, will the Spirit break each insufficient formula as soon as it has shaped itself and compel the thought of man to press forward to a larger discovery and in the end to the largest and most luminous of all. Something of the kind has been happening, but only in a very external way and on the surface. After the material formula which governed the greater part of the nineteenth century had burdened man with the heaviest servitude to the machinery of the outer material life that he has ever yet been called upon to bear, the first attempt to break through, to get to the living reality in things and away from the mechanical idea of life and living and society, landed us in that surface vitalism which had already begun to govern thought before the two formulas inextricably locked together lit up and flung themselves on the lurid pyre of the world-war. The vital *élan* has brought us no deliverance, but only used the machinery already created with a more feverish insistence, a vehement attempt to live more rapidly, more intensely, an inordinate will to act and to succeed, to enlarge the mere force of living or to pile up a gigantic efficiency of the collective life. It could not have been otherwise even if this vitalism had been less superficial and external, more truly subjective. To live, to act, to grow, to increase the vital force, to understand, utilise and fulfil the intuitive impulse of life are not things evil in themselves: rather they are excellent things, if rightly followed and rightly used, that is to say, if they are directed to something beyond the mere vitalistic impulse and are governed by that within which is higher than Life. The Life-power is an instrument, not an aim; it is in the upward scale the first great subjective supraphysical instrument of the Spirit and the base of all action and endeavour. But a Life-power that sees nothing beyond itself, nothing to be served except its own organised demands and impulses, will be very soon like the force of steam driving an engine without the driver or an engine in which the locomotive force has made the driver its servant and not its controller. It can only add the uncontrollable impetus

of a high-crested or broad-based Titanism, or it may be even a
nether flaming demonism, to the Nature forces of the material
world with the intellect as its servant, an impetus of measureless
unresting creation, appropriation, expansion which will end in
something violent, huge and "colossal", foredoomed in its very
nature to excess and ruin, because light is not in it nor the soul's
truth nor the sanction of the gods and their calm eternal will
and knowledge.

But beyond the subjectivism of the vital self there is the possibility of a mental subjectivism which would at first perhaps,
emerging out of the predominant vitalism and leaning upon
the already realised idea of the soul as a soul of Life in action
but correcting it, appear as a highly mentalised pragmatism.
This first stage is foreshadowed in an increasing tendency to
rationalise entirely man and his life, to govern individual and
social existence by an ordered scientific plan based upon his
discovery of his own and of life's realities. This attempt is bound
to fail because reason and rationality are not the whole of man
or of life, because reason is only an intermediate interpreter,
not the original knower, creator and master of our being or of
cosmic existence. It can besides only mechanise life in a more
intelligent way than in the past; to do that seems to be all that
the modern intellectual leaders of the race can discover as the
solution of the heavy problem with which we are impaled. But it
is conceivable that this tendency may hereafter rise to the higher
idea of man as a mental being, a soul in mind that must develop
itself individually and collectively in the life and body through
the play of an ever-expanding mental existence. This greater
idea would realise that the elevation of the human existence
will come not through material efficiency alone or the complex
play of his vital and dynamic powers, not solely by mastering
through the aid of the intellect the energies of physical Nature
for the satisfaction of the life-instincts, which can only be an
intensification of his present mode of existence, but through
the greatening of his mental and psychic being and a discovery,
bringing forward and organisation of his subliminal nature and
its forces, the utilisation of a larger mind and a larger life waiting

for discovery within us. It would see in life an opportunity for the joy and power of knowledge, for the joy and power of beauty, for the joy and power of the human will mastering not only physical Nature, but vital and mental Nature. It might discover her secret yet undreamed-of mind-powers and life-powers and use them for a freer liberation of man from the limitations of his shackled bodily life. It might arrive at new psychic relations, a more sovereign power of the idea to realise itself in the act, inner means of overcoming the obstacles of distance and division which would cast into insignificance even the last miraculous achievements of material Science. A development of this kind is far enough away from the dreams of the mass of men, but there are certain pale hints and presages of such a possibility and ideas which lead to it are already held by a great number who are perhaps in this respect the yet unrecognised vanguard of humanity. It is not impossible that behind the confused morning voices of the hour a light of this kind, still below the horizon, may be waiting to ascend with its splendours.

Such a turn of human thought, effort, ideas of life, if it took hold of the communal mind, would evidently lead to a profound revolution throughout the whole range of human existence. It would give it from the first a new tone and atmosphere, a loftier spirit, wider horizons, a greater aim. It might easily develop a science which would bring the powers of the physical world into a real and not only a contingent and mechanical subjection and open perhaps the doors of other worlds. It might develop an achievement of Art and Beauty which would make the greatness of the past a comparatively little thing and would save the world from the astonishingly callous reign of utilitarian ugliness that even now afflicts it. It would open up a closer and freer interchange between human minds and, it may well be hoped, a kindlier interchange between human hearts and lives. Nor need its achievements stop here, but might proceed to greater things of which these would be only the beginnings. This mental and psychic subjectivism would have its dangers, greater dangers even than those that attend a vitalistic subjectivism, because its powers of action also would be greater, but it would have what vitalistic subjectivism has not and cannot easily have, the chance of a detecting discernment, strong safeguards and a powerful liberating light.

Moving with difficulty upward from Matter to spirit, this is perhaps a necessary stage of man's development. This was one principal reason of the failure of past attempts to spiritualise mankind, that they endeavoured to spiritualise at once the material man by a sort of rapid miracle, and though that can be done, the miracle is not likely to be of an enduring character if it overleaps the stages of his ascent and leaves the intervening levels untrodden and therefore unmastered. The endeavour may succeed with individuals, — Indian thought would say with those who have made themselves ready in a past existence, — but it must fail with the mass. When it passes beyond the few, the forceful miracle of the spirit flags; unable to transform by inner force, the new religion — for that is what it becomes — tries to save by machinery, is entangled in the mechanical turning of its own instruments, loses the spirit and perishes quickly or decays slowly. That is the fate which overtakes all attempts of the vitalistic, the intellectual and mental, the spiritual endeavour to deal with material man through his physical mind chiefly or alone; the endeavour is overpowered by the machinery it creates and becomes the slave and victim of the machine. That is the revenge which our material Nature, herself mechanical, takes upon all such violent endeavours; she waits to master them by their concessions to her own law. If mankind is to be spiritualised, it must first in the mass cease to be the material or the vital man and become the psychic and the true mental being. It may be questioned whether such a mass progress or conversion is possible; but if it is not, then the spiritualisation of mankind as a whole is a chimera.

From this point of view it is an excellent thing, a sign of great promise, that the wheel of civilisation has been following its past and present curve upward from a solid physical knowledge through a successive sounding of higher and higher powers that mediate between Matter and Spirit. The human intellect in modern times has been first drawn to exhaust the possibilities of materialism by an immense dealing with life and the world upon the basis of Matter as the sole reality, Matter as the Eternal, Matter as the Brahman, *annam brahma*. Afterwards it had begun to turn towards the conception of existence as the large pulsation of a great evolving Life, the creator of Matter, which would have enabled it to deal with our existence on the basis of Life as the original reality, Life as the great Eternal, *prāṇo brahma*. And already it has in germ, in preparation a third conception, the discovery of a great self-expressing and self-finding inner Mind other than our surface mentality as a master-power of existence, and that should lead towards a rich attempt to deal with our possibilities and our ways of living on the basis of Mind as the original reality, the great Eternal, *mano brahma*. It would also be a sign of promise if these conceptions succeeded each other with rapidity, with a large but swift evocation of the possibilities of each level; for that would show that there is a readiness in our subconscient Nature and that we need not linger in each stage for centuries.

But still a subjective age of mankind must be an adventure full of perils and uncertainties as are all great adventures of the race. It may wander long before it finds itself or may not find itself at all and may swing back to a new repetition of the cycle. The true secret can only be discovered if in the third stage, in an age of mental subjectivism, the idea becomes strong of the mind itself as no more than a secondary power of the Spirit's working and of the Spirit as the great Eternal, the original and, in spite of the many terms in which it is both expressed and hidden, the sole reality, *ayam ātmā brahma*. Then only will the real, the decisive endeavour begin and life and the world be studied, known, dealt with in all directions as the self-finding and self-expression of the Spirit. Then only will a spiritual age of mankind be possible.

To attempt any adequate discussion of what that would mean, and in an inadequate discussion there is no fruit, is beyond our present scope; for we should have to examine a knowledge which is rare and nowhere more than initial. It is enough to say that a spiritual human society would start from and try to realise three essential truths of existence which all Nature seems to be an attempt to hide by their opposites and which therefore are as yet for the mass of mankind only words and dreams, God, freedom, unity. Three things which are one, for you cannot realise freedom and unity unless you realise God, you cannot possess freedom and unity unless you possess God, possess at once your highest Self and the Self of all creatures. The freedom and unity which otherwise go by that name, are simply attempts of our subjection and our division to get away from themselves by shutting their eyes while they turn somersaults around their own centre. When man is able to see God and to possess him, then he will know real freedom and arrive at real unity, never otherwise. And God is only waiting to be known, while man seeks for him everywhere and creates images of the Divine, but all the while truly finds, effectively erects and worships images only of his own mind-ego and life-ego. When this ego pivot is abandoned and this ego-hunt ceases, then man gets his first real chance of achieving spirituality in his inner and outer life. It will not be enough, but it will be a commencement, a true gate and not a blind entrance.

A spiritualised society would live like its spiritual individuals, not in the ego, but in the spirit, not as the collective ego, but as the collective soul. This freedom from the egoistic standpoint would be its first and most prominent characteristic. But the elimination of egoism would not be brought about, as it is now proposed to bring it about, by persuading or forcing the individual to immolate his personal will and aspirations and his precious and hard-won individuality to the collective will, aims and egoism of the society, driving him like a victim of ancient sacrifice to slay his soul on the altar of that huge and shapeless idol. For that would be only the sacrifice of the smaller to the larger egoism, larger only in bulk, not necessarily greater in quality or wider or nobler, since a collective egoism, result of the united egoisms of all, is as little a god to be worshipped, as flawed and often an uglier and more barbarous fetish than the egoism of the individual. What the spiritual man seeks is to find by the loss of the ego the self which is one in all and perfect and complete in each and by living in that to grow into the image of its perfection, — individually, be it noted, though with an all-embracing universality of his nature and its conscious circumference. It is said in the old Indian writings that while in the second age, the age of Power, Vishnu descends as the King, and in the third, the age of compromise and balance, as the legislator or codifier, in the age of the Truth he descends as Yajna, that is to say, as the Master of works and sacrifice manifest in the heart of his creatures. It is this kingdom of God within, the result of the finding of God not in a distant heaven but within ourselves, of which the state of society in an age of the Truth, a spiritual age, would be the result and the external figure.

Therefore a society which was even initially spiritualised would make the revealing and finding of the divine Self in man the supreme, even the guiding aim of all its activities, its education, its knowledge, its science, its ethics, its art, its economical and political structure. As it was to some imperfect extent in the ancient Vedic times with the cultural education of the higher classes, so it would be then with all education. It would embrace all knowledge in its scope, but would make the whole trend and aim and the permeating spirit not mere worldly efficiency, though that efficiency would not be neglected, but this self-developing and self-finding and all else as its powers. It would pursue the physical and psychic sciences not in order merely to know the world and Nature in her processes and to use them for material human ends, but still more to know through and in and under and over all things the Divine in the world and the ways of the Spirit in its masks and behind them. It would make it the aim of ethics not to establish a rule of action whether supplementary to the social law or partially corrective of it, the social law that is after all only the rule, often clumsy and ignorant, of the biped pack, the human herd, but to develop the divine nature in the human being. It would make it the aim of Art not merely to present images of the subjective and objective world, but to see them with the significant and creative vision that goes behind their appearances and to reveal the Truth and Beauty of which things visible to us and invisible are the forms, the masks or the symbols and significant figures.

A spiritualised society would treat in its sociology the individual, from the saint to the criminal, not as units of a social problem to be passed through some skilfully devised machinery and either flattened into the social mould or crushed out of it, but as souls suffering and entangled in a net and to be rescued, souls growing and to be encouraged to grow, souls grown and from whom help and power can be drawn by the lesser spirits who are not yet adult. The aim of its economics would be not to create a huge engine of production, whether of the competitive or the cooperative kind, but to give to men — not only to some but to all men each in his highest possible measure — the joy of work according to their own nature and free leisure to grow inwardly, as well as a simply rich and beautiful life for all. In its politics it would not regard the nations within the scope of their own internal life as enormous State machines regulated and armoured with man living for the sake of the machine and worshipping it as his God and his larger self, content at the first call to kill others upon its altar and to bleed there himself so that the machine may remain intact and powerful and be made ever larger, more complex, more cumbrous, more mechanically efficient and entire. Neither would it be content to maintain these nations or States in their mutual relations as noxious engines meant to discharge poisonous gas upon each other in peace and to rush in times of clash upon each other's armed hosts and unarmed millions, full of belching shot and men missioned to murder like war-planes or hostile tanks in a modern battlefield. It would regard the peoples as group-souls, the Divinity concealed and to be self-discovered in its human collectivities, group-souls meant like the individual to grow according to their own nature and by that growth to help each other, to help the whole race in the one common work of humanity. And that work would be to find the divine Self in the individual and the collectivity and to realise spiritually, mentally, vitally, materially its greatest, largest, richest and deepest possibilities in the inner life of all and their outer action and nature.

For it is into the Divine within them that men and mankind have to grow; it is not an external idea or rule that has to be imposed on them from without. Therefore the law of a growing inner freedom is that which will be most honoured in the spiritual age of mankind. True it is that so long as man has not come within measurable distance of self-knowledge and has not set his face towards it, he cannot escape from the law of external compulsion and all his efforts to do so must be vain. He is and always must be, so long as that lasts, the slave of others, the slave of his family, his caste, his clan, his Church, his society, his nation; and he cannot but be that and they too cannot help throwing their crude and mechanical compulsion on him, because he and they are the slaves of their own ego, of their own lower nature. We must feel and obey the compulsion of the Spirit if we would establish our inner right to escape other compulsion: we must make our lower nature the willing slave, the conscious and illumined instrument or the ennobled but still self-subjected portion, consort or partner of the divine Being within us, for it is that subjection which is the condition of our freedom, since spiritual freedom is not the egoistic assertion of our separate mind and life but obedience to the Divine Truth in ourself and our members and in all around us. But we have, even so, to remark that God respects the freedom of the natural members of our being and that he gives them room to grow in their own nature so that by natural growth and not by self-extinction they may find the Divine in themselves. The subjection which they finally accept, complete and absolute, must be a willing subjection of recognition and aspiration to their own source of light and power and their highest being. Therefore even in the unregenerated state we find that the healthiest, the truest, the most living growth and action is that which arises in the largest possible freedom and that all excess of compulsion is either the law of a gradual atrophy or a tyranny varied or cured by outbreaks of rabid disorder. And as soon as man comes to know his spiritual self, he does by that discovery, often even by the very seeking for it, as ancient thought and religion saw, escape from the outer law and enter into the law of freedom.

A spiritual age of mankind will perceive this truth. It will not try to make man perfect by machinery or keep him straight by tying up all his limbs. It will not present to the member of the society his higher self in the person of the policeman, the official and the corporal, nor, let us say, in the form of a socialistic bureaucracy or a Labour Soviet. Its aim will be to diminish as soon and as far as possible the need of the element of external compulsion in human life by awakening the inner divine compulsion of the spirit within and all the preliminary means it will use will have that for its aim. In the end it will employ chiefly if not solely the spiritual compulsion which even the spiritual individual can exercise on those around him, — and how much more should a spiritual society be able to do it, — that which awakens within us in spite of all inner resistance and outer denial the compulsion of the Light, the desire and the power to grow through one's own nature into the Divine. For the perfectly spiritualised society will be one in which, as is dreamed by the spiritual anarchist, all men will be deeply free, and it will be so because the preliminary condition will have been satisfied. In that state each man will be not a law to himself, but *the* law, the divine Law, because he will be a soul living in the Divine Reality and not an ego living mainly if not entirely for its own interest and purpose. His life will be led by the law of his own divine nature liberated from the ego.

Nor will that mean a breaking up of all human society into the isolated action of individuals; for the third word of the Spirit is unity. The spiritual life is the flower not of a featureless but a conscious and diversified oneness. Each man has to grow into the Divine Reality within himself through his own individual being, therefore is a certain growing measure of freedom a necessity of the being as it develops and perfect freedom the sign and the condition of the perfect life. But also, the Divine whom he thus sees in himself, he sees equally in all others and as the same Spirit in all. Therefore too is a growing inner unity with others a necessity of his being and perfect unity the sign and condition of the perfect life. Not only to see and find the Divine in oneself, but to see and find the Divine in all, not only to seek one's own individual liberation or perfection, but to seek the liberation and perfection of others is the complete law of the spiritual being. If the divinity sought were a separate godhead within oneself and not the one Divine, or if one sought God for oneself alone, then indeed the result might be a grandiose egoism, the Olympian egoism of a Goethe or the Titanic egoism imagined by Nietzsche, or it might be the isolated self-knowledge or asceticism of the ivory tower or the Stylites pillar. But he who sees God in all, will serve freely God in all with the service of love. He will, that is to say, seek not only his own freedom, but the freedom of all, not only his own perfection, but the perfection of all. He will not feel his individuality perfect except in the largest universality, nor his own life to be full life except as it is one with the universal life. He will not live either for himself or for the State and society, for the individual ego or the collective ego, but for something much greater, for God in himself and for the Divine in the universe.

The spiritual age will be ready to set in when the common mind of man begins to be alive to these truths and to be moved or desire to be moved by this triple or triune Spirit. That will mean the turning of the cycle of social development which we have been considering out of its incomplete repetitions on a new upward line towards its goal. For having set out, according to our supposition, with a symbolic age, an age in which man felt a great Reality behind all life which he sought through symbols, it will reach an age in which it will begin to live in that Reality, not through the symbol, not by the power of the type or of the convention or of the individual reason and intellectual will, but in our own highest nature which will be the nature of that Reality fulfilled in the conditions — not necessarily the same as now — of terrestrial existence. This is what the religions have seen with a more or less adequate intuition, but most often as in a glass darkly, that which they called the kingdom of God on earth, — his kingdom within in man's spirit and therefore, for the one is the material result of the effectivity of the other, his kingdom without in the life of the peoples.

Chapter XXIV

The Advent and Progress
of the Spiritual Age

IF A subjective age, the last sector of a social cycle, is to find its outlet and fruition in a spiritualised society and the emergence of mankind on a higher evolutionary level, it is not enough that certain ideas favourable to that turn of human life should take hold of the general mind of the race, permeate the ordinary motives of its thought, art, ethics, political ideals, social effort, or even get well into its inner way of thinking and feeling. It is not enough even that the idea of the kingdom of God on earth, a reign of spirituality, freedom and unity, a real and inner equality and harmony — and not merely an outward and mechanical equalisation and association — should become definitely an ideal of life; it is not enough that this ideal should be actively held as possible, desirable, to be sought and striven after, it is not enough even that it should come forward as a governing preoccupation of the human mind. That would evidently be a very great step forward, — considering what the ideals of mankind now are, an enormous step. It would be the necessary beginning, the indispensable mental environment for a living renovation of human society in a higher type. But by itself it might only bring about a half-hearted or else a strong but only partially and temporarily successful attempt to bring something of the manifest spirit into human life and its institutions. That is all that mankind has ever attempted on this line in the past. It has never attempted to work out thoroughly even that little, except in the limits of a religious order or a peculiar community, and even there with such serious defects and under such drastic limitations as to make the experiment nugatory and without any bearing on human life. If we do not get beyond the mere holding of the ideal and its general influence in human life, this little is all that mankind will attempt in the future. More is needed; a general spiritual awakening and aspiration in mankind is indeed the large necessary motive-power, but the effective power must be something greater. There must be a dynamic re-creating of individual manhood in the spiritual type.

For the way that humanity deals with an ideal is to be satisfied with it as an aspiration which is for the most part left only as an aspiration, accepted only as a partial influence. The ideal is not allowed to mould the whole life, but only more or less to colour it; it is often used even as a cover and a plea for things that are diametrically opposed to its real spirit. Institutions are created which are supposed, but too lightly supposed to embody that spirit and the fact that the ideal is held, the fact that men live under its institutions is treated as sufficient. The holding of an ideal becomes almost an excuse for not living according to the ideal; the existence of its institutions is sufficient to abrogate the need of insisting on the spirit that made the institutions. But spirituality is in its very nature a thing subjective and not mechanical; it is nothing if it is not lived inwardly and if the outward life does not flow out of this inward living. Symbols, types, conventions, ideas are not sufficient. A spiritual symbol is only a meaningless ticket, unless the thing symbolised is re-alised in the spirit. A spiritual convention may lose or expel its spirit and become a falsehood. A spiritual type may be a temporary mould into which spiritual living may flow, but it is also a limitation and may become a prison in which it fossilises and perishes. A spiritual idea is a power, but only when it is both inwardly and outwardly creative. Here we have to enlarge and to deepen the pragmatic principle that truth is what we create, and in this sense first, that it is what we create within us, in other words, what we become. Undoubtedly, spiritual truth exists eternally beyond independent of us in the heavens of the spirit; but it is of no avail for humanity here, it does not become truth of earth, truth of life until it is lived. The divine perfection is always there above us; but for man to become divine in consciousness and act and to live inwardly and outwardly the divine life is what is meant by spirituality; all lesser meanings given to the word are inadequate fumblings or impostures.

This, as the subjective religions recognise, can only be brought about by an individual change in each human life. The collective soul is there only as a great half-subconscient source of the individual existence; if it is to take on a definite psychological form or a new kind of collective life, that can only come by the shaping growth of its individuals. As will be the spirit and life of the individuals constituting it, so will be the realised spirit of the collectivity and the true power of its life. A society that lives not by its men but by its institutions, is not a collective soul, but a machine; its life becomes a mechanical product and ceases to be a living growth. Therefore the coming of a spiritual age must be preceded by the appearance of an increasing number of individuals who are no longer satisfied with the normal intellectual, vital and physical existence of man, but perceive that a greater evolution is the real goal of humanity and attempt to effect it in themselves, to lead others to it and to make it the recognised goal of the race. In proportion as they succeed and to the degree to which they carry this evolution, the yet unrealised potentiality which they represent will become an actual possibility of the future.

A great access of spirituality in the past has ordinarily had for its result the coming of a new religion of a special type and its endeavour to impose itself upon mankind as a new universal order. This, however, was always not only a premature but a wrong crystallisation which prevented rather than helped any deep and serious achievement. The aim of a spiritual age of mankind must indeed be one with the essential aim of subjective religions, a new birth, a new consciousness, an upward evolution of the human being, a descent of the spirit into our members, a spiritual reorganisation of our life; but if it limits itself by the old familiar apparatus and the imperfect means of a religious movement, it is likely to register another failure. A religious movement brings usually a wave of spiritual excitement and aspiration that communicates itself to a large number of individuals and there is as a result a temporary uplifting and an effective formation, partly spiritual, partly ethical, partly dogmatic in its nature. But the wave after a generation or two or at most a few generations begins to subside; the formation remains. If there has been a very powerful movement with a great spiritual personality as its source, it may leave behind a central influence and an inner discipline which may well be the starting-point of fresh waves; but these will be constantly less powerful and enduring in proportion as the movement gets farther and farther away from its source. For meanwhile in order to bind together the faithful and at the same time to mark them off from the unregenerated outer world, there will have grown up a religious order, a Church, a hierarchy, a fixed and unprogressive type of ethical living, a set of crystallised dogmas, ostentatious ceremonials, sanctified superstitions, an elaborate machinery for the salvation of mankind. As a result spirituality is increasingly subordinated to intellectual belief, to outward forms of conduct and to external ritual, the higher to the lower motives, the one thing essential to aids and instruments and accidents. The first spontaneous and potent attempt to convert the whole life into spiritual living yields up its place to a set system of belief and ethics touched by spiritual emotion; but finally even that saving element is dominated by the outward machinery, the sheltering structure becomes a tomb. The Church takes the place of the spirit and a formal subscription to its creed, rituals and order is the thing universally demanded; spiritual living is only practised by the few within the limits prescribed by their fixed creed and order. The majority neglect even that narrow effort and are contented to replace by a careful or negligent piety the call to a deeper life. In the end it is found that the spirit in the religion has become a thin stream choked by sands; at the most brief occasional floodings of its dry bed of conventions still prevent it from becoming a memory in the dead chapters of Time.

The ambition of a particular religious belief and form to universalise and impose itself is contrary to the variety of human nature and to at least one essential character of the Spirit. For the nature of the Spirit is a spacious inner freedom and a large unity into which each man must be allowed to grow according to his own nature. Again — and this is yet another source of inevitable failure — the usual tendency of these credal religions is to turn towards an afterworld and to make the regeneration of the earthly life a secondary motive; this tendency grows in proportion as the original hope of a present universal regeneration of mankind becomes more and more feeble. Therefore while many new spiritual waves with their strong special motives and disciplines must necessarily be the forerunners of a spiritual age, yet their claims must be subordinated in the general mind of the race and of its spiritual leaders to the recognition that all motives and disciplines are valid and yet none entirely valid since they are means and not the one thing to be done. The one thing essential must take precedence, the conversion of the whole life of the human being to the lead of the spirit. The ascent of man into heaven is not the key, but rather his ascent here into the spirit and the descent also of the spirit into his normal humanity and the transformation of this earthly nature. For that and not some post mortem salvation is the real new birth for which humanity waits as the crowning movement of its long obscure and painful course.

Therefore the individuals who will most help the future of humanity in the new age will be those who will recognise a spiritual evolution as the destiny and therefore the great need of the human being. Even as the animal man has been largely converted into a mentalised and at the top a highly mentalised humanity, so too now or in the future an evolution or conversion — it does not greatly matter which figure we use or what theory we adopt to support it — of the present type of humanity into a spiritualised humanity is the need of the race and surely the intention of Nature; that evolution or conversion will be their ideal and endeavour. They will be comparatively indifferent to particular belief and form and leave men to resort to the beliefs and forms to which they are naturally drawn. They will only hold as essential the faith in this spiritual conversion, the attempt to live it out and whatever knowledge — the form of opinion into which it is thrown does not so much matter — can be converted into this living. They will especially not make the mistake of thinking that this change can be effected by machinery and outward institutions; they will know and never forget that it has to be lived out by each man inwardly or it can never be made a reality for the kind. They will adopt in its heart of meaning the inward view of the East which bids man seek the secret of his destiny and salvation within; but also they will accept, though with a different turn given to it, the importance which the West rightly attaches to life and to the making the best we know and can attain the general rule of all life. They will not make society a shadowy background to a few luminous spiritual figures or a rigidly fenced and earth-bound root for the growth of a comparatively rare and sterile flower of ascetic spirituality. They will not accept the theory that the many must necessarily remain for ever on the lower ranges of life and only a few climb into the free air and the light, but will start from the standpoint of the great spirits who have striven to regenerate the life of the earth and held that faith in spite of all previous failure. Failures must be originally numerous in everything great and difficult, but the time comes when the experience of past failures can be profitably used and the gate that so long resisted opens. In this as in all great human aspirations and endeavours, an *a priori* declaration of impossibility is a sign of ignorance and weakness, and the motto of the aspirant's endeavour must be the *solvitur ambulando* of the discoverer. For by the doing the difficulty will be solved. A true beginning has to be made; the rest is a work for Time in its sudden achievements or its long patient labour.

The thing to be done is as large as human life, and therefore the individuals who lead the way will take all human life for their province. These pioneers will consider nothing as alien to them, nothing as outside their scope. For every part of human life has to be taken up by the spiritual, — not only the intellectual, the aesthetic, the ethical, but the dynamic, the vital, the physical; therefore for none of these things or the activities that spring from them will they have contempt or aversion, however they may insist on a change of the spirit and a transmutation of the form. In each power of our nature they will seek for its own proper means of conversion; knowing that the Divine is concealed in all, they will hold that all can be made the spirit's means of self-finding and all can be converted into its instruments of divine living. And they will see that the great necessity is the conversion of the normal into the spiritual mind and the opening of that mind again into its own higher reaches and more and more integral movement. For before the decisive change can be made, the stumbling intellectual reason has to be converted into the precise and luminous intuitive, until that again can rise into higher ranges to overmind and supermind or gnosis. The uncertain and stumbling mental will has to rise towards the sure intuitive and into a higher divine and gnostic will, the psychic sweetness, fire and light of the soul behind the heart, *hṛdaye guhāyām*, has to alchemise our crude emotions and the hard egoisms and clamant desires of our vital nature. All our other members have to pass through a similar conversion under the compelling force and light from above. The leaders of the spiritual march will start from and use the knowledge and the means that past effort has developed in this direction, but they will not take them as they are without any deep necessary change or limit themselves by what is now known or cleave only to fixed and stereotyped systems or given groupings of results, but will follow the method of the Spirit in Nature. A constant rediscovery and new formulation and larger synthesis in the mind, a mighty remoulding in its deeper parts because of a greater enlarging Truth not discovered or not well fixed before, is that Spirit's way with our past achievement when he moves to the greatnesses of the future.

This endeavour will be a supreme and difficult labour even for the individual, but much more for the race. It may well be that, once started, it may not advance rapidly even to its first decisive stage; it may be that it will take long centuries of effort to come into some kind of permanent birth. But that is not altogether inevitable, for the principle of such changes in Nature seems to be a long obscure preparation followed by a swift gathering up and precipitation of the elements into the new birth, a rapid conversion, a transformation that in its luminous moment figures like a miracle. Even when the first decisive change is reached, it is certain that all humanity will not be able to rise to that level. There cannot fail to be a division into those who are able to live on the spiritual level and those who are only able to live in the light that descends from it into the mental level. And below these too there might still be a great mass influenced from above but not yet ready for the light. But even that would be a transformation and a beginning far beyond anything yet attained. This hierarchy would not mean as in our present vital living an egoistic domination of the undeveloped by the more developed, but a guidance of the younger by the elder brothers of the race and a constant working to lift them up to a greater spiritual level and wider horizons. And for the leaders too this ascent to the first spiritual levels would not be the end of the divine march, a culmination that left nothing more to be achieved on earth. For there would be still yet higher levels within the supramental realm, as the old Vedic poets knew when they spoke of the spiritual life as a constant ascent, —

> *brahmāṇas tvā śatakrato*
> *ud vaṁśam iva yemire;*
> *yat sānoḥ sānum āruhat,*
> *bhūri aspaṣṭa kartvam,* —

The priests of the word climb thee like a ladder, O hundred-powered. As one ascends from peak to peak, there is made clear the much that has still to be done.

But once the foundation has been secured, the rest develops by a progressive self-unfolding and the soul is sure of its way. As again it is phrased by the ancient Vedic singers, —

> *abhyavasthāḥ pra jāyante,*
> *pra vavrer vavriś ciketa;*
> *upasthe mātur vi caṣṭe,* —

State is born upon state; covering after covering becomes conscious of knowledge; in the lap of the Mother the soul sees.

This at least is the highest hope, the possible destiny that opens out before the human view, and it is a possibility which the progress of the human mind seems on the way to redevelop. If the light that is being born increases, if the number of individuals who seek to realise the possibility in themselves and in the world grows large and they get nearer the right way, then the Spirit who is here in man, now a concealed divinity, a developing light and power, will descend more fully as the Avatar of a yet unseen and unguessed Godhead from above into the soul of mankind and into the great individualities in whom the light and power are the strongest. There will then be fulfilled the change that will prepare the transition of human life from its present limits into those larger and purer horizons; the earthly evolution will have taken its grand impetus upward and accomplished the revealing step in a divine progression of which the birth of thinking and aspiring man from the animal nature was only an obscure preparation and a far-off promise.

OTHER TITLES BY SRI AUROBINDO

Bases of Yoga (New U.S. edition)	p	6.95
Bhagavad Gita and Its Message	p	15.95
Dictionary of Sri Aurobindo's Yoga (compiled)	p	11.95
Essays on the Gita (new US edition)	p	19.95
Gems from Sri Aurobindo, 1st Series (compiled)	p	8.95
Gems from Sri Aurobindo, 2nd Series (compiled)	p	12.95
Gems from Sri Aurobindo, 3rd Series (compiled)	p	10.95
Gems from Sri Aurobindo, 4th Series (compiled)	p	8.95
Growing Within	p	9.95
The Human Cycle: The Psychology of Social Development (new US edition)	p	14.95
Hymns to the Mystic Fire (new US edition)	p	17.95
Ideal of Human Unity (new US edition)	p	17.95
Integral Yoga: Sri Aurobindo's Teaching and Method of Practice (compiled)	p	14.95
The Life Divine (new US edition)	p	29.95
	hb	39.95
Lights on Yoga	p	2.95
Living Within (compiled)	p	8.95
Looking from Within (compiled)	p	6.95
The Mother (new US edition)	p	2.95
A Practical Guide to Integral Yoga (compiled)	p	7.95
The Psychic Being: Soul in Evolution (compiled)	p	8.95
Rebirth and Karma (new US edition)	p	9.95
Savitri: A Legend and a Symbol (new US edition)	p	24.95
The Secret of the Veda (new US edition)	p	15.00
The Synthesis of Yoga (new US edition)	p	29.95
	hb	34.95
The Upanishads (new US edition)	p	17.95
Vedic Symbolism (compiled)	p	6.95
Wisdom of the Gita, 2nd Series (compiled)	p	10.95
Wisdom of the Upanishads (compiled)	p	7.95

available from your local bookseller or
LOTUS LIGHT PUBLICATIONS, Box 325, Twin Lakes, WI 53181 USA
414/889-8561 • www. lotuspress.com

SECRET OF THE VEDA by Sri Aurobindo

In this ground-breaking book, Sri Aurobindo has revealed the secret of the Veda and illustrated his method with numerous translations of the ancient hymns. *Secret of the Veda* has been acclaimed by scholars and yogins as the ultimate key to revealing the hidden sense and secret inner meanings of the original spiritual revelation of the Veda. The Rig Veda provides an inner spiritual and psychological practice to achieve realization. It is the foundation upon which the Upanishads were later developed.
Now in it first US edition.

Sri Aurobindo
Secret of the Veda

LOTUS PRESS PUBLICATIONS   ISBN 0-914955-19-5 581p pb $19.95

ESSAYS ON THE GITA by Sri Aurobindo

The Bhagavad Gita stands alone in the spiritual tradition of humanity by being at the same time a Scripture, a teaching , a poetic utterance and a practical guidebook to the problems of life in the world. For this reason, the Gita is a powerful aid to anyone who wants to integrate the life of the Spirit with the issues of life in the world. It does not "cut the knot" but systematically works to untie it. In so doing, it helps us clarify the issues alive within ourselves. Sri Aurobindo understood these issues and in his famous *Essays on the Gita* he was able to reveal many subtle and hidden aspects of the teaching of the Gita. He entered into the spirit of the original and created a commentary that has stood the test of time in its lucidity and value for anyone wishing to truly understand the Bhagavad Gita. *Essays on the Gita* has been widely acclaimed for opening up the deeper sense of the Bhagavad Gita.
Now in its first US edition

Sri Aurobindo
Essays on the Gita

LOTUS PRESS PUBLICATIONS   ISBN 0-914955-18-7 588p pb $19.95

THE MOTHER by Sri Aurobindo

Sri Aurobindo has created, in this small book, a powerful guide to the practice of spirituality in life. To discover this gem is to gain a constant companion whose guidance remains forever meaningful. Its power of expression and meaning are so concentrated and far reaching that many have called it "Matri Upanishad", the Upanishad of the Mother. Sri Aurobindo's Matri Upanishad is the text which reveals this power and energy of creation in its universal and personal sense, providing both truth of philosophy and truth of yogic experience at one and the same time.

Sri Aurobindo
The Mother

Now in its first US edition

LOTUS PRESS PUBLICATIONS   ISBN 0-941524-79-5 62p pb $2.95

SAVITRI: A LEGEND AND A SYMBOL by Sri Aurobindo

Savitri is an inner guidebook for the soul. These mantric verses imbue even the body with potent spiritual resonance. In this epic spiritual poem, Sri Aurobindo reveals his vision of mankind's destiny within the universal evolution. He sets forth the optimistic view that life on earth has a purpose, and he places our travail within the context of this purpose: to participate in the evolution of consciousness that represents the secret thread behind life on earth. Sri Aurobindo's verses describe the origin of the universe, the appearance of sentient beings and the stages of evolution, as well as speak to many of mankind's unanswered questions concerning pain and death.
Now in its first US edition

Sri Aurobindo
Savitri
A Legend and a Symbol

LOTUS PRESS PUBLICATIONS   ISBN 0-941524-80-9 816p pb $24.95

available from your local bookseller or
Lotus Press, PO Box 325, Twin Lakes, WI 53181 • 414 889-8561
www.lotuspress.com

REBIRTH AND KARMA by Sri Aurobindo
In depth study of the concepts of rebirth, karma and the higher lines of karma.
One of the best introductions to this area we've ever found.

LOTUS PRESS PUBLICATIONS   ISBN 0-941524-63-9   190p   pb $29.95

Sri Aurobindo
Rebirth and Karma

LIFE DIVINE by Sri Aurobindo
The Life Divine is Sri Aurobindo's major philosophical exposition, spanning more
than a thousand pages and integrating the major spiritual directions of mankind into
a coherent picture of the growth of the spiritual essence of man through diverse methods,
philosophies and spiritual practices.

Sri Aurobindo
The Life Divine

LOTUS PRESS PUBLICATIONS   ISBN 0-941524-61-2   1113p   pb $29.95

THE INTEGRAL YOGA
Sri Aurobindo's Teaching and Method of Practice
by Sri Aurobindo (compilation)
"These carefully selected excerpts from the writings of Sri Aurobindo provide a
wonderfully accessible entre into the writings of one of the great masters of spiritual
synthesis."
    Ram Dass

Sri Aurobindo
The Integral Yoga
Sri Aurobindo's Teaching and Method of Practice

LOTUS PRESS PUBLICATIONS   ISBN 0-941524-76-0   416p   pb $14.95

SYNTHESIS OF YOGA, US EDITION by Sri Aurobindo
In The Synthesis of Yoga Sri Aurobindo unfolds his vision of an integral yoga
embracing all the powers and activities of man. First, he reviews the three great
yogic paths of Knowledge, Works and Love, along with Hatha Yoga, Raja Yoga and
Tantra, and then integrates them all into a great symphony. "Truth of philosophy is
of a merely theoretical value unless it can be lived, and we have therefore tried in
the The Synthesis of Yoga to arrive at a synthetical view of the principles and methods
of the various lines of spiritual self-discipline and the way in which they can lead to
an integral divine life in the human existence".

Sri Aurobindo
The Synthesis of Yoga

LOTUS PRESS PUBLICATIONS   ISBN 0-941524-66-3   899p   hb $34.95
LOTUS PRESS PUBLICATIONS   ISBN 0-941524-65-5   899p   pb $29.95

available from your local bookseller or
Lotus Press, PO Box 325, Twin Lakes, WI 53181 • 414 889-8561
www.lotuspress.com